I KILLED

KILLED

TRUE STORIES OF THE ROAD

FROM AMERICA'S TOP COMICS

COMPILED BY ✳ **Ritch Shydner** AND ✳ **Mark Schiff**

CROWN PUBLISHERS ☀ NEW YORK

Published in the United States by Crown Publishers,
an imprint of the Crown Publishing Group,
a division of Random House, Inc., New York.
www.crownpublishing.com

Crown is a trademark and the Crown colophon is a
registered trademark of Random House, Inc.

Library of Congress Cataloging-in-Publication Data

I killed: true stories of the road from America's top comics /
compiled by Ritch Shydner and Mark Schiff.—1st ed.
I. Standup comedy—United States—Miscellanea.
I. Shydner, Ritch.   II. Schiff, Mark.
PN1969.C65I3   2006
792.702'8092273—dc22   2006013087

ISBN 13: 978-0-307-34199-0
ISBN 10: 0-307-34199-2

Printed in the United States of America

DESIGN BY BARBARA STURMAN

10 9 8 7 6 5 4 3 2 1

First Edition

This book is dedicated to all the Sheckys, Redds, and Phyllises
who worked the road before there was a road.
And to Steve, Jack, and Johnny,
who gave them a place to sit down and tell us what happened.

CONTENTS

❋

Plus bits and pieces from . . .

ORNY ADAMS ✴ TIM ALLEN ✴ KERRY AWN ✴ IAN BAGG
✴ GREG BEHRENDT ✴ JOHN BIZARRE ✴ LEWIS BLACK ✴
ALONZO BODDEN ✴ PAT BUCKLES ✴ KATHY BUCKLEY
✴ BRETT BUTLER ✴ RED BUTTONS ✴ TOM CALTABIANO
✴ MARK CORDES ✴ DAVE COULIER ✴ JIM DAVID ✴
PHYLLIS DILLER ✴ TOM DREESEN ✴ MACK DRYDEN ✴
JEFF DUNHAM ✴ JIM EDWARDS ✴ DAVID FELDMAN ✴

The thing about being a comedian is, the very first time you do it you're introduced and walk out onstage as a *comedian*. There's no school, there's no training, there's no beginning. You start right in the middle of your career. You can't try it out—you can't figure it out in advance. You just start doing it. It's like if you said you wanted to be a surgeon and they went, "Okay, here's the knife, start cutting this guy up. And do it so that when you're done, he feels better."

FOREWORD

✳

Jerry Seinfeld

It's a pirate job. You want to be a pirate? You're a pirate. There are no "trainee pirates" with little paper hats on so everybody knows. Knock a tooth out and get on the boat. And I believe it was the brain-crushing simplicity of the comedian's life that was one of the most attractive things about it for me as a young man. I remember at the age of twenty feeling very overwhelmed by the infinite gray areas of accomplishment and futility in the occupations I saw around me. But standup comedian—there was nothing gray about that. It's a swimming-with-your-knife-in-your-teeth kind of job.

And it never really changes much from that. I've spent a long time at every different level of the profession. I know them all. I remember them all. I spent years at the bottom. I spent a lot of years in the middle. And I've played the best places there are. And I can tell you honestly, it's pretty much all the same. It works when you're the one who gives a damn whether this is really happening or not.

I've performed with the actors, the musicians, and the singers— and I'm sorry, but it's just not the same for them. That little bit of padding on the knees and elbows makes a difference. Standup comedy doesn't belong in the arts section; it belongs on the sports pages. There's not that much to interpret. Everyone in the room knows how the game turned out. You learn to partially block out what it is you're actually doing, because the audience always outnumbers the comedian by a huge amount. "Why should this one person be talking while the rest of us sit here quietly?" Someone better justify that arrangement real quick or there's going to be trouble.

I don't think comedy is a particularly lofty profession, but it is one of the Great Jobs. And there are only four Great Jobs in the world: baseball player, race-car driver, professional surfer, and standup comedian. Given that these jobs pay handsomely and also involve an enormous amount of fun, I suppose it makes sense that they're tough to get into.

I'm not going to say standup comedians are special people, because they're not. I don't think there *are* any special people. Everyone's sneezing and farting and burping and coughing. That's what enables you to walk in front of three thousand people and say, "All right, now I'm going to tell you all what to think."

If you're cut out for it, I don't think there's any downside to being a comedian, although you do have to travel. And travel, combined with the intrinsic silliness of the profession, always seems to lead to bizarre occurrences. While on the road, every comedian will be involved in numerous surreal, uncomfortable, irrational events. It's not optional. Every comedian has stories. They can involve albinos, foreign embassies, the tiny little padlock that comes with the luggage, anything. Up to now, these stories have only been used to make other comedians laugh or to relate on a talk show. But thanks to the publication of this book, they're finally being put to productive use.

I applaud the great effort Mark and Ritch made to gather together these amazing stories. To assemble *I Killed,* they conducted literally hundreds of hours of interviews with dozens and dozens of comedians, which is wonderful, because it would have been terrible if these hideous experiences had gone to waste. I don't know why, but it seems right that if one person has to go through some twisted freak drama, another group of humans should be able to enjoy that they didn't. And even more important, in the great tradition of the comedic arts, they should be able to laugh richly and enjoyably at that miserable human being's expense.

Thank you and good night.

JERRY SEINFELD
March 6, 2006
New York City

✳ Mark Schiff

AND FURTHER DELAYING TACTICS

✳

Sometime in 2004, I was in Savannah, Georgia. It was around 2:00 in the afternoon. I was at a "comedy condo," taking a bath and getting ready for my nap, when Ritch Shydner called and said, "Let's do a book of comic road stories." I said, "Why not?" After all, I'd been on the road for almost twenty-five years and was looking for a way to spend more time at home, fighting with my wife and arguing with my kids. What better way to get off the road than to write a *book* about the road.

Truth is, I love my wife. In 1988, I was on the road and spent a total of ten hours in San Antonio, Texas. When I left San Antonio, I had a paycheck and the phone number of the woman I was to marry. Today, that woman and I have three great kids. Thank you, road.

Unless you're flying in private jets and riding in limos—or are very young with few attachments—the road is hard. The food is bad, and the bars of soap are tiny. Despite that, few things are more exciting than the road and the people you meet. I once flew to Italy to work for fifteen minutes. I traveled to England, where I got paid $15,000 even though the show was canceled. I found myself in Lexington, Kentucky, where a cop told me I had an hour to get out of town or I'd be arrested. I played the Knesset in Jerusalem, Israel, and a few days later, a country-western bar in Texas where mechanical bulls bounced up and down. One time, my wife had to leave our baby with a waitress while she was taken to the hospital (for an allergic reaction) because I was onstage.

It's stories like those that you'll find here, though believe me, much, much more *bizarre*. Most of the contributors are American. I had the pleasure of interviewing hundreds of comics for their stories.

At one point, my friend and fellow comedian Hiram Kasten accompanied me to Jan Murray's house. Jan is in his eighties now. When we got there, the housekeeper said he would be right out. Jan then yelled from the bedroom, "I'm just getting ready. I'll be out in five minutes." Five minutes later, he came out in his boxer shorts and T-shirt. Funny people are funny any time of the day and at any age.

I Killed's contributors all swear on a stack of 3:00 A.M. pancakes that these stories are true. You decide. I would estimate that 99 percent of the comics in this book started at nightclubs or comedy clubs. So while reading, if you want to pay homage to them, get a bottle of cheap wine (but pay $75 for it), deep-fry a pound of mold-tinged mozzarella, place thirty lighted cigarettes next to your chair, and with the windows shut tight, sit back and enjoy these frequently hilarious glimpses into how hard it is to keep smiling while trying to make others laugh.

✳ Ritch Shydner

Like those of most professional comics, my earliest performances were for classmates and neighborhood friends. I liked the way their laughter made me feel. Eventually I needed a bigger and steadier supply of laughter than my friends could provide. Once I discovered I could get guffaws from a group of strangers, I set out each night in search of a stage. I soon heard tales of "The Road," a place with an endless supply of fresh crowds. That began my twenty-year odyssey through bars, conference rooms, and outdoor stages, looking for The Big Laugh.

The life of the standup comic is defined by the road. It leads either to stardom or to starvation. As Bob Dylan said, "Sacrifice is the code of the road." Not that I was looking to give up anything.

I saw more of the country, did more drugs, and had more brief intimate encounters than your average serial killer.

Road stories are a common currency among comedians. Several times it occurred to me that someone should record these stories. Three years ago I was catapulted into action when a lack of showbiz work brought me face-to-face with the horror of a Real Job.

I quickly called Mark Schiff, a friend I had met in the New York standup scene of the late seventies. Like me, Mark has three kids, so I knew he was up for anything that might make him money and get him out of the house.

We approached every comedian we knew or knew of and received contributions far more generous—both in terms of length and candor—than we asked for. Even when the story was being recorded over the telephone I could see the joy on the face of the comic making me laugh. One story led to another, then to three and a new tape. Gathering the stories for this book reconnected me to what I love about standup comedy and the people who do it. It's all about the funny—giving the laugh or having it.

Back in 1985 I was driving through the South, listening to late-night radio. A guest made this statement: "Jazz and standup comedy are the only two original American performance art forms." I don't know if it's true; hell, the next guest talked about Bigfoot. But there does seem to be something in American mythology about the single person taking on long odds, whether it be the solo aviator, the cloistered inventor, or the lone assassin. Standup might not deserve the attention of the Civil War, but this book is a pretty good look at the life of the comedian over the last fifty years.

. . .

To learn more about the book,
visit www.standupstories.com.

I KILLED

HEY, MR. COOPER!

✳ Larry Miller

One of the first lines or jokes I ever wrote in standup was a reflection about high school. The bit was this: if you go back to your old high school reunion, whether it's after five, ten, or fifty years, whatever it is, you'll still feel a formal obligation to call all your former teachers "Mr." or "Mrs." You could be Secretary of State—and you'd still do that. After making that observation, I'd look off in the audience and point, as if I were spotting someone, and say, "Hey, Mr. Cooper, remember when we set you on fire?"

Now, it was a joke, a line. It wasn't great, but it always worked. The bit was a good part of my act, and I always enjoyed doing it.

So I was working in Philadelphia at The Comedy Works. My friend Todd Glass, a comic and part-time agent, came by the club, and he told me he'd booked me for a late-night gig after I finished my set at The Works. He said it was at about two or three in the morning, somewhere out in New Jersey. It was a high school prom and it paid about fifty bucks. It's dough, so you go! Honestly, I had no other way of earning that kind of money legally, so I accepted the gig and Todd's offer of a ride.

Most people think of New Jersey as just turnpikes, but this was in a rural place. It was more like rural Indiana than New Jersey or New York.

It turned out the people at the school had a great idea. Instead of having the kids leave their prom for a drunken high-speed chase for the Jersey Shore, they gave the kids the whole school for their prom; they could decorate it any way they wanted, have different rooms and games—whatever they wanted. The ultimate or penultimate moment was going to be a comedy show in the audi-torium. Since there were so many kids, they had to bring in extra folding chairs.

I went up to do my set at about three in the morning. I wasn't worried that the audience was tired. They were nice, well-mannered kids—it was a rural place.

I decided to myself, because I'm so clever a comic, that I'd open with the bit about Mr. Cooper, because it would create a little bond between the kids and me. So I was onstage, and I was supposed to do about a half an hour. I said, "Hey, I was in high school. I found out that when I went back, as you'll see when you go back, you'll still call all your old teachers 'Mr.' or 'Mrs.'" Then I used the line, "Hey, Mr. Cooper, remember when we set you on fire?"

Not only were there no laughs, but a wave—a palpable wave—of unmistakable hatred hit me like the waves you see coming off a radiator in the summer. I felt the hatred, almost saw it in the air; it nearly made me take a step back—it was that strong! I blinked a couple of times and just kept doing the rest of the set. I'm a pretty good comic, but because I felt what I felt, I started to weave a little. But, you know, I was digging out at negative thirty just to get back to zero.

After twenty-five minutes of really pretty solid work, changing bits and switching gears, I could tell there was *no* bond with the audience—just scattered breaths now and a couple of what you might call semi-laughs. I'd done yeoman's work just to dig myself back out, and then I got offstage.

I thought, *What in the world happened?* Then Todd came run-ning up to me and said, "Come on! We gotta get outta here!"

I said, "What's wrong?"

Todd told me the story. Apparently they had had a beloved Mr. Chips–type teacher named Mr. Cooper, who had died just days before in a fire. He was killed in a fire!

And I'd used that line, "Hey, Mr. Cooper, remember when we set you on fire?" Now, what are the odds of that happening? How many double sixes in a row was that? A million?

The president of the student council and the prom king and queen had stormed up to Todd during the show and said, "You can tell your friend we don't appreciate the jokes about Mr. Cooper!"

Todd said, "What?"

The student council president and the prom king and queen explained.

Todd said, "You don't think the guy researched your school for weeks beforehand just to find the one thing that would offend you so much, let alone open with it?"

But they were still really mad. In fact, they were turning into villagers in a Frankenstein movie. They were bubbling with anger.

After Todd explained all this to me, I just started to laugh. I couldn't stop laughing. It was nervous laughter. It was like laughing at a funeral when you can't stop. I couldn't stop laughing!

Todd said, "Larry, come on, it's not funny! I gotta get you outta here!"

Todd had to half-drag me down to the car because I was laughing so hard. We started to pull out, and now we saw, coming down the hill, the irate "villagers." They were rushing toward us, a whole sea of people. There was a minister or a pastor from the town who held them back about thirty feet away and said, "No, wait, this isn't right! Stop it!"

Then I heard, "We gotta get him!" There was no reasoning with them!

I heard the pastor say something like, "Forgive him! His punishment will come later!"

But now I started to laugh again, and I couldn't stop. I wasn't laughing at them, but at the circumstances.

We drove back to Philadelphia like the two idiots we were. I was about twenty-five years old, and Todd, the agent, was nineteen or twenty-one; we were kids. They'd paid Todd up front, so we had about fifty-three dollars. I gave Todd his ten percent, which was $5.30.

I thought, "Look at us—we're big businessmen now! We're in show business!"

MY FIRST ROAD TRIP

✳ Ron Shock

In the summer of 1983, Bill Hicks, Bill Silva, and I left Houston for a little road tour. I'd just met these guys—I was the new guy on the Houston comedy scene and not yet accepted. I was older than the rest, so I obviously couldn't be funny. I was happily married, so therefore I couldn't possibly be fucking funny.

The first gig was two days at this redneck discotheque in Lake Charles, Louisiana. They used to book us into another place in Lake Charles, but the owner had found his wife in bed with one of our comics.

The first night was a Wednesday, which was also Ladies' Night, free beer for the ladies. So you got a lot of drunken women and horny guys dancing. Their first clue they were going to see comedy was when the owner stopped the music at ten-thirty and announced over the PA, "I paid a lot of money for these comics, and I sure hope you think they're fucking funny. Here's the first one, Ron Shock."

I got on stage and the first thing yelled at me was, "Blow job, blow job!"

I responded with what I thought was a decent and logical question: "Are you asking, or are you offering?"

This pissed the heckler off. He rushed the stage, grabbed me, and said, "I'm askin'."

I replied, "Well, you're not my type."

Everybody was cheering him on, but I knew he was just bluffing. It was bad. I left to indifference, and Silva went up. They hated him. Of course, Hicks took the stage and turned on them—fortunately, no one was listening. We barely got away.

But this little adventure was only beginning. It was a two-day gig, so we called the agent and said, "We can't go back there. It isn't that they don't think we're funny. They hate us. They're gonna physically hurt us if they see us again." Of course, this agent said, "It's Shock's fault. He's new. He doesn't know how to handle a crowd."

We said, "You don't understand!"

He said, "No, *you* don't understand. If you don't do the gig tomorrow night, you can blow off the rest of the trip and you'll never work for me again." This was before the great comedy explosion of the mid-eighties, so there wasn't any work.

We were sitting in the hotel room. I wanted to go back. I didn't know these guys and, more important, they didn't know me. Hicks and Silva were both practically chanting, "What're we gonna do, what're we gonna do?" I said, "Well, you know, guys, we're gonna die tomorrow. We're gonna get shot or something. I'm an old-time hippie and I've always said if I knew the day I was gonna die, well, I'd be trippin'. I'd wanna take some LSD because the transition from life to death is gonna be a lot easier."

Hicks said, "You'd do that?"

"Bill, I always carry LSD with me for just that purpose."

Hicks didn't hesitate. "Can I have some?"

Silva's eyes just popped, because he couldn't believe this conversation.

I was probably just letting my alligator mouth overload my

hummingbird ass, but now I'd been called on it. And this was Bill Hicks, who I already knew was a genius, so I had to carry it through.

Hicks and I agreed to take LSD the next day before the show. Silva was shocked. "You guys aren't gonna really do that?"

I couldn't pussy out at that point. "Fucking-A I'm gonna do it."

Bill was right with me. "Fucking-A I'm gonna do it."

The next day we packed the cars, so we could get out of town as soon as the show was finished. We had two cars and Bill's pet ferret. Bill and I each took half a tab. I'd never done this type of acid. Maybe trying it for the first time while performing for hostile strangers wasn't my best idea ever, but it was my best idea at the time. Of course, as it always goes with this sort of thing, the acid was stronger than I expected. Bill and I got inside the club and the shit started coming on. People's faces were taking on rather grotesque shapes and melting. It was the usual: people turning into lizards, ghouls, and demons, just the sort of thing to get into a bit of relatable humor.

Bill and I were scared. This wasn't a good idea. A guy came in and sat down at the table next to us. He had a cut over his eye, blood pouring down his face. This was not something you want to see just before performing comedy, and never while tripping on acid. He'd gotten in a fight on the way in the door. The night before had been a packed ladies' night, so this crowd was a third of that, and all male. There wasn't a woman in the whole joint, except the waitresses, which didn't bode well.

Bill Silva went first. No sooner had he gotten up there than a guy at the bar yelled, "You better be funnier than you were last night, 'cause I got my gun with me tonight." He pulled back his coat to show a pistol stuffed in his waistband.

It was the Wild Wild West, without the Indians to take the heat off us. Silva said, "Gosh, I wish you hadn't said that."

Hicks and I could only manage to say the same thing we'd been saying since we'd entered the bar on acid: "Aw, fuck!" We were right on the edge of losing it. "They're armed. They really are fucking armed." As God as my witness, a waitress came up and said, "Don't worry, boys, I've got my gun, too." She proceeded to show us this little .22 that she had tucked under her blouse.

Hicks and I were over the edge. The waitress was armed. The guy next to us was bleeding. Silva was being threatened onstage.

I use the word "performance," but I honestly can't say that what happened next fits any definition of that word. I don't remember what Silva did. I don't remember what I did. I only remember that when Hicks went up, Silva got the money from the guy.

Somebody unplugged Hicks's microphone. A sober Bill would have lost it at that point, but tripping Bill went past threatening them and into assaulting everything they held dear and their entire way of life. It was brilliantly funny, not that any of those people understood anything other than that they were fighting words. Silva and I were in the back, trying to get Hicks's attention. We're waving our arms and mouthing, "We've got the money; let's go!"

Finally, Bill saw us and repeated his exit of the night before: a loud "Fuck you," a microphone toss, and a defiant walk through the crowd. They were so stunned by his audacity it was like the parting of the Red Sea.

Bill came out the back door and we headed for my truck. Silva was in his car. I'd locked the keys in my truck. The crowd of angry, gun-toting locals was coming out the back door. Bill and I picked up rocks and were bouncing them off my truck window. Silva jumped out of his car and confronted the mob. He was telling them it was all a joke. Hicks and I finally found a rock big enough and broke out my truck window. We motioned Silva and we all drove away.

That was my very first road trip.

THIS AIN'T MY FIRST GIG

✳ David Tyree

In 1988 we were picked up at the Laughton, Nevada, International Airport by the club owner in his 1957 Ford Ranchero.

Now I knew this was Laughton, the gambling resort for people who don't have the gas money to get to Vegas, so I didn't expect a stretch limo. But this Ranchero wasn't even a this-is-my-impress-people restored ride, but rather more like an all-I-got run-down piece of shit.

The three of us jammed into a front seat designed to accommodate two people starved down from the Depression and World War II, not their fat-ass kids. There was no air conditioner, but at least the windows worked, so we enjoyed the dry 120-degree desert air blowing in our faces.

The owner informed the middle act and me that he didn't have the money to put us up in a hotel "per se," but he'd renovated his attic to comfortably accommodate entertainers of our status.

This club owner had a pencil-thin mustache and wore a green, western-style leisure suit. He reminded me of that cartoon character Snidely Whiplash, from the old Dudley Do-Right cartoons. I tried to keep in mind what my grandma said: "Don't judge a book by its cover." But sweating in this Ranchero and listening to him talking about attics and "entertainers of our status," I got the feeling this book was nothing *but* cover.

Upon entering his abode we were led down a long hallway, where we had to climb pull-down stairs and literally stoop and walk back into a dimly lit corner of the attic. The renovation of this attic was probably adding the cord to the stairs so you didn't need to jump up to pull it down. There was no toilet, no phone, and no television. At least a prison cell has a bowl. I was waiting for him to promise to play his TV loud downstairs so at least we could listen to our favorite shows. We were pissed and wanted to leave, but neither of us had any money. Besides that, we were ten miles from civilization, with no car.

Just as we were thinking that things couldn't get any worse, the owner told us to be careful because his house was surrounded by cottonmouth snakes and at least a million of the largest tarantulas on earth.

What did we do? Hell, we were road comics—we unpacked!

The other comic and I settled in for a nice relaxing stare at the ceiling when the club owner stuck his head through the attic hole to inform us that his refrigerator was empty. Not to worry, though, he had a lake on his property and plenty of fishing poles. Add a little tarantula and snake meat, and there you had a well-balanced diet! I'd never done a gig where I had to trap my food. I was getting a feeling what it was like for the pioneer comics of the old Wild West.

Despite all of the aforementioned, everything was going smoothly. The shows were good and the audiences were great. We were having fun. We'd stop at McDonald's after the shows and pick up enough food for the next day. The waitresses were pretty and friendly.

Saturday night—payday! After the shows, the owner, Mr. Whiplash, called me into the office. He was sitting at his desk, smiling and twirling his mustache. He said, "Do you like the little blonde?" One of his waitresses was a twenty-five-year-old blonde with a fabulous figure.

I think my response was, "She's aw'ight."

Then he said, "You can have her if you want. She's attracted to black men, but she's never been with one. You could be her first."

Before I could say, "Sounds good," this pimping-ass motherfucker said, "You can fuck her all night, and we'll just call it even."

I leaped to my feet, acting all pissed off. "She's not a piece of meat, and for that matter, neither am I! No way am I gonna accept sex as payment for a week's work! You ought to be ashamed of yourself for even suggesting it! Now give me my money!"

Sheepishly, Snidely counted out the cash and handed it to me. He apologized, then told one of his male employees to give me a ride back to the attic. Still faking, I exited in a huff.

Outside the office, I had to smile. Shit, ain't no pussy worth two thousand! Besides, the little blonde had been giving me blow jobs in the bathroom since Tuesday.

MY RIDE IS HERE

✳ Ant

Early on in a comic's career, you get calls from weird bookers offering these crazy jobs. In 1995 I got such a call. "We need you to be in Arkansas in twelve hours. It pays $200, and you have to provide your own airfare and hotel." I would never again take a gig where it cost me more to get there than the pay, but back then I just needed stage time.

Twelve hours after I hung up with the booker, I landed in Arkansas, where I was met by Archie Whiteman, "pronounced Wit-man."

We drove through Harrison, Arkansas. On the Welcome sign to the city, where you usually expect to see "Knights of Columbus" or "Elks Lodge," a slogan read, "Proud Home of the KKK."

If you don't know, I'm this huge queen. When I was born, I

skipped maiden and princess and went right to queen. I started thinking, *I know the KKK doesn't like blacks.* So I asked my driver, "Does the KKK hate gays, too, or *just* the blacks and the Jews?"

The driver said, "I think it's just the blacks and the Jews. Although there is talk of adding Koreans to the list."

I was thinking, *Oh, I'm safe because I probably don't have to bump into any of those KKK people!* Now, I hadn't put it together that because this was a small town, there was one lodge where *all* the town's entertainment performed.

We pulled up to this lodge, where the show was being held. There was a line around the block.

I said, "Holy shit, what are all those people doing here?"

The driver said, "They're here to see *you.*"

I said, *"What?"*

The driver said, "You're Antler!"

I said, "No, I'm not Antler! I'm just *Ant.* Antler is another comic out of New York who's this huge racist comic."

The driver said, "Oh, well, have a good show."

About an hour later I was on stage, and for the first half of my act I just talked about old people, credit-card debt—standard stuff.

Then as usual I came out of the closet onstage and talked about being gay. The reaction was horrible.

This huge man named Bubba was sitting in the front row—and I only knew his name was Bubba because it was tattooed on his left arm. He looked at me, and I couldn't tell whether he was smiling or angry, because he had no teeth—probably from years of crystal meth abuse. He climbed up on the stage and literally picked me up off the stage, and I started screaming, "Rape, rape! It's a hate crime!" as he was carrying me out of the theater.

Bubba then threw me in the back of his beat-up black Toyota pickup truck and said, "We've gotta get you out of here, little buddy, or they're gonna *kill* you!"

LIFE WITH RODNEY

✳ Robert Schimmel

Once I went to visit Rodney Dangerfield when he was getting out of the Pritikin Center. So I went to see him and he was sitting at a table. The first thing I noticed was how odd he looked. Despite having been there two weeks, he looked like he'd actually gained twenty pounds.

I saw he was eating this Pritikin navy bean soup and a salad, which was just a quarter of a lettuce wedge with sliced tomato. He squeezed a little lemon on it and added freshly ground pepper, and he had a bottle of Evian water.

Rodney said, "Bob, I'm on the Pritikin diet now."

I said, "Wow, Rodney! I can't believe it! This is unbelievable!"

He said, "Yeah, I got the navy bean soup and I got this lettuce. I'm doing the whole thing." Then Rodney said, "I got to take a piss. This diet makes you piss every four minutes. I'll be right back."

About fifteen minutes passed; Rodney had not come back. So I went to the kitchen to get a glass of water, and I noticed Rodney was leaning against the refrigerator; he had a turkey leg in one hand and a Miller Lite in his other hand. He stared straight at me and said, "Want a bite?"

I said, "Rodney, what happened to the Pritikin diet?"

Rodney said, "I'm eating that, but the weed gets me hungry. See, if you eat the Pritikin shit, it makes the other stuff healthy."

Oh, as to the bottle of Evian, I found out later it was filled with Absolut vodka.

About two weeks later I was onstage at Governor's Comedy

Club in Long Island, when a waitress passed me a note that said Rodney Dangerfield was in the audience.

So I said, "Ladies and gentlemen, we have a special guest in the audience—Rodney Dangerfield." The crowd went nuts; Rodney came up onstage and said, "Hey, how about Robert Schimmel? A real funny guy." After watching Rodney tear apart the room for fifteen minutes, I wasn't so sure how funny I was by comparison, but I reclaimed the stage anyway, and finished the show.

As I came off stage, Rodney said to me, "You want to have dinner with me after the show? This Pritikin shit has got me so weak, I gotta eat twice as much."

I said, "Yeah. Let me get my pay first."

The club's owner, Jimmy, gave me a $500 bonus. "That's for having Rodney come in." He added, "I didn't know Rodney was going to be here, but I don't care. You know what? I couldn't buy this kind of advertising! These people are going to go home and say, 'Hey! We saw Rodney Dangerfield at Governor's.'"

It occurred to me that no one was going to say they saw Robert Schimmel. All right, I did get an extra five hundred bucks to smooth over my dented ego.

I got in the car with Rodney, who said, "So how much did we make?"

I said, "What do you mean?"

Rodney said, "You didn't get anything extra because I stopped in?" And I said, "Yeah."

Rodney said, "It has to be like three hundred or four hundred bucks."

I said, "Five hundred."

Rodney said, "Where's my half?"

I gave Rodney half the money.

Rodney said, "Hey, Robert! Where do you want to go to dinner? By the way, you made an extra $250, so dinner's on you."

At dinner that night, Rodney asked me if I wanted to go to Vegas with him. He said he was working on a movie and doing a show. So I invited my mom and dad, thinking that when my parents saw me hanging out with Rodney Dangerfield, they'd finally believe I was in show business. My parents are Holocaust survivors and have an okay sense of humor, but I was a bit concerned because Rodney onstage live is *not* the same Rodney who performs the nice TV material on *The Tonight Show.*

When Rodney walked out on the stage at Caesars Palace, the first thing he said was, "Chicks dig Sylvester Stallone so much that when he jerks off, the girl he's thinking of comes."

My dad was laughing, but my mom was not. Then, all of a sudden, my dad stopped. After being married for fifty million years, he knew that it was not worth having a good time if he had to pay for it later because my mom disapproved.

Mom would have likely scolded Dad at home afterward: "Why did you laugh at that filth? You embarrass me when you encourage a grown man to talk like that. This is why our son talks the way he does!"

After the show, Rodney said, "I would love to meet your parents. Bring them up to the dressing room."

My dad had to go to bed because he wanted to get up for the free breakfast, so I took my mom. I knocked on the dressing-room door and Rodney opened the door wearing a silk robe with a playing-card design on the fabric.

But who would even notice the playing cards? Rodney's robe was wide open; you could see his dick and what looked like two old punching bags swinging between his knees. His hair was all messed up, his eyes were fire-engine red, but that was probably due to the big fat joint hanging from his mouth.

However, Rodney acted as if he were dressed in a tux and meeting the Queen of England. He smiled and offered my mom his hand—the same one that had probably scratched his balls just two seconds before he opened the door.

"You must be Bob's mom," Rodney said. Then he added, "Where's your husband?"

My mom said, "Oh, he went to bed."

Rodney, in his best Rodney voice, said, "So what are you doing later, baby?"

Rodney, a joint in his mouth and his balls nearly touching the floor, flirted with my mom.

A few weeks later, I remember hearing my mom on the phone, telling her friend how big Rodney's *schmeckle* was.

A LOST LOVE

✳ Jay Leno

Back in the early 1970s, before I was married, I met this girl at a nightclub in New York. We went out a few times. One night she said, "We'll go to my place. My roommate won't be home tonight."

So I said, "Fine," and we went back to her place. As she'd done every other time, she asked me to tie her to the bed.

Up to this point, I'd always refused; this was partially because I'd never done well with knots, even failing the Boy Scout badge test. There was no way I could call my old scoutmaster. "Hey, Mr. Strickland. It's Jay Leno. This girl wants me to tie her to the bed. What knot should I use? A 'slippery hitch'? Yeah, that sounds about right for the job. What do you recommend for a mouth gag? A tennis ball? That's not too big? Okay, if you say so. Thanks. And,

Mr. Strickland, I just wanted you to know I never believed what the other kids said about you."

Finally, though, this particular night I agreed to tie her up. And, really, when you come right down to it, if it means having sex, most guys would tie themselves to a crop duster.

A little while later, I looked at the clock and saw it was two-thirty in the morning. I remembered I had to go move my car to the other side of the street because of alternate-side-of-the-street parking regulations for street cleaning. Those cars not moved were towed. Plus, this was New York City. If you tried to stop them from towing you, they'd shoot you and leave you in the street as a warning to others. Maybe the laws have changed, but back then, if you were lying dead in a parking space, you still had to put money in the meter, or they towed your body.

Before I left to move my car, I started to untie the girl, but she said, "Just leave me here, and go move your car."

Despite being tied to a bed and shouting various instructions to me, this woman nonetheless had the presence of mind to realize I needed to hurry if I was to reach the street in time to beat the tow truck.

I said, "Okay," and went downstairs to look for a parking space. This was New York, where parking was never easy, as illustrated so clearly in the movie *Godzilla*. The giant monster attacked Manhattan, the city was evacuated, and yet there was still not a single empty parking space to be found.

After a half hour, I finally found a spot to park. Then I walked back to the woman's building, just in time to realize that I'd forgotten her apartment number and her last name. I felt so stupid! Maybe this was the last-name-optional seventies, but even those first Dutch traders knew that to do business in New York, they had to memorize the Indians' apartment numbers.

Unfortunately, the tied-up woman lived in one of these buildings which you either needed a key to enter, or someone had to buzz you in. I just stood around outside the building, waiting till someone came out. Every time someone did exit, I'd try to sneak in. Of course, it was now about 6:00 A.M., and any tenants exiting the building would get me to back off with a deadly New York "Watch it, pal" stare. Still, I waited for an opportunity to quickly slip inside before any questions were asked. And exactly what was I going to offer in the way of an explanation anyway? "Hey, I left this girl tied up because I had to move my car. Will you let me back in so I can go finish killing her and robbing her place? And maybe I can do you later this afternoon."

Finally, after a couple of hours, I just started hitting buttons until someone was drunk enough, or lonely enough, to buzz me in.

I walked around on floors I thought might be the one she lived on, passed all kinds of doors I thought might be hers, and called out, "Susan? Susan? Susan? Susan?"

Plenty of people in other apartments heard me calling for her. I could here these old people yelling from behind their doors, "Who's out there? What do you want?"

The thought never occurred to me that even if I did beat the odds and found the woman's apartment, there was no chance of her opening the door—because I'd left her tied to her bed.

That's a bridge I never had to worry about because I never came close to crossing it. I continued wandering the halls for what seemed like hours when I decided to abandon my futile efforts and leave. I knew the tied-up woman had a roommate who'd return home soon and be able to free her, a task that was likely not a first.

A week later a woman approached me at a club and said, "Jay, I'm Susan's roommate."

I said, "Really? She all right?"

The roommate said, "Oh yeah! She didn't get untied till I came home from work that night."

I said, "Oh, I am *so* sorry."

The roommate said, "No. She really wants you to call her. She thought that was like the greatest thing that ever happened!"

Good Advice

✳ **Dave Coulier** I was working PJ's, this crazy strip club in Anchorage, Alaska, in 1983. A heckler lost an exchange with me and threatened me with a gun. As they pulled him away he was still waving the gun and shouting, "I'm gonna shoot your ass." A few minutes later I was offstage and still shaking when the bouncer consoled me with this line: "Unless the bullet actually hits you, you got nothing to worry about."

✳ **Maryellen Hooper** One night I asked this woman seated in the front row, "So, when are you expecting?" She said, "Expecting what?" All I could say was, "When are you expecting ... *to kick my ass?*" I learned my lesson. I don't care if I see a baby's head coming out of a woman, I'm not asking.

✳ **Phyllis Diller** I always told my tech guy to put the spotlight on any hecklers. They're only brave because of the anonymity of yelling at you from the darkness. Once you hit him with a light, the heckler loses all his power. My theory was if you want to be onstage with me, you've got to be lit. Of course, most hecklers were pretty well lit to begin with.

✳ **Bob Saget** Once an off-duty cop jumped on stage at the Punchline in San Francisco and put me in a headlock. I sent him scrambling off the stage when I shoved the mike up his ass. If an audience member grabs you physically, just shove the mike up his ass. It's a piece of metal and it's connected to electricity.

JOKE'S ON ME

✳ Mack Dryden

In 1984 I was working in Houston with Bob Saget and Jim Samuels. Saget and Jim had this gag where they'd make eyes at each other and pretend they were having a torrid affair. They said the most hideous, salacious things to each other. Samuels had these ostrich boots. One night between shows, Bob went into the bathroom. He noticed Samuels's ostrich boots under the next stall.

Saget said, "There's nothing that I'd like better than a nice, warm cock up my ass right now."

And, of course, the other stall was not occupied by Jim Samuels, but instead a cowboy from Houston, who had on the same ostrich boots as Samuels. This Houston cowboy barked, "What'd you say, boy?"

Saget came flying out: "Oh, it's a joke. Just joking, sir."

THE 200-POUND HECKLE

✳ Bob Goldthwait

It's funny when comics talk about being heckled. I learned during my stint as the opening act for the music group Nirvana that heckling can take many different forms.

Before the show in Chicago, a Christian group handed out little

Bibles to all the kids entering the arena. I'm sure the thought was that during musical breaks the kids would thumb through the little Bibles and get religion. It's hard enough to hear God talking when you're alone, sober, and in the woods. But when you're on X and Boone's Farm wine and jammed in with ten thousand screaming fans, all being blasted by lasers and guitars at jet-plane-level decibels, it's impossible to even spell the word *God*.

The Nirvana crowd had already proven they could hit me with M-80s, shoes, and beer-soaked blue jeans. So nailing me with a tiny souvenir Bible was a no-brainer, a perfect match for their mental condition. It didn't matter how the drugs affected their aim, they launched a hundred at a time and easily nailed me in a shotgun-blast pattern. Then they truly set a new standard for heckling when they launched a teenager at me. No amount of comedy-club heckler training could ever have prepared me for the sight of a pie-eyed teenager flying toward me. He struck me square in the back and the crowd roared. I really expected an appearance from the lions.

I don't know what prompted my next joke. It wasn't one of mine, or anyone else's, either, and for good reason. It was probably my primitive self-defense mechanism reaching for any weapon available. In this instance it was the news that Michael Jordan had retired from basketball after his father had been found dead with a gunshot to the head. I blurted out to my new ten thousand worst enemies, "Hey, Chicago, I feel bad for your Michael Jordan, but for forty million dollars a year, I'd shoot my own dad in the head!" It wasn't a joke so much as a mass kick between the legs, a nuclear mutation of the classic "Fire!" shout in a crowded theater.

The noise bursting from that crowd couldn't even be classified as booing. I was rolled over by a tsunami of primitive verbal rage. Clear voices yelling "Kill him!" popped out at me from this wall of fury. The only thing I can compare it to is the chattering birds make when they see a worm they're about to kill.

Security guards placed a towel over my head, rushed me into a waiting van, and drove me to a waiting jet at O'Hare Airport. I remember passing Kurt Cobain, who was watching from the side of the stage. He was laughing his ass off. Of course, he hired me for the rest of the tour. It always paid to make the band laugh.

THE MARK OF A GENIUS

✳ Jackie Martling

Sometime around 1980, I was on the road, making money from a self-produced comedy album. After finding out that I'd produced a comedy album of my own, Jackie Mason got the bug to do his own album, about the upcoming presidential election.

He asked me, Richie Minervini, and Barry Mitchell to help him write the new political stuff. One morning we were sitting in Jackie's second-floor Park Avenue apartment throwing around ideas when I offered a joke or an idea—I wish I could remember what it was—and his eyes lit up.

He looked at me and said, "That's genius. Do you know that's genius? *You* are a genius. What an idea. You, my friend, are a genius."

We were all still pretty new to this whole comedy thing, and this icon was calling me a genius. I was feeling ten feet tall.

A few minutes later, Jackie said, "Let's go to the corner and get some lunch."

We got on the elevator, and the elevator operator took us from the second floor to the lobby.

As we were getting off the elevator, Jackie turned to the elevator operator and said, "Did you just bring us down here? Did you do that? Mister, you are a genius. You, my friend, are a genius."

GET IN THE CAR

✴ Margaret Smith

One night I got a ride from the club to the hotel with some waitress. So she's driving and I noticed her hands on the steering wheel and her knuckles were all swollen and bloody, and there was gauze stuck to 'em.

I said, "Oh, were you in an accident?"

She said, "Nooo. You know, I just got into a fight last week." She told me about beating this girl bloody.

I was just thinking she could drop me off anywhere when she pounded the steering wheel and exploded, "Aawww, Jesus, I passed where I'm supposed to turn in!!!" It was pretty apparent she had an anger problem.

I said, "That's all right. I can get out here and walk back."

"No, you won't. I'll take you!"

I asked her why she beat the girl up.

She said, "'Cuz, you know, she was one of them girls that thinks she's better than everyone else."

I tried to play along and said, "Oh, one of those girls."

"Yeah, one of those."

I think I said, "Well, you know. I'm sure she deserved it."

I didn't know what to say, you know? What am I going to say? Not one of those girls with the self-esteem. Not those bitches.

Not in New York Anymore

✳ **Alonzo Bodden** I was in Beaumont, Texas, probably doubling the black population. While I was onstage, a big redneck was leaning against the bar talking shit, and I just ripped him apart. After the gig, several people congratulated me for ripping this guy. "Just because he runs the Klan, he thinks he's the big man around here." Thank God it was a one-nighter.

✳ **Lew Schneider** My first road gig ever was a one-nighter in Mishiwaka, Indiana. It was a giant bar with a wrestling ring in the middle where we performed. It was me, then Tim Lilly, and finally John Wing. They threw penny firecrackers at Lilly and me. Wing got cherry bombs and M-80s. I think they hated me the most but were saving the heavy ammo for the headliner.

✳ **Conrad Lawrence** I was working this Texas shit-kicking bar in 1989 when this little scrawny guy walks up to the stage, pulls a knife from his pocket, and cuts the mike cord. He turns to the crowd and yells, "Show's over. Let's dance!" The music was playing and people were dancing before I got off the stage.

✳ **Joey Novick** We were three New York comedians in the Deep South, and the directions given to us by the club were, "Go past the Italian restaurant." We drove back and forth for an hour till we realized the "Italian restaurant" was a Pizza Hut.

SHAQ CAN STOP BULLETS

✳ **Carlos Mencia**

Around 1996, Freddie Soto was on The Comedy Store stage and some black guys were making fun of him, heckling him bad. I really liked Freddie. He was young, but you could see he had something. I walked up onstage in the middle of his act, looked at the hecklers, and said, "Listen, he's an amateur—it's amateur night. Be nice. I'll be up here in about three minutes, fuck with me." I left the stage, Freddie finished, and the emcee introduced me.

As I walked to the mike, one of the black guys yelled out, "What are you gonna do? Some of your taco-bender jokes?"

I said, "No, actually I'm gonna do some nigger jokes."

He said, "Whut?!!"

I told him, "Hey, you can't get racial on me and think that I'm not gonna get racial on you. I'm not fucking white, I'm from the ghetto, so if this is what you fuckin' want, let's fuckin' do it."

The audience went with me, so I started picking on them.

It turned out that the hecklers were Dr. Dre, Snoop Dogg, and The D.O.C., who had lost his voice in a car crash. He was one of my favorite artists, so I knew all of his music. He tried overpowering me, but I had the mike and he had this raspy little frog voice. I told him, "So why'd you stop rappin'? You should have used a voice box." I started singing all of his songs as if I had a voice box. I put the mike to my throat and did one of his songs—I think it's called "Torture of a Masterpiece." I had the beat and the words down, and the audience was just going fucking nuts.

Then I hear, "I'm gonna bust a cap in your fuckin' ass," and it was real. It didn't sound funny, it didn't sound like we were kidding, ha-ha. It sounded like, "We're gonna fuckin' shoot you."

I started to get scared, and then from the other side of the room I heard a deep voice: "Naw, you ain't, bitch. You started that shit, view it." I looked over, and there was just this mass of darkness. It was just getting bigger and bigger and bigger. When I finally got to focus, I realized it was Shaq, who then told them to shut the fuck up.

I sort of crept over to Shaq's side of the stage. I wasn't stupid enough to nail the guys anymore. I just did a couple of quick ha-ha jokes and it was time for "Thank you and good night."

Like five years later, Dr. Dre was at The Comedy Store. He came up to me and said, "You're incredible. You're one of the funniest guys out there. I also want to apologize because we were gonna shoot you that night. If Shaq hadn't stepped in, you were gonna get shot."

I didn't know what to say. The man complimented me, but then said Shaq was the only thing that had kept me from getting shot onstage.

That's when I realized that jokes can be some powerful shit. Not as powerful as Shaq, but enough to get your ass shot.

A TIP FROM BOB HOPE

✳ Dan Bradley (as told to Jason Dixon)

This story, dating back to 1981, was told to me by Dan Bradley, who died in 2001.

Dan had just started his comedy career and was working as a bellman at a prestigious hotel in Minneapolis. Dan learned that Bob

Hope, his comedic hero, was coming to town, and arranged to be the one who picked up Mr. Hope at the airport.

Bob traveled with a masseuse and a ton of gear. Dan made two trips in a cargo van before Bob settled into his suite. Dan had dealt with a few arrogant and unapproachable stars, so he was happily surprised by Bob Hope's talkative, friendly nature.

Not only did Dan move all of Bob's luggage, he also ran a few errands for the star. He definitely anticipated a huge tip when at the end of the day he said, "Well, ya know, if there's not going to be anything else, I *do* need to be going along." Bob Hope knew what Dan was intimating and palmed Dan some money. "Here, kid, that's for you."

Not wanting to appear greedy, Dan shoved the money into his pocket without looking to see how much it was. As soon as Hope had closed his hotel room door, Dan looked at the tightly folded money and noted that it was a five-dollar bill. All Dan's good thoughts about this comedy legend disappeared faster than a gallon of Hope's Texaco gasoline in a speeding Cadillac.

All the way to his pitiful piece-of-shit car, Dan cursed Bob Hope.

Dan remembered seeing a TV special featuring Bob Hope's mansion, which resembled a James Bond–type villa, yet Hope had given him only a measly five dollars for a full day's work! Dan had envisioned a generous tip that would pay his rent and save him from eviction. A five-dollar tip wasn't even going to buy enough beer to get Dan drunk enough to forget his hero had just stiffed, stuck, and stabbed him.

However, when it came to forgetting ream jobs, a hazy blur was better than a clear memory, so Dan stopped to buy a six-pack of beer. Withdrawing the Hope tip from his pocket, Dan noticed it was not only doubled up, but very thick. Opening the folded five-dollar bill, Dan discovered three $100 bills. Immediately he felt remorseful about his unkind thoughts.

The next morning Dan went into work. Bob Hope was in the

foyer practicing his putting. As soon as he spotted Dan, Bob lit up. "I got you! I got you, kid! Man, I bet you were cussing me up one side and down the other!"

Dan thanked him for the tip and said, "I didn't want to tell you this yesterday, but I'm an aspiring standup comic. Can you give a guy who's just starting out any advice?"

Hope putted the ball and said, "Don't fuck the waitresses."

Dan blurted out *What?* He was completely confused, having heard that for a comedy club waitress to fuck a comic was a sign he was actually funny.

Hope lined up another putt and explained, "Don't fuck the waitresses. You see, kid, there are two kinds of comics: There's the kind who work on their act and the kind who work on the waitresses. The kind who work on the waitresses are *never* going to be comics. But the kind who work on their act, at some point, get to fuck *all* the waitresses they want."

ONLY SUPERMAN ONSTAGE

✳ Daniel Tosh

In 2002, I emceed a Battle of the Bands at a college in Lakeview, Florida. I thought it would be fun, kind of like *American Idol*, and I could make fun of each band a little bit after it had performed.

What I didn't realize was that the only people who showed up at these things were friends of the people performing. They don't want to hear some stranger belittle their friends right after they've performed.

The show was going on and we were having a good time. Then

some guy really just went into me, heckling and screaming at me. So I went right back into him. He wouldn't quit, so I had them turn the houselights up and offered him a microphone if he wanted to continue. It wasn't a fun exchange, like in a comedy club. This was pretty angry and violent.

He said, "Who the fuck do you think you are?" I was just like, "I'm the guy who they're paying a lot of money to make fun of your friend's shitty band."

Onstage, a comedian can be fearless. You get all that laughter from so many people and start to feel superhuman, invincible. So I didn't hesitate before I said something like, "I'll kill you and all your friends." I was so drunk with thoughts of immortality that it never occurred to me somebody out there might be saying, "Okay. We're gonna wait outside for this guy afterwards."

Sure enough, the show ended and I was walking outside to the car with my little college-girl student sponsor, who noticed very quickly that, "Hey, there's that guy." And there was the heckler with a crew of guys. He was probably about fifty yards away from me, screaming, "Come on, let's fight, motherfucker!" I yelled back, "Oh, no. I'm busy," and told the student, "Okay, let's go to the car. Now. Quickly." The entire group started running toward us. And that's when I transformed from the powerful comic to the scared little pussy who had needed to become a comic in the first place.

Seconds after we took off, they were on our bumper, and I realized that the student was driving me to my hotel and got a big dose of pure fear. "Hey, you *do* know these guys are really trying to kill me, right?" She kept right on driving the speed limit, straight to my hotel. Suddenly this carload of guys pulled into the lane next to us, screaming for us to pull over. She began to realize that maybe something unusual was happening. "What are we going to do?"

"Well, for starters, we're not going to pull over."

Then the guy who wanted to kill me waved a gun out of his window, and she still stopped at the next red light.

By now I'd stopped trying to look cool and was just yelling at her, "Run the light! They're pointing a *gun* at us!" And she said, "No. I could get a ticket." I was trying to enlighten her: "Yes. Yes. We *want* police now."

Finally she got it, ran the light, and started speeding and ducking into backroads trying to lose them. After watching this fresh-faced college girl turn from law-abiding citizen to demonic driver, I'm convinced everyone has the ability to lead a high-speed chase, given the proper motivation.

I guess the heckler and his posse were pretty motivated, because they stayed right with us. Suddenly my driver screeched to a halt in front of my hotel and smiled at me like, "We made it." Meanwhile, they were pulling up right behind us, and I started yelling, "Go! Go!" Finally I called 911 from my cell. Conscious of the fact that they play those recordings back, I was trying not to act too scared. "Oh, yes. Hi. Well, you see, we seem to have some crazies driving next to us with a gun. We really could use your help. We're going to stay in the car just driving around until a cop intercepts us." And that's what happened—a patrol car showed up, my pursuers took off, and another cop went and followed them. I said, "That's it. I'm not staying at that hotel." The 911 operator said, "Yeah, the cop just found them circling your hotel."

When I got into the police car, the college girl reacted just as if we'd driven back to the hotel from having a tuna melt, instead of being chased there by gun-toting lunatics. She just smiled at me and said, "Okay, it was nice meeting you. Hopefully you can come back next year."

So I had a police escort take me to the hotel and go up to my room with me and pack all my stuff. I even got a police escort back to the freeway, where I drove to my brother's house in Orlando. And I curled up in bed with him and cried. For the next six months, all hecklers got from me was a smile, "God bless you," and the next joke.

Leave the Folks at Home

✳ **Carrie Snow** My parents were in the audience one night when I had this big old truck driver heckling me. I told him to stand up and show me his rig. He did. Even through all the laughter I heard my mother say, "Oy, vey."

✳ **David Feldman** I was middling at the Tropicana in Atlantic City in 1997. After the show my mother came backstage and said to me, "This was worse than Daddy's funeral. Daddy's funeral I understood. He had been sick. His death made sense to me. This I could not comprehend. I don't know who was in the crowd. I don't know why they hated you so much. I don't know what you did to deserve this. Why, God, why?" Only my mother could take a bad set in a crappy casino lounge to such biblical proportions.

✳ **Joan Rivers** When I first started, I talked onstage about being single and my bad dates. I could hear my mother in the audience talking to people near her: "It's absolutely not true. She never dated a married professor. No, no, no, no, no. She had plenty of dates."

✳ **The Sklar Brothers** We came back to our hometown, St. Louis, from L.A. and brought our parents to see us perform. The emcee started our introduction, "These next guys are here all the way from L.A. . . ." A drunken woman in stretch stirrup pants yelled, "Fags!" She still holds the record for our quickest heckler.

BLAME THEM FOR MY FUNNY

✳ Bob Marley

Once I brought my parents with me on the road to Martha's Vineyard, to work a gig at this good blues club, the Hot Tin Roof, owned by Carly Simon.

So we're driving down there from Maine. My dad's sitting in the front seat, and my mother's in the back, complaining the whole way, "I'm hungry. Are you hungry? I'm hungry. Who's hungry? I'm hungry. You hungry?"

My dad says to me, "Will you do something about this?" He points to the backseat like my mom's the "this." It's not "her," "your mother," or "my wife," it's "this." She's a situation to him, like a flat tire.

My mother sees Dunkin' Donuts. "Dunkin' Donuts. Donuts? Dunkin' Donuts. Donuts? Dunkin' Donuts." She just repeats the phrase, like a small animal might if it had the power of speech.

My dad goes, "Okay, we're fucking going to Dunkin' Donuts."

I get her a couple of muffins. But when we finally get on the boat for Martha's Vineyard, my mother's off again. "I'm hungry. You hungry? Hungry?" I'm in hell, an hour from show time and as far away from funny as you can be.

She sees a snack bar on the boat. "Oh, a snack bar, they have clam chowder. Oh, I love clam chowder. Love it, love it, mmm, mmmm, love it."

My dad looks at me and says, "There she goes, spend, spend, spend. Puts us in the fucking poorhouse." I'm thinking, *Do you really think the clam chowder's gonna break you?*

So then she eats three bowls of clam chowder in a forty-five-minute boat ride. We get off the boat and we're walking down the wharf. This representative from the club, holding one of my eight-by-ten promo pictures, greets me and we all start off for the hotel. From behind, all I hear is, "Oh, oh, sweet Jesus, no."

My dad doesn't even turn around, he just says, "Well, here it comes."

I turn around and my mother is straddling one of the benches on the wharf. She's not sitting. She's not standing. She's teetering back and forth, like she's jumping high hurdles and got caught. I ask, "What's wrong?"

She says, "Oh, I had the chowder and those muffins and... I think some of those muffins are starting to peek out of my ass."

My dad yells, "What!?"

She goes, "They're peeking out of my ass."

My dad says, "Well, get off the bench and walk across the street to the hotel."

She's still rocking back and forth on the bench, moaning, "I can't get off this bench, there'll be a big surprise." We just watch her.

She then says, "I feel greasy."

My dad barks, "You feel what?"

She repeats, "I feel greasy."

My dad is all sympathy. "You can feel upset, you can feel tired, but you cannot feel a viscosity." That's what he said, "a viscosity," like she's motor oil.

So we go to move her, and the person from the club is looking at us like, *What the fuck is going on? Who are these people?*

Sure enough, as soon as we get her off the bench, she shits her pants, all over the wharf on Martha's Vineyard. I wish to God that were the end of the story.

Of course, my parents come to the show. I get up onstage and start my act, and my dad's sitting there waving at me. I'm making believe I don't even see him. I'm just looking away, pretending, *Okay, I don't see him, I don't see him.* Finally he yells, "Hey, hey boy."

I try to act as if he's just another audience member I've never met. "Yes, sir?"

He says, " 'Sir'? Who the hell's 'sir'?"

I finally break down and acknowledge him. "Hey, Dad. How are you?"

He says, loud enough for the whole audience to hear, "This stuff's not funny. You want something funny? Tell 'em how your mother shit her pants today on the wharf."

SOMETHING I SAID?

✳ Jerry Seinfeld

This story happened in 1979 while I was onstage at Catch a Rising Star in New York City. With its bare floors, hard walls, and poor air-conditioning, almost any sound became a distraction at Catch. The only noise comedians tolerated was the urgent pleading of a fellow comic trying to convince a waitress to go home with him.

Five minutes into my set, I heard a guy in the audience talking loudly, trying to be funny or to entertain the other people at his table. I've never quite understood why people go to comedy clubs and try to be funnier than the comedian. In my fifty-plus years, I don't think I ever heard a loud talker say anything helpful or informative.

When someone in the audience talked during my act, my solution was to stop talking, a technique I learned from my schoolteachers. So I just stopped talking and the rest of the room followed my lead and looked at the disturbance. A normal person usually became very uncomfortable at suddenly becoming the center of attention and stopped talking. It didn't work for me that night.

So I stopped waiting for him to shut up, and went on with my act. Then a drink glass, one of those thick, sixteen-ounce tumblers, whizzed past my head and shattered against the brick wall behind me. It was like one of those western movies where the guy throws a bottle at the mirror behind the bar and shatters all the glass. Everybody froze and just watched the two of us. Actually, more people had their eyes on him than on me, since he was a proven lunatic.

When someone throws a glass at your head, they can't even lie about it afterward. What can they say, "These glasses sure are slippery"? At least at Jewish weddings, the groom steps on the glass, rather than throwing it at fifty miles an hour at the rabbi's head.

I froze onstage, not out of fear, but from anger. That was stupid of me, because regardless of my mood, lots of motion would have been a better strategy to cope with my transition from comedian to target. For a long minute I just held the stage, looking forward to seeing this guy tossed out of the club.

About a minute later, the emcee came up on the stage and said, "Jerry, come on, let's go! You gotta get off!"

I said, "Me? I'm not going anywhere! Why the hell do I have to get off?"

Then the audience got into it. "Throw that guy out! Don't throw Jerry out—throw the guy out!"

The dispute went back and forth, but the emcee was adamant. He said, "Come on, Jerry! Let's just go! Get off the stage!" This was quite a change from the usual, "How about a hand for Jerry Seinfeld, folks?"

Maybe it was the absolute fear in the emcee's eyes and the panicked cracking of his voice that finally convinced me to get off the stage. Anyway, there certainly was no way I was getting the act back on track, so I just shrugged and walked off.

The audience was still applauding for me while the club's bouncer and bartender hustled me out of the club and around the block.

I said, "What the hell is going on here? This guy throws a glass and I get thrown out! If he throws a table, does he get to manage the club?"

It was then explained to me that the glass-thrower was a gangster, a hit man for the mob. Nobody wanted to throw *him* out, so I had to go.

A few months later, Joe Piscopo dealt with the same guy from the Catch stage. The thug grabbed Joe and broke his nose. A few hours later Joe returned from the hospital with his face all bandaged up, only to find this mobster still sitting in his seat enjoying the show.

I went on to have a TV show. Joe starred on *Saturday Night Live*. Obviously, this guy had an eye for talent.

NO LOVE FROM A LLAMA

✳ John Bowman

Back in '89, this friend of mine set me up on a blind date. He said we had a lot in common. Actually what he said was, "Dude, she's just like you but with tits." As terrible as that sounded, I called her anyway. What we had in common was we were both desperate enough to trust my pal Eric the Fucking Surfer.

She asked that we meet in public, which indicated that the

kind of dates she'd experienced tended to need witnesses for the after-date litigation.

We decided to meet at the zoo. The first thing in the zoo was a petting zoo, and the first animal we encountered was a llama. I didn't know that the llama's defense mechanism involved a stomach designed solely to collect bile. When the beast is threatened, it just fills up its throat with this toxic goo and spits it at whatever offends it.

I had a reasonable expectation that at the zoo I would see some dangerous and unfamiliar animals, but protected by a fence, a moat, or at least some plastic sheeting. There might be a thing where you put in a quarter to look at them from a safe distance. I certainly wasn't worried about the animals in the petting zoo.

So I had no fear when this llama ran to this little three-foot-high fence, made eye contact with me, and started to make a gurgling sound in its throat. Its lips were moving. Trying to be funny for my date, I said, "That llama wants a kiss."

She said, "Oh look, he's puckering up his lips."

I started mimicking the llama's lip movements and throat sound. Which of course in llama language meant, "Let's throw down, bitch."

I found out later he had not attacked anyone in eight years. What that meant was he had accumulated eight years of bile waiting for one stupid motherfucker to walk up there and go "Oooo" back to him.

So I kept getting closer. The girl was laughing. I was thinking this was the perfect start to the date; she was enjoying the only side of my personality that is at all desirable.

I found out later that the llama could have nailed me from a hundred yards away. But I turned it into a slam-dunk contest by getting about two feet from the fence and doing a funny little cabbage-patch dance. I kind of remember my last words were, "I'm turning him on."

It was like one of those terrible accidents when you see everything in slow motion. I actually saw something coming for my face, and instead of a decent defensive reaction, like closing my mouth and eyes or turning away, I went slack-jawed and wide-eyed. The bile not only filled my eyeballs but shot down my throat. It lifted me off my feet. I landed on my back, completely blinded, choking and vomiting. What followed was a smell that I still can't describe. I would have huffed a skunk's ass to get away from that llama stink. A week later I noticed that flies still buzzed around my head.

As I was lying on the ground, somebody said to my date, "Did the llama attack your husband?"

Her response was, "He ain't my fucking husband."

She had already abandoned me. Gone was the five minutes of llama-inspired laughter we'd shared. They took me to the zoo vet to swab out my eyes, so she was forced to give me a ride home. She said that the smell was making her ill. I had to ride all the way back with my head out the window, my ears flapping in the wind like a dog—a blinded, stinking, unwanted mutt taking its final trip to the pound. She didn't really stop to let me out; I had to jump from a still-moving car.

I had to go onstage that night. My whole face was red. My eyes were swollen half shut. I stunk so bad when I entered the bar, the waitresses yelled en masse, "You gotta go stand over there."

I spent the whole next day washing my hair with tomato juice. It supposedly works for skunk stink but only enlivens llama fumes.

Comics love things like this because it turns into material, and for eight years the Llama Stink bit owned fifteen minutes of my act. But if given the choice, I would rather have been ass-raped by backwoodsmen or lost a leg to a shark as fodder for new material than what I endured to get the llama jokes. Even now, the memory of it instantly turns my stomach and fills me with the pain of having lost a chance at love—or at least some decent road pussy.

Payday

✳ **Billy Riback** After a show the owner said, "I gotta pay you in cocaine." He flashed it to me and said, "There's much more than the $250 in here." I said, "I will not be able to walk into Ralph's or Von's, or whatever grocery store I use, and say, 'I'd like the veal chops; here's some coke.' Give me the cash or I call the police." I got the cash.

✳ **Greg Otto** After my show at a Texas club, the owner came over to pay me and said, "You're making $1,300, right?" I told him, "No, $1,500." He said, "Well, I gave it a shot."

✳ **Jeff Garland** My best stiffing ever was in East Lansing, Michigan. After the first night, the club owner told me he was sending me home without pay. Then he asked me where I played in Chicago. "If I'm ever in town, I'd love to see you perform. You're not right for my audience, but I think you're funny."

✳ **Dick Martin** In the 1950s, there was a guy named Red Andrews who ran the Riverside Club in Casper, Wyoming. After the show, we were in the office to get paid. Red was on one knee, putting cash away in his safe, and said, "I'll send you a check." Sure, like we'd be taking the stagecoach back to Wyoming after the check bounced. My partner, Dan Rowan, put his foot on Red's head, pinning it to the top of the safe, and said, "No, we want the cash now." He kept his foot on Red's head until Red finished counting out our cash.

ALABAMA WAITRESS

✳ Barry Marder

Sometime in the 1980s I was working at a comedy club in Birmingham, Alabama. I think the name of the club was The Laugh Bag. Or it could have been Gasps. It didn't matter. I was just another comedian, a Jewish Willy Loman, schlepping his bag of jokes from bar to bar. I still had some physique in those days and was down to a normal weight. Now I'm heavy. The last shirt I bought was an XXL. I thought to myself, "my God, I'm up to Roman numerals already. The next size for me will be XXLCVM."

I had my eye on this sexy waitress who worked at the club. All week we were flirting with each other. Lots of winking. I had to have sex with her. Ask any comic on the road: By the third day in any club you want to have sex with the waitresses. I wanted to get into her pants. (Today I can't even get into my own pants. So why would I want to get into anyone else's pants?)

I hung around this waitress a lot. She said "You're not gonna stalk me, are you?" I said, "Stalk you?! I don't even have enough energy to run my own errands. Do you think I want to figure out what you're doing all day and show up there?" We continued to wink at each other a lot. (Actually, she thought I was winking at her a lot. I explained I had conjunctivitis.)

I think her name was Ruth Anne. Or Ann Ruth. Or Otto. She told me she was depressed about her father and looking forward to a wild weekend, wanted to have some fun. She said her father had diabetes and had to have part of his foot removed. I said, "Tell him, don't be a pessimist. Be an optimist. Look at the shoe as half full.

Don't sweat the petty stuff." Or was it don't pet the sweaty stuff? Whatever it was I told her something.

Saturday night I waited for her in my car like a disgusting creep in a comedy club parking lot. I think the name of the place was Tickle My Balls. Or maybe it was The Laugh Sphincter. Or it could have been The Belly Spoonge.

I was ready for a night of amour. I'd even gone to a bakery and brought a nice dessert for our after-sex celebration. Yum.

She got in my car. I had use of the comedy club car for the week. And if you know the comedy club cars used by comedians—well, let me just tell you this—they are *filthy*. There's so much sex and porn left over from last week's headliner that you could actually register the car as a sex offender. I once saw a cockroach commit suicide on the dash. He pulled out a tiny rope and hung himself from the air freshener.

By now I was hotter than a Pepsi from a hotel vending machine. I had to have this woman. I think her name was Sally Ann or Lisa Lou or Spoongy. She had hair coming through her shirt. I remember that.

Yes, the hotel room was filthy. All comedy club hotel rooms are filthy. The first thing I did when we got to the room was shoot the comforter. Hey, it moved! I emptied my gun into it.

I remember the outfit she had on. Black panties and a T-shirt that said Aloha Ha's. Or maybe it said The Chortle Guffaw. I wore a crotchless Burger King outfit.

We made glorious love. Every position imaginable. I was going at it for a good forty-five minutes, really getting into a steady rhythm. I said, "Honey, you are so moist tonight." And she said, "You fell onto the rum cake twenty minutes ago." (Mess-eee!)

When we were done we just laid there in bed, like two complete lovers. (Or a dog and a shoe.) As was required by the Rules of Road Love, now that we'd had sex, I was required to find out who she was. So I asked her about her life and she said her father was a racist, a bigot, and hated everybody. I said, "What would your father do if he found out you made love to a black man?" She said, "Oh, Barry, he would kill me. He would just take me out by the barn and shoot me dead." I said, "What would your father do if he found out you made love to a Jew?" She said, "He would kill the Jew."

That's why you don't ask who the person is until after the sex.

THE PISSED-OFF PIRATE AND ME

✳ Cathryn Michon

The first time I did standup was a lot like the first time I had sex: it was painful, it was over a lot faster than I expected, and I was anxious to try it again so I could finally understand what all the fuss was about.

Being a woman doing standup means you're constantly thrusting yourself into a position where no matter what you do, the people watching would like you better if you just took your shirt off. Well, to be more precise, half the audience would like you better if you took your shirt off. The other half doesn't understand what someone so skinny and blond has to complain about.

The brilliant writer Samuel Johnson said, "A woman preaching is like a dog walking on his hind legs; it is not done well, but you are surprised to find it done at all."

Clearly, what this teaches us is that Samuel Johnson was a dick.

His point is well taken, however. Standup's a lot like preaching, and there are very few people, men or women, who enjoy being preached at by a woman. This is because, for most people, the first person who ever preached at them was a woman. Most likely that woman was the one who made them feel bad about crapping their pants, which, up until her bossy interference, had been rather a convenient system. And they still resent it, and her, and anyone who reminds them of her.

Thus, as you see, the entire human race is programmed to heckle women comics. Or that's how it often feels to me, anyway.

Generally people go to comedy clubs to hear bitter white guys complain about their penises, because what could be more delightful? Sometimes they like to hear a bitter black guy brag about his penis. On rare occasions, they'd like to hear from a bitter guy who's, say, half-Irish and half-Chinese talk about how he gets really drunk and then an hour later he's sober again, and then have him complain about his penis.

All this reminds me of an excruciating gig I had once in Cleveland, where I had to follow a guy who received a spontaneous standing ovation for a joke called "The Pissed-off Pirate." Since my mom always reads any book I write or am featured in, I'll have to euphemistically synopsize the joke: it was a description of this comic's favorite sex game, which he called "Pissed-off Pirate" and which involved enticing your beloved to perform an act of presidential-level satisfaction on you, and then at the penultimate moment removing oneself from the dental cavity and aiming at her eyes while simultaneously kicking her in the knee, thus causing her to clutch her eye and hop one-legged around the bedroom like, well, a pissed-off pirate.

After he told this charming joke, I got up to do some material about how women sometimes have low self-esteem. When the audience didn't actually rip me limb from limb, I counted it a major victory.

IS SHE STILL DRUNK?

✳ Alex Cole

I went into show business in about '78. My childhood friend Mike was laying asphalt at the time—hardworking guy, long hair, Fu Manchu. He came with me on a tour of Illinois one-nighters and nooners. I had a big La-Z-Boy chair mounted in my van. Mike stayed drunk in that easy chair for the whole two weeks.

One night we were drinking in Chicago when we heard of a bar that served alcohol till four o'clock in the morning. We headed over to find an ugly bar in a nasty section of town, packed with young drunks trying to hold off the hangover.

Right before closing time I saw Mike with this equally trashed chick. They were just hanging on each other and laughing. I couldn't understand them, so I just whispered to Mike, "Hey, you got to dump the girl 'cause I have a noon show in Quincy tomorrow and we got to get some sleep. I'll go pull up the van."

I pulled up the van, and as soon as the door opened the girl piled in and Mike was right behind her. After that, it was three young drunk people in a cheap motel room in pre-AIDS America— you connect the genitals.

I woke up naked on the floor, with a mouthful of small dead furry animals. I kicked Mike. "Hey, get up. We got to drop her off where she lives and get to the show." Mike went into the bathroom and the girl woke up and smiled at me with hair in her face. I said to her, "Hon, I'll drop you off at home. Me and Mike got to go. Where do you live?" She babbled incoherently and laughed, making no sense.

I went into the bathroom and told Mike, "That chick can't talk." Mike said, "Bullshit." He started talking to her, then he looked at me and said, "She's retarded."

The night before, all three of us were retarded. The difference was the next morning two of us sobered up.

So we got her in the van and started heading out of town, and Mike said, "Well, we can't take her to the gig. What the hell do we do with her?" I said, "She looks Italian; let's drop her in Little Italy." We pulled over to a corner and Mike told her, "Hey, go check that pay phone for change." The girl got out and we slammed the door and took off. We made the gig by noon.

That's a terrible story that I'm going to burn in hell for. I do like telling it, plus she was a terrific lay.

POKER FLATS DID JUST THAT

✴ Marcie Smolin

So I get a call from a booker. "I have this great gig for you. It's a resort, swimming, horseback riding, a spa. It'll be like a mini-vacation." I'd be the middle act on the mini-vacation gig, along with Jason Stuart, the headliner, and Claudia Lonow as the opening act. Jason Stuart is a very out gay comic; I, following the trend of the time, was sporting Madonna-style lingerie onstage; Claudia's big closing bit was a Jewish-girl rap. The three of us were definitely colorful.

We drive up to the resort, called Poker Flats. The lake for

swimming consists of an oil slick with one old moldy duck gasping for air, the horseback riding is actually done on an ancient mule, and I don't want to know what the spa was.

We check into our rooms and notice bullet holes in the doors of two of our rooms. We should have left then.

We go down to do the show. There are no women in the audience, and all of the men look like members of ZZ Top.

So Claudia's onstage doing her set when suddenly one of the guys in the audience stands up and yells, "Whoooeee, I'm in the mood to kill me a Jew." I go over to the manager and mention that he should perhaps go deal with that, and he says, "Well, little missy, I can't do that, he's the warden of the state prison."

I get onstage, and they assume I'm a stripper and start yelling, "Take it off...take it off." I somehow finish my act with all my clothes on.

Jason takes the stage and suddenly they're just silent. It's almost as if they're all stunned by their first contact with a real live gay man.

After the show I go to the ladies' room in the lobby. As I come out, two guys from the audience come up to me and say, "We really liked your show. We want to show you how much." At which point they unzip their pants and expose themselves to me.

I run and find Claudia and we go to talk to the manager of the club. We tell him what happened and he says, "Oh yeah, I should have told you girls to stay away from the ladies' room. We've been having a little problem with rapes in there."

Later we decide to go sit outside by the poolside bar. We're on our way out when the manager stops us and says, "You may not want to sit out there. We've been having a little problem with stabbings."

So we go to our respective rooms, but apparently the front desk has given out our room numbers and people start banging on our doors. The three of us spend the night huddled in one room, with all the furniture barricaded against the door, which, if you remember, had several bullet holes in it.

After a long night, we venture outside and call the booker to complain. He tells us that if we don't do our show that night, he won't pay us for the previous night. None of us can afford to walk away from the money. So, before the show, we pack the car and park it behind the back door to the stage.

Claudia and I get the same sort of Kill Jews/Stripper heckles as the first night. And this time they're ready for Jason, too. With the place quickly getting the vibe of a Nazi bonfire rally, Claudia and I run to the car, turn on the engine, and honk. Jason literally dashes off the stage, jumps straight into the car, and we speed out of town with crazy ZZ Top zombies taking off after us.

It was definitely a "mini-vacation."

FUNNY GOES TO THE FRONT OF THE LINE

✳ Brant von Hoffman

It was like 1979. Larry David called me up to go to a Yankees game. He said, "When you get there, don't buy the tickets until I show up. Just wait for me."

When I got there, it was a very short line to buy tickets. I stood there for a while waiting for Larry, watching the line grow longer. By the time he showed, the line was a mile long. I was pissed at him, but he said, "Don't worry, I can get right to the front of the line. I do a thing that, well, I don't do it often, but I can act retarded."

Larry wasn't bald yet; he had curly hair that went straight out, a style comedian Freddy Roman referred to as the "Jew-fro." He was wearing these round glasses and an old army jacket.

All of a sudden he sort of hunched over and changed his walk as he went to the front of the line. Right in front of the ticket booth, the next people in line to get their tickets were a quartet of couples who put the "yup" in yuppie. Larry lumbered to the ticket booth right past this patch of happily chattering, yellow Lacoste sweaters. One of them must have said something, because Larry turned around and gave them this look, the strangest mix of stupidity and psychosis. They moved back and started talking among themselves, I guess hoping Larry would just buy his tickets and not attack or drool on them.

Larry got the tickets, shot them one more look, and shambled toward the gate. I stood away from him until the last minute, when he slipped me my ticket and we entered the stadium.

I'M THE MOTHERFUCKING MAN

✳ Chris Rock

I got this gig in Chicago back in my first year of *Saturday Night Live*, when I wasn't married. As soon as I got off the plane, it felt like one of these promoter gigs, where *someone* was making money, but it wasn't me.

This guy who was waiting for me at the airport said, "Hey, man, welcome to Chicago. Whatever you want, don't worry about it. I can get you anything you need. You want to get high, I can get you that. You want some girls, I can get you that. You want to go to a club, I can get you into any club. I'm the motherfucking man in Chicago. I'll get you whatever the fuck you need, because I'm the mother-fucking man in Chicago."

This guy checked me into the hotel. He had the key to my room, and he checked me in and everything was kind of smooth. I had nothing to do that night because my gig wasn't till the next evening, so he said, "Okay, you take a little nap, and I'll come back and get you at around eight. We're going to go have something to eat, and then we're going to hit some clubs. And it's going to be hot, because I'm the motherfucking man in Chicago."

So we went out to eat, then went to a couple clubs. There weren't any girls after me, because Chicago has a baseball team, a football team, and a basketball team. Any town with sports teams meant I wasn't getting laid. Not by the good pussy, anyway.

We were at this one club, and we were checking out these two girls in the distance.

"Hey, you want me to go get those girls?" the guy said.

I said, "Whatever."

He said, "I'm going to get them girls. You know why? Because I'm the motherfucking man in Chicago."

So he walked over to these girls and said something to them. I have no idea what he said. He came back and told me, "You're going to see them bitches later. We've got about two more clubs to hit. Don't worry about it! I'm the motherfucking man in Chicago."

We went to about two more clubs, but no girls were talking to me. They were all after whoever the fuck was playing ball at that time or whoever was the local Chicago rapper. Those bastards were all getting laid, but I was just Pookie from New Jack City—only local crackheads were attracted to me.

But at the end of the night when the guy was dropping me off at the hotel, who was there waiting but those two girls.

"Ahh! I told you them bitches would be here. That's right. Like I told you, I'm the motherfucking man in Chicago."

We went up to the room and hung out, just the girls and me. The next thing I knew, I was fucking two girls—one was balling me and one was sitting on my face. I couldn't fucking believe it. I was thinking, *That guy* is *the motherfucking man in Chicago! That big, fat, Don King-looking motherfucker* is *the motherfucking man in Chicago!*

While I was fucking both these girls, I heard the fucking door jiggling. I was thinking it was room service.

I had forgotten that the Motherfucking Man in Chicago had my room key. So the door opened and this big, fat motherfucker came in and grabbed one of the girls. "Hey, it's my turn!" he said.

The girl started blowing him right next to me. I thought, "This is the most disgusting thing!" I couldn't fucking believe it. My dick shriveled up.

Then he came on her face. It was the worst shit ever.

The three of them left, I assumed to do cocaine or whatever. I drew the line at coke. I would have a few joints, but I wasn't cokey.

At about three in the morning I was getting ready to go to sleep when I heard a knock on the door. I looked through the peephole, and it was the girls. I thought, "Ah, maybe they left something."

I opened up the door and said, "Hey, what's up?"

One of the girls said, "Where's your man Rodney?"

I said, "Hunh, who's Rodney? Oooooh, *that's* his name? I don't know where he is."

"Where's your motherfucking man Rodney? He said you was his motherfucking friend."

"I don't know."

One of the girls said, "Rodney told me you was going to give us a thousand dollars. You was gonna give both of us five hundred apiece! We're not leaving until we get our motherfucking money. I don't give a motherfuck."

This was the sweet girl who'd seemed so into blowing me just a few fucking hours ago.

She said, "You don't pay me, I'll yell rape out this motherfucking window. You'll go to jail, motherfucker. I don't give a fuck! Fuck this shit! I'm from Cabrini-Green, motherfucker! I ain't right in the head!"

All I could think was, "What the *fuck* is going on?" I was just panicked out of my mind. I ran downstairs and tried to call Rodney, but of course he was nowhere to be found.

Eventually I got $300 out of my agent. I said to the girls, "Here! Take it." I handed them the $300. Sweet girls that they were, they left after that.

I think that was the last time I went to Chicago.

A NIGHT AT THE PRECINCT

✳ **Brett Butler**

In 1984, I was the middle act for John Fox in Lexington, Kentucky. After the show, John was going out with the club manager, a third-rate Linda Evans, a poor man's Jane Fonda. She had that aerodynamically shaped hair; it looked like a good gust of wind might lift the little woman off the ground. I was about forty-five days off alcohol and drugs. So there was no way I was going out with John, who at the time was moonlighting as Satan's drug taster.

After the show I stopped by the store, where I bought a box of Wheat Chex and a quart of milk. John and the manager drove me back to the condo, where they handed me the keys to the front door before kicking me to the curb. Off they went to distract each other from life's miseries. In the throes of my detox, I preferred that explanation for their activities rather than "fucking each other's brains out."

I climbed the steps—just a long enough walk for them to drive out of shouting distance—and quickly discovered that the keys didn't work. It was the dawn of the cell-phone era, where only world leaders, Hollywood agents, and Colombian drug lords carried those fifteen-pound, gasoline-powered phones. There was no way for me to get in touch with John.

There I was, standing outside a condo on the outskirts of Lexington, Kentucky, at two in the morning with no money. It was the moment when I first realized that I needed to plan my life a bit better.

I carried my little box of cereal and my milk to a phone booth and called the police. They sent a patrol car and brought me to the precinct. The night-shift sergeant didn't even look up from his paperwork, as if providing shelter for a woman and her breakfast food was a normal police function. He told me, "You can sit in this chair, but you gotta go before the shift changes."

I sat down, my cereal and milk in my lap. On the next chair was a case filled with virtually every drug I'd just stopped doing six weeks before. Fortunately, I was just sane enough to realize that even if I wanted to trade my Wheat Chex for the dope, a police station might not be the best place to score.

Just before the 7:00 A.M. shift, the night guy said, "I gotta take you back to that place. You'll be all right; the sun's coming up."

They dropped me off at the condo. I crawled into a ball at the top of the steps and fell asleep, using the box of Wheat Chex as my pillow. An hour later I heard a car door slam and saw John coming up the steps. I looked at him, and his look told me that he realized he'd left me without a key. Instead of an apology I heard, "Oh my God, you need to put a tampon in your ear to suck the blood out of your eyes."

Weird, how it's possible to be that furious at someone and still laugh.

Politically Correct

✳ **Richard Jeni** I was at a club in San Antonio. A big cowboy said, "We never seen a New York Jew." I said, "I'm not a Jew." He said, "Close enough."

✳ **Carol Leifer** I was in the South one night and I did a joke about the pope giving homosexuals a lot of work. And this guy yelled out, "He does not." I said, "Come on, who do you think designs all his outfits?"

✳ **Kathy Buckley** As a deaf person, I carried a flashlight with me onstage. If I got heckled, I put the flashlight on the heckler's lips so I could lip-read what he was saying. One night this guy was heckling me, so I said, "Come on, put your lips on my light." The guy said, "I can't see it. I'm blind." I said, "Great, leave a blind man to heckle a deaf woman."

✳ **Steve Moore** ·I'm working in front of a redneck crowd, and they're just mean as hell. I don't know if they know I'm gay, but I'm wearing a bow tie and an accordion. So I say, "Hi, how's everybody feeling?" They're all grumbling, so I say, "Anybody out there from the South?" And some guy at the back yells, "On your knees, faggot." I say, "Anybody from the North?"

✳ **Margaret Smith** One guy yelled out, "Could you go a little slower?" I said very slowly, "Why, do you have a learning disability?"

✳ **Tom Caltabiano** A black comedian from Philly, David P. Hardy, was heckled by a guy at the front table who was there with his family. Finally the guy said, "What's your name, man?" David Hardy answered, "You can call me Dad." The guy said, "How 'bout I call you 'nigger'?" Finally they dragged the guy out screaming, but his family stayed for the rest of the show, laughing their heads off.

HENNY WORKED CLEAN

✳ T. Sean Shannon

I was on a plane from L.A. to New York to tape an MTV show. I had frequent-flyer miles, so I got bumped up to first class and I ended up sitting next to Henny Youngman. I was wearing a comedy club T-shirt, so Henny said, "Hey, you do comedy?"

I said, "Yeah, I'm a comedian."

He then lectured me for about fifteen minutes. "The key to longevity is being clean. You have to be clean, because if someone books you and you work dirty, that person gets in trouble and they're not going to use you again. And the reason I've lasted so long is because I'm clean."

Just after he finished the lecture, a stewardess walked by and Henny said, "Hey, where's my fucking drink?"

THE PERFECT INTRO FOR SAM

✳ Ralphie May

In the fall of '89, I'm seventeen and doing Houston "open mikes," shows where anyone can get onstage. Sam Kinison's coming into town, and the local radio station has a contest to open for him for a hundred dollars. I win the contest, probably because every other local comic is too smart to want to face Sam's crowd. A hundred dollars isn't coming close to covering *that* hospital bill.

Sam, his brother Bill, some chick, and I are in the limo on the way to the venue. Sam's like, "Kid, are you nervous?" I'm like, "Naw, I'm not nervous." Sam digs a little deeper. "Kid, there's thirty-five hundred people there and not one of 'em paid to see you." And I'm going, "Okay, I may be a little nervous." He goes, "It's understandable. You're young. Here's what you do. If for any reason you're not doing well, just start yelling at the audience. It's what I do. Call 'em all the most disgusting names you can think of, all right? Just shit all over 'em, all right? And I guarantee you they'll love it."

He's my Comedy God. I'm lapping up all this advice like a starving puppy. "Really, Sam?" He's like, "Yeah. Yeah, they'll love it."

I go onstage nervous as hell, but I'm doing okay till about four minutes in, when I flip a punch line and a setup. I'm thinking about that screwup and mess up the next joke. I don't know how to recover because I'm so new, and my show grinds to a total halt.

I just flash into Sam's advice and I go, "Hey, you stupid cocksuckers, you couldn't get these jokes if I wrote 'em down for you, you stupid Ned Beatty pig-fucking muthafuckers. You're a bunch of fuckin' illiterate dogs. Fuck your mothers, you fucking dog people. You dirty cocksuckers. I hope you all die, you fuckin' pricks." I turn an audience of thirty-five hundred comedy fans into a lynch mob. They're instantly booing in unison, as if they'd worked together before.

I start to cry and leave the stage when suddenly the crowd does a one-eighty and begins to cheer wildly. Just as I disappear into the wings, I turn to see Sam, with another microphone, "Can you fuckin' believe that kid comin' out here and talking to you good people like that? That fuckin' asshole will never be in comedy again. I'll fuckin' see to it. That piece of shit's gonna die. You mutha-fucka, die! Ohhhh-ohhh!"

Thirty-five hundred people are on their feet cheering for him like he's just given them all winning lottery tickets. All I know is I just heard an icon of standup comedy say I'll never do standup comedy again. I got driven there and have no money. So, while I'm dialing my mama to come pick me up, Bill, Sam's brother, hangs the receiver up and goes, "Kid, Sam thought that was the funniest shit of all time. He never thought you'd have the balls to actually do that. It's fucking hysterical. You set him up perfect. Listen to this fucking crowd. It's the hottest we've had ever. He got a standing ovation when he came out. He loves you. We're thinking maybe we can have you do this for the rest of the tour." Sam's great to me at the after-show party. Hell, he's great to everybody; he tips the pizza delivery boy three grams of cocaine.

I never heard another word about being Sam's sacrificial open-ing act. Even the best jokes are usually funny only the first time.

LEFKOWITZ COMEDY

✳ Pat Cooper

I got a job doing a gig at the Lefkowitz Bungalow Comedy in the Catskills. I drove out and the guy at the Bungalow said, "Yes?"

I said, "I'm here to do a show."

He said, "Fine."

I did the show.

Monday I got a call from the agent. "Where the hell were you?"

I said, "What are you talking about?"

He said, "How come you didn't do the show?"

I said, "I was there. I went to Liebowitz Bungalow Comedy."

He said, "Schmuck, it was *Lefkowitz* Bungalow Comedy."

The Liebowitz guy had never said I was in the wrong place. He let me go out and entertain the audience. Afterward he gave me a hug and a kiss and said, "Thank you. Come back anytime."

MAN OVERBOARD

✳ Ray Romano

Working a cruise ship can be very dangerous, not because of the weather or the pirates, but because the cruise is a mandatory seven days. If you have a bad show on the first night, you're stuck on the ship with the audience for the rest of the week. I know acts that bomb and hide in their cabins for the rest of the cruise.

I did a show on a ship that didn't go well at all. I spent the rest of the night weighing my chances of making it to shore with a stolen lifeboat. I was walking through the narrow hallways of the ship and about to make a turn, when I overheard a couple talking around the corner.

"Where do they get these comedians from? I mean, who pays this guy?"

"I know. He's soooo unfunny."

I turned, and there they were. We had to squeeze and shimmy past each other in the narrow corridor. They avoided looking at me like I was Medusa.

I know that the stench of a bad comedy set lasts longer than the fragrance of a killer show, but in that moment I learned that people would rather hug a wet leper than acknowledge the presence of a bad comic.

I know what happened to the *Titanic*. God answered the prayers of the comic who bombed the first night out. He chose death in the freezing North Atlantic waters over facing his critics in those narrow ship corridors.

THE SHOW MUST GO ON

✳ Rita Rudner

When I was starting my career in comedy in the early 1980s, the paying gigs that were available rarely took place in legitimate comedy clubs. We honed our craft in restaurants or bars, and many places in the New York City area started offering their patrons Comedy Night, to go along with Ladies' Night, Two-for-One Shooters Night, and Club a Drunk Off a Bar Stool Night.

One such establishment had devised the unfortunate gimmick of placing large kegs of unshelled peanuts between its tables. It was impossible to judge whether the person performing was funny or not, because the moment a comedian took the microphone, he or she was pelted with nuts. I took my turn through this ha-ha gauntlet because I needed the stage time and the fifty dollars. I proudly bore the peanut-shell marks like dueling scars. Another time I opened my set on Hell's Angels Night by asking the audience, "Have any of you ever been to the ballet?" I did my twenty and took home my fifty.

It really was the only way up the ladder. No one puts an untested comic on the Carnegie Hall stage, for good reason.

On the New Year's Eve of the new millennium, many entertainers were offered a great deal of money to perform their acts, myself included. Y2K disaster rumors were rampant, and boarding a plane was considered an act of bravery. There were no incidents reported anywhere in the world that night, except for the establishment in which I was booked—that hub of terrorist activity known as the Ritz-Carlton Hotel in Palm Beach.

I missed the first bomb scare because I was taking a shower in my hotel room. The second happened about ten minutes before I was scheduled to go onstage.

I was seated at a table in the ballroom, admiring the ice sculpture of a huge dollar sign riding in a Rolls-Royce, when I noticed thin women wearing expensive designer gowns dashing toward the exit. When I see rich people running, I follow, and so I joined the taffeta conga line to the parking lot across the street from the hotel.

The worried president of the Ritz Carlton tiptoed over to me.

"What do you want to do about the show?" he whispered furtively.

Everybody has heard the saying, "The show must go on." Every comic knows the end of the saying: "Otherwise, the performer will not be paid."

I told him most sincerely, "I want to do the show, of course."

I stood on a crate, and an accommodating customer turned on his car headlights, pointing them in my direction.

Comedy does not normally do well outdoors, and if you add bomb-sniffing dogs and helicopters with searchlights, getting a laugh becomes an Olympic event. But after cutting my comedic teeth entertaining bikers and peanut-tossers in Jersey for fifty dollars, serving jokes to a huddled mass of frightened rich people under a starry Florida sky was child's play.

THE REAL ANDY KAUFMAN HAS STOOD UP

✳ Bob Zmuda

Andy Kaufman's alter ego was this obnoxious lounge singer, Tony Clifton. Because the press was beginning to pick up that it was actually Andy hidden underneath the Clifton makeup, we decided I was going to start doing Clifton. I had the voice down, and I was already writing for the Clifton character. I was a bit reluctant, but Andy got so excited. "Zmuda, you've got to do it. It's perfect."

Andy told his manager, George Shapiro, "George, you start booking Clifton, but it has to be Zmuda. But don't tell anyone. The only people that know are you, me, and Zmuda. That's it." So I went on Merv Griffin and David Letterman as Clifton. Everybody involved in the production thought I was Andy, because I would show up in full makeup.

On one of my appearances as Tony, Letterman turned to me (or to Tony) during a commercial break and said, "Andy, if I didn't know it was you, I would swear it was somebody else." Letterman never knew. And Andy sat at home watching all these appearances on TV, laughing his ass off.

Eventually, Harrah's Casino in Lake Tahoe called George Shapiro to book Tony Clifton for a ten-day run. George told the guy, "You have to realize that it's not Andy Kaufman." The guy was thinking George was putting him on. "Oh yeah, we get the whole thing. We understand Tony is Tony, blah, blah, blah. But we want him anyway." So George said, "Well, okay."

To help pull off the illusion, Andy came to Tahoe and walked around the Harrah's casino as himself during the day to be seen by all the employees. They asked him things like, "Andy, what are you doing?" Andy would tell them, "I came up to see Tony Clifton perform." And they went, "Oh, oh, sure, Andy." He loved it.

Then, of course, Andy would be nowhere to be found around showtime. He'd be back in Carson City, or at the brothels, because he loved the hookers. A couple of times he attended the show in disguise, wearing a long wig and beard, and changed his voice and heckled Tony Clifton, saying, "We know you're Andy Kaufman. Why are you doing this to the public?" He'd make an ass of himself until Harrah's security threw him out. He was happy, because his goal was to be thrown out of the room. The casino people had no idea that they were throwing out the guy they'd hired to perform.

Every night I performed there, I noticed that about halfway through the show, the back doors of the theater would open and a showgirl from Caesars would run in to watch me. She was a fucking knockout in one of those Brett Wall productions over at Caesars— "Bottoms Up" or some shit—one of these burlesque things. She was a big Andy Kaufman fan, so every night, as soon as she got offstage, she ran next door to our theater and talked her way past the security people to see the remainder of Tony's act. So I thought to myself, "Hmmm. I'm Andy Kaufman, aren't I?" On one of the last nights, I sent a message that Tony Clifton would like to meet her.

We hit it off. Of course, I didn't drop the Tony Clifton because she thought it was Andy Kaufman under the makeup. If she'd known it was Bob Zmuda, she'd have been out of there. Nobody fucked Bob Zmuda. Who fucked that loser?

But she did fuck Tony Clifton for the last two days of his run. I never ever took the makeup off. I told her, as Tony, "There's not enough prosthetic pieces for the run, and that's why I can't take this makeup off. It has to be used for the next couple of days."

When my run at Harrah's was over, it was time for me to pack up and go to L.A., and she asked me for my phone number. I couldn't give her Bob Zmuda's, so I gave her Andy Kaufman's. I didn't even take her number down. It was over.

A few months later Kaufman called me from L.A. He was hysterical. "What am I going to do? What am I going to do? I just got a call from this Tahoe broad, she's at LAX right now and wants me to come pick her up." She was in town for a couple of days and wanted to stay with him. I said, "Well, what's the bad news?" "But," he said, "I don't even know her." I said, "Andy, you slept with her for two fucking days."

So he picked her up at the airport and took her to his place. Every couple of hours he called me for information on her, like her brother's name or where she was born.

Now, what's amazing about this whole thing is that Andy was Jewish, and of course circumcised. I'm a good Catholic Polack boy from Chicago, and uncircumcised. She never said a word about it. Women pay far less attention to our penises than we do.

THE REAL HIGH

✳ **Ritch Shydner**

In 1990, Sammy Shore—former opening act for Elvis Presley, father of Paulie, and ex-husband of The Comedy Store's founder, Mitzi Store—had a grand opening for his new comedy club, which he was calling Sammy's Last Stand. For the opening, Sammy comped all his buddies and cajoled the younger comics—including me—to put on a free show for them.

When I got to the club, Sammy said to me, "Milton Berle's coming. He's really old and sick and it's the first time he's been out since his wife died. We're going to try to get him onstage, maybe help his spirits. But he won't be able to do more than two, three jokes, so you gotta close the show."

I was already cocky enough to try following the reigning champ, Jay Leno, so closing the show after a seventy-eight-year-old man was not going to be a problem.

The show started, and after an hour watching some of the best young comics of the time hit the audience with their best stuff, I was anxious to get up there before these guys squeezed the last bit of juice from the crowd.

Then Sammy introduced Uncle Miltie, who came in holding some guy's arm for support. Sammy gave a five-minute introduction for Milton. It served a dual purpose, as a reminder to the crowd of this great man's showbiz achievements and to give Milton time to hobble feebly onto the stage. It played like a living eulogy. Finally Milton took the stage to a standing ovation.

Miltie started speaking in this soft, weak voice: "Ladies and germs. I just wanna..." He seemed to lose his thought. "I can't be here long. I don't feel well." The place went completely silent. Everyone was on edge, as if he might keel over right there and then. I started to get ready to take over for him. Then Miltie took a deep breath. "I went to see my doctor today. He gave me a strong laxative. Now I'm sitting pretty!" The place broke up. It was a dumb old joke, but it got a big laugh. The old master had set us up perfectly.

Milton straightened a bit and began firing off one line after another. Within ten jokes, this little old man was seven feet tall and breathing fire.

Within three minutes I realized I was not going anywhere near that stage. He was going to leave that audience a smoldering ruin. I sat down next to Kevin Pollack to watch the Master, whose jokes-per-minute ratio was about three times higher than anyone else's there that night.

The place was rocking when Milton taught us another lesson. Right after a huge laugh, he said, "Well, folks, I got to go." The audience screamed, "No!" I swear I thought I saw a little, sly smile on Milton's face as he took a puff off a two-foot-long cigar. He had just played them for the first of what would be three encores. Then it hit me. Where'd he get the cigar? He didn't have a cigar when he got up there.

At one point he got feedback from the microphone and said, "Gee. I hope they're our planes." The audience loved it. Pollack and I looked at each other. We realized he'd just done a saver from 1945, and it still got a laugh. It didn't even matter what he said now. The audience was now a single organism, breathing and laughing to the old man's rhythm. He did an hour. People were screaming and cheering as he left the stage. By the time he made it to the back of the room, he was again just a frail old man greeting a growing line of well-wishers.

Sammy ran to me. "You ready to go on?" Sammy probably didn't understand, because nobody had ever asked him to follow Elvis, or maybe he just wanted to see my comedic balls kicked so hard they rang the top of my skull. But there was no way I was going to try to follow that act. I told him the show was over and got in line to meet Uncle Milton.

The club died three weeks later.

Milton Berle kept joking until March 27, 2002.

ENTERTAINING THE MOB

✴ Allan Havey

I'd been doing standup about three years when I got a call from this cheesy booker I'd met at the Improv in Manhattan. He had a private party in Westchester he wanted me to work with two other comics. We were to get one hundred bucks apiece, and there was the possibility of a tip depending on the performance.

"Remember, you go last," he said. He was adamant about this. I told him no problem.

The big night came and I was picked up by the other two comics. We'd never met. We made small talk for a while, and all of a sudden the guy in the backseat said, "I'm going on last." I told him the booker wanted me to close the show, but he wasn't buying it.

"I'm a headliner. Headliners go on last."

I repeated what I'd just said. He didn't budge.

We pulled up to this beautiful Italian restaurant, and when we told the maître d' we were the performers, he snapped his fingers and we were whisked to a table. This was my first time being whisked. The waitstaff bowed and scraped. We felt like royalty as they laid out, gratis, the most incredible meal I'd had in my life—

antipasti, salad, soup, pasta, and a veal scallopini that transcended all previous culinary sensations. Topping all this was my first tiramisu. Suddenly I loved show business. This was heaven.

After dessert we waddled down to the basement and entered the showroom. The packed room was literally split down the middle, with gangsters on one side, civilians on the other. The first comic went onstage and did as well as you could expect, considering the gangsters wouldn't shut up. They paid attention for a while and then started laughing and talking among themselves. The comic onstage had sense enough to ignore this. He played to the civilians and took his bombing like a man.

The "headliner" standing in the back with me had no such sense. "Why doesn't somebody shut those guys up?"

I looked at him like he was out of his mind. "I don't think that would be a good idea."

"You scared, Havey?"

"To death."

The "headliner" and I watched the opener sacrificing joke after joke, all dying in vain. The gangsters were in their own world. The show was a nightmare to us, but the gangsters were having a great time, and really, all that ever mattered was that the audience had a great time.

Finally the "headliner" said, "Hey, you know, if he was that specific about you closing, I don't want to argue."

"Oh, really?"

"I'll go on next, it's no big deal."

"I thought you were a headliner."

Mr. Chickenshit couldn't hear me. He was too busy frantically signaling the comic onstage to bring him up instead of me.

Mr. Hotshot went up, opened with nothing, and followed that with even less. The gangsters were of course talking away, but now the civilian side of the room was dead, too. The rapidly shrinking act of the ex-headliner was nothing but old Woody Allen jokes with shitty timing. Eight minutes in, one of the gangsters turned to the comedian onstage. "Hey, comedian. Off." He gestured with his hand like you would beckon a collie. The nitwit on stage ignored him.

"*HEY!*"

I was standing behind the gangster, so I couldn't see his expression, but I noticed his neck had just grown two sizes bigger, with one visible pulse on his jugular vein the size of a tree root. The comic went white and left the stage. Didn't even say good night. No intro for me. He just walked off and disappeared. He might've made his own door.

The room was still. You heard nothing. The gangster looked at me.

"G'head."

The only sound in the room was my footsteps. I reached the stage, and it was an angry room. I used an old trick and gave myself a Madison Square Garden heavyweight-champ intro. A hacky device, but it worked. It got the crowd going, and I launched into my best stuff right at the top, putting everything I had into it. It was working. I was getting laughs, steady and building. Even some of the mob guys were into it. This went on for a while and I started feeling cocky. I decided to work the room. I did a lame joke about one of the waiters' jackets, and the gangsters howled. I got cockier. I was on fire. I had raised the dead. This guy up front was wearing a plaid jacket. He had a thin, curly mustache. I pointed this out, saying, "You look like Barney Fife and Salvador Dalí after a ride on a Tilt-a-Whirl."

The place went ballistic. I had the whole room now.

And then I saw her. This old lady up front was smiling at me. She was wearing a horrible wig, her natural hair sticking out at the bottom. In addition to this, she had a ridiculous corsage on that was almost twice her body weight. This was going to be fun.

"What's your name, sweetheart?"

"Marie."

All of a sudden, out of the far corner of my eye, I saw this HUGE man stand up. His hands were hanging down at his sides and his head was slightly tilted. The mobsters around him froze.

My ass tightened and sweat instantly poured down my back. Fear racked my body. The little men in my brain sent a quick signal: Abort! Abandon! Get the fuck out! My tongue turned to sandpaper. I kept going.

"What's the corsage for, Marie?"

The giant whispered to a goon next to him. His head was so enormous, I heard his brow furrow.

Marie piped up, "Today is my birthday."

I gave her a big smile. "Happy Birthday!" I addressed the crowd, "How about raising a glass to Marie on her birthday!" I again gave her my biggest smile. "Marie, you remind me of the fine women of my parish." I quickly segued into my Catholic hunk. I delivered it smooth as silk, but my heart was kicking the shit out of my insides. The goon sat down and the other mob guys relaxed. I finished with my altar boy hunk and got the hell off.

I headed for the door. Fat chance. The mobster grabbed me by the arm.

"Hey, you."

He reached out and pinched my cheek so hard I felt my Achilles tendon tighten.

"You made my mother's night! You got some class!"

His buddies were standing around, smiling and patting me on the back. He still had a hold on my cheek. His hand had the girth of a first baseman's mitt. He pinched harder.

"If you woulda said one bad word about her, I was gonna take you out of here and put you in a fucking oil drum."

He turned and yelled to the far side of the room.

"HEY, ANTHONY! ANTHONY? WHAT DID I TELL YOU I WAS GOING TO DO TO THIS GUY?"

A voice from the back:

"YOU WERE GOING TO PUT HIM IN AN OIL DRUM."

Everybody was laughing hard. He was bouncing me up and down by my cheek in a playful, carefree manner. I stood on tiptoe so my neck didn't snap on the upswing.

"I was going to put you in an oil drum! You got a lot of class! You made my mother's night. Mom . . . Hey, Mom!"

My nervous system had reached Code Blue. I was either going to shit or vomit. The gangster finally released me, and Marie came over and gave me a hug. She smelled of ricotta cheese and Lysol. I gave her a birthday kiss on the cheek.

"Hey! Who said you could kiss my mother!"

Everyone froze.

The big guy laughed. "Just bustin' ya balls."

As I headed up the stairs, an old fat guy with suspenders said, "You're smart, leaving now. Vic doesn't stay happy for long."

I got outside and the other comics were waiting in the car, with the engine running. I held up my finger for them to wait, and walked to the side of the restaurant.

I threw up in the bushes, that beautiful meal gone. A chunk of veal sizzled on a floodlight as I wiped my mouth and walked to the car.

The beautiful thing was they stiffed Mr. Showbiz. He whined that we should pitch in some coin to him. Fuck him. I got no tip. I was sure the booker took that.

Hitting the Big Time

✳ **Jonathan Katz** I used to book a club in New Haven. Opening week, the ad in the paper read EVERY WEEK, 3 NY COMMIES. The first week the audience was three people with red shirts on.

✳ **Kevin Pollack** I'm waiting in the kitchen of a restaurant/ club and here's my introduction: "Ladies and gentlemen, we're out of Thousand Island, and now here's Kevin Pollack."

✳ **Andy Kindler** I get to the comedy condo, and there are no knives and forks. So I go to the club and say to the owner, "You know, I got to the condo and there are no knives and forks." He goes, "You're damn right there's no knives and forks. And you know why? Because the guys last week took them! Okay?" I just stood there, grateful the comics hadn't taken the toilet.

✳ **Sue Kolinsky** I was playing at the Punch Line in Atlanta and staying with one of their favorite headliners in the comedy house. We were watching TV. It was cold and we had the fireplace going. As the fire went down, the headliner just started breaking all the furniture in the room and throwing it in the fire.

✳ **Tim Allen** No matter what the comic ordered at Dangerfield's, it became a Coca-Cola and a club sandwich. A strip steak and vodka on the rocks came back a Coke and a club. I was so new that I kept thinking, *That's one weird bartender.* I figured he just wasn't really listening to me. I'd tell him one thing and then a club sandwich shows up. Finally, one night he asked me and I said, "I guess I'll have the club." He gave me one of those New York smirk-smiles and said, "There you go, sport. Now I think you're getting the idea."

✳ **Sinbad** I would go to the Greyhound bus station with no money. I'd look for the bus driver, hoping he might have a kind heart, and try to beg a free ride. I made a little list of everybody who ever helped me. After I made it big, I took every bus driver I could find to dinner.

EARLY DIGS

✳ Paula Poundstone

When I started out, the clubs didn't offer a place to stay, typical ill treatment for comics "paying their dues." I took Greyhound buses around the country even to audition at places. When I came to work the club, if there wasn't a couch available, I'd check the Greyhound schedule for a town four hours away, book a round-trip ticket, and in this way I got eight hours' sleep. I carried a small Swiss Army knife for protection. I could stab attackers and then open a bottle of wine to celebrate.

In 1983, I came to Zanies in Chicago. The owner knew I didn't have a place to stay and let me sleep in the office above the nightclub. He said, "Don't tell anybody." There was no chance of that; I was as embarrassed about it as he was.

Everybody finished telling their jokes and I pretended that I was going someplace else. When they finally closed the bar, I snuck upstairs into this little cubby with a teeny black-and-white television set. I was very afraid of the dark, and this place made a lot of weird noises; every time the ice dropped in the ice machine, I levitated about a foot off the floor. I slept in my clothes, but finally got relaxed enough to take off my sneakers.

Then I heard someone calling my name from outside the building. No one knew that I was staying there, other than the club owner. I grabbed my sneakers and thought that as much as I liked this club owner, I wasn't stopping to lock the door.

Then I heard a knocking on the window. I was two stories up and totally freaked out. This voice was just insistent: "Come to the window." So I went to the window, the kind of move that always gets you killed in one of those psycho-slasher movies. This guy was standing on the cement wall in the alley, using a two-by-four to tap on the window. I recognized him: Mike Farrell, one of the nicest comics in the world.

He'd stayed in the office the week before me. He was a total road comic—without a gig, he was homeless. So, when his Wisconsin job had fallen through, he'd decided to come back, knowing that I was in the cubbyhole apartment and possibly sympathetic to his plight.

He had to stay with me, because by then I was so scared I couldn't possibly have stayed by myself. In fact, I think he toured with me for a year after that, until I was able to get comfortable again.

FOR THE KIDS

✳ Tom Papa

I got hired to play a high school in New Jersey. I had to do an hour show; at the time I only had about thirty minutes of material, so I brought along my friend Kyle Dunnigan to open for me.

When we got there, one of the teachers told us we had to keep it clean for the kids, nothing dirty. The teacher who was telling us this was a knockout. She was our age, and stunning. I fell in love.

Two minutes into his set, Kyle was bombing. These were high school kids. They didn't want New York comedians; they wanted a clown. In order to save himself, Kyle broke out his guitar and launched into a song about the St. Patrick's Day parade. The song was filthy—hysterical, but filthy—sung in an Irish brogue from the point of view of a gay Irishman pleading to be allowed to march in the parade.

I figured that Kyle was going to clean it up. One of his verses was, "Hey diddy-high, hey diddy-hoo, if your cock be the ladle, me ass be the stew," which he now sang, proudly. The chorus was, "We're proud and we're Irish, we're drunk and we're gay," a lyric that Kyle now had the entire student body of boys and girls singing along with and clapping. I got a little insight as to how the Nazis took over so easily.

Kyle finished his song and brought me on.

I came out and told some jokes. I started bombing. The kids didn't want my little jokes about cats and dogs; they wanted to sing that gay Irish song again. What fun was I when the last adult on-stage had them screaming "cock" as if it were okay?

Unfortunately, unlike Kyle, I didn't have a guitar, so I started working the crowd. I was just grabbing at anything I saw.

In my desperation, I focused on the hot teacher in the back of the room. I started making some jokes about how sexy she was, and how, if she were my teacher, I'd go nuts. And how the boys in the school must think of her every night as they...you know. As I said, I was desperate!

I wrapped up my set, went backstage, and two students gifted us with cookies wrapped in colored construction paper decorated with hearts and stars and unicorns. In glitter, the cookie package was inscribed with the words "Thanks for Performing at Our School."

Just then, another teacher informed us that the principal wanted to see us in his office.

We went down to the principal's office; the principal, dressed in a Winnie-the-Pooh tie, started yelling at us, "These are children! Cock in the ass? Whacking off? What were you thinking?"

The entire time the principal was yelling at us, he had our check in his hand and was waving it back and forth. If I hadn't been holding my unicorn cookie tray, I would have grabbed my check and run.

We started begging for forgiveness and apologizing like crazy. Somehow we persuaded the principal to give us the check. We ran to our car, buzzed back to the city, and deposited the check immediately.

The rest of the night, Kyle and I spent laughing at what we had done and worrying that the man in the Winnie-the-Pooh tie was going to call our moms and tell them what perverts they had raised.

TANKING IT

✳ Don Barnhart Jr.

I was just getting started in the business when my friend said I should set up a showcase at the Improv in Los Angeles. Sure, why not? I had nothing to lose. I'd been emceeing at a club for a while and had already been going up at the local bars during the band's breaks. I'd done a week on the road in Oklahoma as a feature act when the opener got snowed in. I figured I was ready.

When we got to the Improv the night of my show, the place was packed. The best of the best were doing their thing—Leno (pre-*Tonight Show*) was tearing the crowd up.

We were watching from the back of the room, squished together in the corner. My dad and my best friend were there to cheer me on. As it got later, the crowd was still overflowing. Then George Wallace came in. I'd known him from my hosting days at the Comedy & Magic Club in Hermosa Beach, California. As he was being introduced, he looked over and gave me a big thumbs-up. He knew this was my big day.

George is one of the best. And the crowd knew it. They were seeing a standup in perfect form. He was in the zone. He even had to stop a couple of times to wait for the crowd to stop laughing.

Then Budd, the owner of the Improv, walked in. With a nod of his head, he told the emcee it was time to do the showcase. The emcee walked up to me and said, "You're up. What do you want me to say in your introduction?" "Uh, whatever you think is fine," I replied. I had no credits for him to list.

As I waited in the wings, George was coming off the stage. He looked at me and said, "They're not putting you up now, are they?"

I nodded. He smiled and told me the secret of comedy: "Just try and have fun."

I wish I could say that I killed. Or even did well. But I didn't. I bombed. Not in the I-had-a-bad-set or the-crowd-really-blew-tonight way; I truly just died onstage. I had no act. I was out of material in the first three minutes. I was trying to work the crowd like a host does..."Any birthdays?"...Silence.

I didn't give up, either. I kept right on bombing. I had twelve minutes to fill and I wasn't going down without a fight, even though I was out on my feet after the first thirty seconds. I could feel the sweat streaming down the back of my neck, and it got worse. I started to leave my body.

I looked down and I could see myself. My mouth was moving but nothing was coming out. At least nothing that was getting laughs. Why wouldn't I just bail?

Wait a minute. I just got a laugh...and another one. There was hope. I was starting to get them, but it was coming from the back of the room. I knew that sound. It was my dad's laugh. The worse I died, the funnier it got...for him. As he said later, "I wanted to just shoot you and put you out of your misery, but I couldn't. It was so painful watching my boy up there, I couldn't help but laugh." I've always had that kind of love and support from my family.

I don't know what I talked about, but I kept on and finally got the signal to get off the stage. "Thanks for putting up with me. You probably won't ever see me again," I said as I left the stage for the long walk to the front bar. The audience laughed the biggest laugh I had heard the whole time I had been up there.

Hmmm, wow. I was honest and not contrived. I poked fun at my own situation and the crowd laughed. Before I could finish my thought, George Wallace walked up to me and asked how it went. I asked him, "Didn't you just *see* that? What do you think?"

George didn't have to say anything then, but he did. He said, "It doesn't matter what I think. It matters what *you* think, Donny boy.

Tonight was the best thing that could have happened to you. You will now either get out of the business and lead a normal life, or you'll work so hard this will never happen again."

Fifteen years later I was at the Montreal Comedy Festival. Backstage was a young comic shaking in his shoes, with tears in his eyes. "How did it go?" I asked.

"Didn't you just see that? I just took a nosedive in front of everybody," he replied.

"Did I ever tell you what George Wallace said to me?"

WELCOME TO MY WORLD

✳ Jeff Foxworthy

It was 1984, and I was just beginning my career in comedy, which meant I was working the road.

I was also early into my relationship with my soon-to-be wife, which meant meeting her parents. At the time I wasn't certain how long I'd last in standup or with my new girlfriend, but I knew I loved them both.

I was more than a little nervous when my future in-laws decided to drive from New Orleans to a comedy club in Montgomery, Alabama, to see what their daughter's new boyfriend did for a living.

All I really knew about my future wife's father was that he wore suits, both to his job and to church. My family didn't even wear long pants to court appearances. I fully expected him to put my job telling jokes in the same category as a carnival-ride operator.

This particular weekend, I opened for one of the all-time road dogs, Ollie Joe Prater, a comic who worked loud, fast, and foul. He was five feet five inches tall, whether standing on his feet or lying on his side. With his cowboy boots, hat, long hair, and beard, Ollie Joe was Yosemite Sam come to life, only with serious drug and alcohol problems.

He once told me that instead of taking antibiotics for a urinary infection, he figured if he could get a fresh dose of syphilis, it might destroy the first infection. By the end of his career, Ollie Joe was so fat that moving even a few feet at a time winded him. The club owner's solution was to seat Ollie Joe onstage before the crowd arrived. He was given a bottle of whiskey and then covered with a sheet. Eventually he actually learned how to smoke while under the sheet without setting fire to it. The opening acts were forced to perform in front of what appeared to be a giant, wheezing, smoldering piece of covered furniture.

Anyway, I hit the stage. Within four jokes into my act, a woman heckled me. This was my first female heckler and an important lesson for a young Jedi comic.

The lesson: You cannot make a drunken woman shut up. If you're married, you know you can hardly make *any* woman shut up. Now imagine a drunken woman you don't even know, yelling from the dark...forget it!

A drunken male heckler can be embarrassed into shutting up. If a man gets too obnoxious, despite all the alcohol disabling his rational thought, somewhere deep in his reptilian brain lies the knowledge that to continue heckling might mean no sex that night. There is no such fail-safe mechanism in a woman's brain. She knows that no matter how drunk she is, or how insufferable her behavior, there is *always* the possibility of sex.

Eventually this woman got bored with heckling me, or passed out, or went to the parking lot to conceive a child. Whatever the reason for her silence, I managed to drag the audience back to my act and finished respectfully enough to keep my Jester's License.

As I left the stage and the master of ceremonies introduced Ollie Joe, I heard him mumble from under the sheets, "I'll take care of these fuckers."

I spotted my future in-laws and the love of my life sitting deep in the center of the crowd, and knew there was no way to save them without a smoke bomb and a line from a Chinook helicopter.

Ollie Joe downed five shots of Crown and smoked almost a pack of cigarettes before he did one joke. Oh, he cursed. He yelled. He made off-color toasts, but not one joke.

When he finally started his act, I longed for the lewd toasts. His act was just filthy, as blue as can be. If they arrested Lenny Bruce for what he said, the gas chamber seemed appropriate for what was crawling out of Ollie Joe's mouth. Thomas Jefferson was about to make an emergency trek from his grave to take back Freedom of Speech. I was in the back, with my head in my hands, thinking it could not get any worse, again showing how little I knew about the world of comedy.

My woman heckler resurfaced in the middle of Ollie Joe's classic piece "Pissing in Public Places." Ollie Joe was a big fan of alliteration. I don't remember what she said to Ollie Joe. I don't think anybody knew what she said that night. She spoke a seldom-heard, backwoods dialect of drunkenese.

What I do remember is the lesson Ollie Joe inadvertently taught me that night: if you get too mean with a woman heckler, the crowd turns on you. I think it's tied to that same rule that requires "women and children first." You don't want to get caught bumping a mother and child out of the lifeboat or laying the "C" word on a Southern lady in public.

Ollie Joe, however, held to *none* of those rules. As a result, the comedy crowd turned into a lynch mob in seconds. It happened faster than a knife fight in a phone booth.

People left. Ollie Joe sent them out the door with things like "Fuck you, you fat bitch," and "Eat shit, old man." Little mementos to help the crowd remember a meaningful night of shared humanity.

Finally, Ollie closed with a blanket blessing: "Fuck all of ya." He left the stage. All I thought was, "Oh, thank God it's over." But it wasn't. The death rattle of comedy was just beginning. The master of ceremonies returned to the stage and pleaded with the nine people still in the room, "Ladies and gentlemen, *that* was a show-business legend. And you should be ashamed at the way you have treated this man. If he dies tonight, it'll be on your heads. I think if we put our hands together, we may be able to coax him back up here."

The stragglers who'd been unable to get out fast enough clapped politely, very slowly and lightly. That was all it took to coax Ollie back up for another twenty minutes of free booze. He started his encore by telling these nine unfortunates where to stick it.

After the show, my future father-in-law said that if Ollie Joe was my competition in this funny business, I should do okay. I asked his daughter to marry me the next day.

Soon after, Ollie Joe moved on to Showbiz Heaven, where I last heard he was fired as Elvis's opening act.

Keeping the Peace

✳ **Larry Reeb** I was standing in the back of a club, waiting to go onstage, when two women started fighting. I tried to break it up and this old lady punched me right in the head. As soon as I got hit in the head I heard, "Please welcome Larry Reeb."

✳ **Greg Behrendt** One night a guy was heckling Bill Hicks, who stopped the show and said to him, "Look, I don't have any fancy comeback lines. What will happen is you'll continue to talk and I will dig the heel of my boot into your skull." The crowd was silent for a minute before bursting into laughter. The next night I was opening the show and a guy heckled me. I tried Hicks's approach. "Dude, if you don't stop talking, I'm going to kick the shit out of you." The guy stood up and ran toward the stage. I was saved when someone tackled him. I learned that night I was no Bill Hicks.

✳ **Brett Butler** I was onstage when out of the corner of my eye I saw a guy get up out of his chair, crouch, aim a gun at me, and fire a shot. I heard a loud bang, my knees went weak, and then—proof of what narcissism exists in our profession— I thought, *But I'm not finished with my show.* It turned out to be a blank from a prop gun.

✳ **Ian Bagg** I was onstage and these Native American guys were playing pool. I told them to turn off the light and quit playing pool, because I was doing my show. This one huge Native guy yelled out, "You've broken the peace." I asked them, "Was there an eighteenth-century treaty guaranteeing Indians unlimited pool-playing?" Then one of the Indians yelled out, "Way to go, white guy, you broke it again." I said, "If it makes you feel better, I'll buy you a casino."

COMIC MATERIAL

✳ Dennis Miller

One time, around 1984, I was standing outside the Pittsburgh Comedy Club with Richard Belzer, who was having a cigarette. A thirteen- or fourteen-year-old kid came driving by on his bicycle. We watched as the club's young car parkers started hassling this kid on the bike. Not really brutal, like Crips and Bloods, more like "Our Gang" stuff. But they slapped him around a little, being a little mean, taking his bike, riding it around. The car parkers were bigger and a little older, so the kid's only recourse was incessant complaining. "Hey, give me my bike. Come on. Give me my bike. Come on, guys…"

Finally they gave the kid his bike. Belzer turned to me and said, "Well, there goes the next great standup comedian." That, I think, speaks to me—the roots of comedy, what kind of pain is required to ascend the standup ladder. In the more brutal sense, it was a display of what it takes to form the personality and mentality to become a standup comedian.

GOODNIGHT CHARLIE

✳ Ophira Eisenberg

In 2003, I was booked for a week at Charlie Goodnights in Raleigh, North Carolina. I was thinking, *This time I'm not going to let road loneliness get to me.* I hate road loneliness—it's like being the unpopular one in a threesome. But I was determined that Raleigh was going to be different. I was going to be motivated and write jokes every day. Then, when I got to my hotel room, I panicked. Within five minutes, depression had completely taken me over. I called my boyfriend, but it went straight to voice mail. A voice in my head told me, *He's the popular one in a fivesome.* I stared at the TV and considered starting smoking again.

By 7:45 P.M., I was at the club on the desperate side of early. Finally I hit the stage and I was transformed into everyone's best friend for forty-five minutes. I left the stage sporting a nice comforting buzz. I wanted to keep the high going, so I headed to the bar. When the bartender told me the comedians drank for free, I showed my self-control to the door.

Several drinks later, I found myself scanning male faces at the bar, looking for someone to flirt with, someone to play with. Of course, I didn't want to cheat on my boyfriend, but my drunken brain was telling me that I might have to. Loneliness was stalking me, and I had to survive to do another show in twenty-three hours. I spotted my target: a tall, lanky one who seemed like the silent type. I grabbed my beer, wandered over to him, and said, "Are you like the dark horse of this place or something?" This was my opening line. I'd just found out that it's tougher being a guy than it looks. Still, I'm a woman and he's a guy, so my lines don't matter. He smiled, and soon it was clear my dark horse was actually a just-out-of-college dark pony.

We went to the dark pony's apartment. One gravity-bong hit later, and I felt my hands turn to ice. My skin itched and my clothes felt too tight, my head was heavy and hot, and I felt really, really dumb. I started getting paranoid: *He doesn't think I'm funny, and maybe he doesn't think I'm pretty and women aren't respected enough in comedy and I don't have enough female role models and maybe I should wait another night before I make out with him and I shouldn't be here at all and I should have a stronger relationship with my manager...* But my train of thought was interrupted by the dark pony offering me another hit.

I realized that I was too fucked up to fuck the dark pony.

Minutes later we were in his car. I was feeling a bit better and recognized that I had a small window before I talked myself out of the whole thing. We stopped at a red light. I placed a hand on his leg...my boyfriend was miles away...he looked at me intently... *God, he's young*...we started kissing. We both had dry mouth, so it wasn't fabulous, but I found it exhilarating. It was like robbing a bank and being called pretty at the same time. Hands started going, clothes were stretching...and the light turned green.

He stepped on the gas and I noticed I was smiling and stared out onto the road ahead of us, trying to maximize the rush I was getting from speeding and cheating.

He rolled down the window and screamed. He turned to me and said, "Man, I am so glad I did a little crystal meth before I left the apartment."

For God's sake—I have friends who are starting families and saving for a house with a backyard and I should have been at home with my boyfriend, writing a pitch for a reality show...Instead there I was, breathing in what was probably crack-laced pot through a Canada Dry bottle and swapping DNA samples with a meth addict. I was no longer stoned. Now I was gloomy.

We got to my hotel. He offered me a cigarette, which I took. He was still good for something. In seconds I was back in my hotel room, where I started. Nothing much had changed, except I'd made out with a powder monkey and smoked a cigarette. My self-esteem clicked one notch lower, then two more notches until "Failed Suicide Attempt." I still had some breathing room.

I slept most of the next day and then slowly made my way to the club, hungover and looking a little rough. I said hi to the hostess as I walked in.

"I heard you had one crazy night last night," she said sourly. I guess that's how this town works—that's how it stays exciting. Everyone's in everyone's business. I tried to order a Diet Coke from her but couldn't seem to get her attention. Whatever.

Then the show started. The crowd was pumped and I was trying to harness all the energy I had left for them. I was onstage feeling good, and I started in on my dating jokes:

"I go on a few dates a month...just to remind myself that I have no standards..."

It got a good laugh, but I heard a "Yer fulla shit!" from a female voice in the crowd.

I searched for the heckler and I saw...I saw it was one of the waitresses. What the hell? She was standing there staring at me, tray in hand. Defiant. I looked at her, she looked at me, and the audience looked at us both. I didn't get it right then and there, what the connection was, but I needed a comeback:

"She's just bitter because I'm talking about her boyfriend!" It got a great laugh, and she had fire in her eyes and whipped her blond head around and walked away. What the fuck was that? I continued with my act while trying to figure out what had just happened. Why would she do that? Does she have a thing for the dark pony or...oh my God...I *was* talking about her boyfriend! Holy fuck! She's going to kill me!

I kept telling jokes. I knew I was going over my time, but I didn't want to get off and deal with my future. The red light started flashing; finally I had to wrap up. I got off and headed to the bathroom. I'm a coward. I went into a stall to sit and think.

She came into the bathroom. Fuck. "Ophira." I wondered if she had a gun pointed at my faded yellow stall.

"Yeah?" Why don't I know her name? Fuck. Where's a scrawled number for a good time when you need it?

"Never ever come near my boyfriend again." Simple. Succinct. Sweet.

"Seriously—I didn't know, I had no idea, I..." I'm a fucking cowardly fool. What does she know? Did he tell her?

She said something else—something like "Have a nice week," or "I'm going to kill you in your sleep," but I couldn't hear it because my head and heart were pumping too hard. She left. The brevity of the talk freaked me out. It made her all the scarier. I quietly emerged from my stall after a long while and took a seat at the far end of the club to order my comp meal. No waitress approached my table or seemed to see my subtle waving. This is her revenge, I realized: I can't eat, and I can't drink. I was blown away.

The rest of the week was tough. I was invisible to the venue. I just arrived, did my set, and left. It was a particularly lonely week. At the end I got paid and honestly I think I got a little screwed. But I didn't say anything.

I knew Raleigh was going to be different, just not this kind of different. I don't know what the going rate is for male prostitutes, but I'm pretty sure the dark pony cost me a lot more for a lot less. Thanks for the one trick, pony.

ZIPPITY-DOO-DAH

✳ Rusty Warren

In 1965 I was new to the business, a kid just out of college, maybe twenty-three. I was working a little nightclub in Omaha, Nebraska. I played piano and sang risqué songs. There was no dressing room. I dressed in the ladies' room, put my music under my left tit, and went to work.

After the show one night I was changing out of my show clothes when the boss, a pockmarked Norwegian from Minnesota, walked in without knocking.

So I covered myself up and said as casually as I could, "Hi, did we do good tonight?"

He said, "We did fine. Now you're gonna do better."

He unzipped his fly, and out flopped this dead-looking mole. When you're really scared, I think you either laugh or faint. I started to laugh. I just pointed at it and said, "Would you like me to invite your wife? She's at the cash register. Maybe she can help me identify the deceased." I just kept going. "You want me to applaud? What do you want me to do?" I was so nervous, I just said anything that came into my mind. "I've seen them before. It's not the sort of thing that just shows up uninvited. To tell you the truth, I've seen better."

He got so angry and so embarrassed he left without zipping himself up. I heard some waitress scream in the hallway. Then I heard his wife yelling. I slipped my music back under my left tit, snuck out the back, and hit the road.

THE COMIC STRIPPER

✳ Eddie Brill

One time I had to work at Hilarities Comedy Club in Cuyahoga Falls, near Cleveland, Ohio. I hated it because it felt like a dungeon, and the audience hated the fact that I was from New York City. I was sitting in the office during the week, hanging out, and I heard customers on the speakerphone saying, "Where's this comedian from?" When the reservationist said "New York," you heard a loud *click*.

The guy opening for me was this black guy who was a total hack. All he did was pander to the crowd, and they ate it up like you wouldn't believe. He was the hack of hacks—Hack Wilson, Gene Hackman, Buddy Hackett, and this guy. The audience loved him.

Then I'd come out and it was like, "Hey, you wanna think for a second?" and the crowd's like, "Hunh? Bring out the pandering guy." It was just awful.

But after one of the shows, the second show on Saturday, these five girls came up to me and said, "Look, we really enjoyed the show and this is my friend's bachelorette party and we'd like you to strip for us."

I blurted, "What?"

They came back, rather matter-of-factly, "Well, you know, we enjoyed the show and now we'd like you to strip for us."

I said, "What do you think, comedians are like monkeys and whatever you want us to do, we're your entertainment for the night?"

She whipped out what was supposed to be an irresistible lure: "I'll give you a hundred bucks."

I was doing my best to curb my anger. "I don't care if you give me a thousand dollars, I'm not gonna strip for you."

So I went to the other comedian and said, "Hey, you'll never guess what happened." I told him the whole story about these girls, and he was laughing as to the stupidity of such a proposal. My disdain for him as a panderer was washed away by our moment of shared contempt for the girls' offer.

A half hour later I found him behind the club, stripping for the girls.

STATE FAIR COMEDY

✳ Richard Lewis

I think after thirty-five years of standup still one of the most horrifying road gigs, gigs period (but also one that really gave me my balls), was opening up for Sonny and Cher. Night after night they had a bad-postured Jewish comedian, unknown basically, in front of ten or fifteen thousand people, either outdoors or indoors. To even try to describe the rashes that I had and where they were would be impossible.

At a fairground in Allentown, Pennsylvania, the thousands of people were separated from the stage by a racetrack. So they were easily about a quarter of a mile away from me. Not more than twenty yards behind me was like the highest, most frightening first drop of the roller coaster. So I also had to time my punch lines for my own hearing with the screams from the people with their arms lifted.

I was supposed to do a half hour, then Sonny and Cher were to do an hour, at four in the afternoon.

They had two speakers, monitors that were forty feet high. My friend Homerun Johnny stood twenty feet to my left, just watching me. I did my lines, and the audience was so far away I couldn't even hear any laughs. I wouldn't even consider it bombing. I would consider it like an experiment. I raced through thirty minutes of material in about eight minutes. As soon as I left the stage, Homerun Johnny and I ran through the back of the fairgrounds. He wanted to put on a disguise because he didn't want to be associated with me.

Every now and then these little angels pop up. Some guy approached Homerun Johnny and me. He looked like a regular salesman, like a blender salesman in a suit and tie. He was a nice guy, not hostile. He said, "Hey, I just saw your set."

I said, "Yeah, it was pretty tough. I only did about eight minutes, but it was impossible because I couldn't hear myself because of the roller coaster. I couldn't see the audience. I couldn't hear the laughs. Fuck it."

He was laughing when he said, "Let me tell you something. I saw Cosby here last week."

Of course, Cosby was headlining. This was 1976 and Cosby was already a big star.

The guy continued, "Cosby was supposed to do about an hour and a half. He did about thirteen minutes."

I just started laughing. I went, "Fuck this." I was making about $100 and Cosby was making about $200,000 and he only did four more minutes than I did. They're lucky I did a minute, these lucky bastards. It might sound strange, but hearing that Cosby also had a rough time at the fair gave me the confidence to go out and do a decent second show.

PEER LAUGHTER

✳ Billy Martin

In 1989, I played a Comedy Caravan club in Florida. On this particular week, "accommodations" meant a condo, an apartment where headlining and middle acts would cohabit and share in a creative exchange. It was also a place where the middle act and the headliner bonded over the mutual objective of making the opening act's life a living hell.

I was the middle act. Headlining was a comedy duo from the Midwest whom I'll call Dell and Mel. Their hook was that one was really, really fat and the other one was really, really, really fat. Get it?

Dell and Mel would be introduced as a comedy team, "one fat, one skinny," and then Dell, the smaller of the two, would take the stage. With the audience naturally presuming he was the fat one, Dell would explain, "Oh no, you ain't seen fat." And, with that, ominous music would blare through the showroom and Dell would pull out two flashlights and, like an airline employee working the tarmac, he would wave the two beacons to guide his four-hundred-pound-plus partner, Mel, down the center aisle and onto the stage. It was actually quite a spectacle, and quite funny.

Back at the condo, Dell and Mel took a liking to me and missed no opportunity to point out that I was "one funny motherfucker... offstage!" Then they would both laugh and laugh until one of them would slip into a coughing fit.

Both men were so big that they had to sleep upright in chairs, not unlike many of my audiences. Also, they both snored so loudly that, three rooms away, I could barely hear myself masturbate.

Worst of all, both Dell and Mel had sleep apnea. Their snoring would rattle the walls, leaving me longing for the quiet of, say, a NASCAR event. Mid-snore, their throats would close off and they'd simply stop breathing for what seemed like an eternity. Ten seconds. Twenty seconds. Half a minute. Forty-five seconds... Breathe, dammit!

There I'd lie in the darkness, contemplating the awful ramifications. What if one of these guys died? What if he suffocated in his sleep? Would the show go on tomorrow night? Would the surviving Dell-and-Mel member go on without his recently deceased partner, or would he withdraw from the gig altogether? And, in that case, would the owner bring in a new headline act or would he bump me up to headliner? *I hope that prick club owner doesn't think he's going to headline me through the weekend and still pay me middle-act money.* I had no problem hearing my mind masturbate.

Oh, and the condo had no toilet paper! No toilet paper, but hundreds and hundreds of clean, new towels wrapped neatly in bundles with white string, "acquired," no doubt, from some unsuspecting motel or linen truck. The towels were stacked in the closets, in the upstairs hallway, and in the bathroom. It didn't take long before Dell and Mel were using them for all manner of purposes.

I believe it was Saturday afternoon when I was headed into the bathroom, only to be met by Mel, the bigger one, who was on his way out—naked. Lovely. As much as it sounds like a gross exaggeration, the man was so huge that at first I didn't see him. Honestly. His hulking brownness filled my peripheral vision so completely that, for the briefest second, I just thought the door was closed. I was just about nose-to-chest with this flesh mountain when I realized he was no door, and that certainly was no doorknob!

I stepped aside, aided, I believe, by Mel's fingertips pushing against my chest. As I began to enter the bathroom and he began to saunter coolly away, I just couldn't help myself. I had to take a glimpse of the rear view. In my defense, something like that is like an accident on the side of the highway. As much as you know you shouldn't look and as much as you resolve you're not going to look, there's something involuntary that takes over, something much bigger than the human will, and you take a peek.

I took a peek. And that's when I saw it—a white towel hanging from Mel's backside. Yes, like a terry-cloth tail. It looked like he'd sat on someone who was trying to surrender. Or like he was some sort of towel dispenser. Either way, I was faced with a dilemma. What to do? What was proper etiquette here? Do I say nothing, trusting that Mel will discover the towel on his own? Do I speak up? You know, nonchalantly say, "Yo, Mel, my man, you got a towel in your ass!"

I opted for a third, more thoughtful choice. I would just oh-so-quietly step on the end of the towel, allowing Mel to walk away from it with no one the wiser, saving the man his dignity. Or so I thought. The towel was wedged up there a lot farther than I had anticipated, and instead of just quietly dropping to the floor, it kind of jerked out of his rump. Mel, feeling something going on up inside his ass, wheeled around to find me wincing sheepishly directly behind him. This giant, nude man's eyes burned with anger, and his ham-sized fists began to clench. Forget my trip to the bathroom; I was peeing then and there.

But then a broad smile swept across Mel's face, followed by a deep, hearty laugh that made his bare belly bounce. He had waited for me. This man, after his shower, had decided to stuff a towel in his ass, and then wait there naked until I came into the hallway—just to see how I would react.

That was funny, and that was being on the road.

True Love

* **Bob Zany** I was onstage talking to this woman in the audience who said she just got engaged. So I said, "When did you know he was the one?" She said, "When the stick turned blue."

* **Nick Hines** My first road gig, I asked the audience if anyone was in an angry relationship. One guy said, "I am!" Then his wife hit him across the face and he fell off his chair. She then tried to blame me. It was a bad night for that guy, and he didn't make the twenty-five bucks I made.

IS THERE A COMIC IN THE AUDIENCE?

* Tom Stern

I managed Mark Schiff for a brief time in the early eighties. At that point I was an inveterate pot smoker, a white Rastafarian with a trust fund. I never made him any money or did anything else that a manager should do, except write with him and tell him he was a genius. About a week before Mark was going to do the Letterman show, he said to Jerry Seinfeld, "You know, Tom's a great guy, he's really funny. I really like him. But he smokes pot twenty-four hours a day and he doesn't have an answering machine. Do you think he's a good manager?"

Jerry said, "You need to fire him. Make it fast."

Mark called me in the Bahamas, where I was vacationing from not working, to announce that my income of zero would be maintained, but not by working with him.

We remained friends and nothing changed, because I kept smoking pot and helping him with his act. I just couldn't call myself his manager. A few days later he said to me, "I've got a gig at the Playboy Club. Do you wanna come?"

I said, "Sure. Look, just this one last time, will you tell them I'm your manager, because I'll probably be able to get a free meal."

So, for old times' sake, we got there, and Mark introduced me as his manager. I proceeded to order five entrées.

Mark went in front of a whole bunch of accountants who I assumed were at the Playboy Club for blue comedy and near-naked women, but what they got was Mark Schiff talking about his childhood.

Mark was bombing in a way that's hard to describe. It's not only that the audience wasn't laughing, but that you could see his whole world crumbling. It's not just that he was sweating; he looked like a guy having a nervous breakdown.

After about ten minutes of absolute death, Mark said to the audience, "Does anybody here know a joke?"

Somebody in the audience said, "Yeah, I do."

So Mark went running into the audience, held the microphone out, and the guy told a joke, getting a gigantic laugh.

Mark said, "Anybody else?"

This guy yelled, "Yeah." So he told a joke and got a huge laugh.

Now the audience was in a better mood. They'd actually had some laughs, and they really liked Mark because there's something about the humility and the way he's dealt with the situation. They applauded him as he got back onstage.

I was thinking, "All right, he's turned it around."

But when he went back into his act, instant death. Five minutes of more death, he couldn't take it anymore. He said, "Thank you and good night," and walked offstage.

I was eating my pasta, but across the room I heard Mark talking to the owner, who definitely looked like he'd gently rolled a couple of bodies into car trunks. He was giving Mark a very stern expression and gesturing with his hands. I knew Mark well enough to see that he was getting defensive and very agitated. Through the din of the bar noise, I could hear Mark say from a hundred feet away, "Well, then, talk to my manager."

I literally stopped in mid-bite, with a huge slew of pasta hanging from my chin, as I stared straight ahead. Mark motioned to me and I came over.

The owner said, "I don't understand your client. I'm not paying him. That's the worst act I've ever seen."

To which I said, "I'm sorry you didn't enjoy it. Mark is a unique performer. He's not for everyone."

He said, "What was he doing up there? He got the audience to tell jokes."

"Well, that's what's unique about Mark. He shows the audience how funny they are."

He said, "That's the craziest thing I've ever heard. What happened in Buffalo? I heard he was great, that's why I hired him."

I said, "The people in Buffalo were the funniest audience Mark ever worked in front of."

The guy was not buying it. "I think you're fulla crap."

I was full of food and confident, so I said, "You can think whatever you like; Mark is a unique performance artist, pay him his twelve hundred dollars."

Finally, the guy paid up.

Mark still didn't pay me a commission—*and* he dressed me down for telling the owner that Buffalo was the funniest audience ever.

DON'T WORRY IF THEY SUCK

✳ Paul Reiser

It was 1987 or '88. I was opening for Melissa Manchester on a two- or three-week tour. I had a great time, with great shows and great audiences. There was one venue I specifically looked forward to, the Concord Hotel in the Catskills, a legendary place, a famous showroom. Everyone played the Concord: Alan King, Shecky Greene, Buddy Hackett, Don Rickles, Morty Gunty, everyone. To me, this was a career landmark, a notch on the belt of a "real comedian."

When we were driving over to the show, Melissa Manchester sat next to me, the first time she did that the whole tour. She said, "Now listen, don't worry about tomorrow if it stinks. It's not your fault."

I said, "What are you, kidding? It'll be great. It's the *Concord*."

She said, "Well, yeah, but sometimes the audiences there can be a little...tough."

I said, "Please. These are my people. They'll love me."

She said, "Okay, but just so you know—the guy who opened for me last year left the stage crying."

I was still confident. I couldn't wait to go out there and hit it out of the park.

When I walked out onstage—death. Thirty seconds in, I was thinking, *Oh my God, this is horrible. They hate me.* Every joke, every bit—as it started to come out of my mouth, I was thinking, *Oh, they're just going to hate this, too.* Everything—death. There were a few people scattered around the room laughing, but forty people out of 2,500 is not really good.

There's a phenomenon that happens when you're not doing well: your material kind of shrivels. It disappears on you. A half hour of your best stuff is over in seven minutes. Because there are no laughs, no ad libs, no finding new little sidebars, no playing. You just keep jumping to the next bit, hoping that this one will get them. But it didn't. Because, as I mentioned earlier, they hated me.

Now, I have no great desire to perform somewhere I'm not wanted. I've always felt like, "Folks, if you'd rather not hear my jokes, then for God's sake, let's just call it a night and cut our losses." But this was a big gig for me. I had a specific job to do: I was there to "warm them up" for Melissa. It was my job to entertain for twenty minutes. So I stayed there and sweated it out. I was tap-dancing. I was telling joke-jokes. I was doing jokes about how they're not liking the jokes I already told them, thinking this would pop the tension, put them on my side. No. More death.

It's no secret that the audiences there were largely old. Even if they were young, they'd act like old people. So they'd give them these little wooden mallets—like you get in a crab house—and they were supposed to bang on the table with the mallets, because they were too tired to actually clap. Or laugh. So even if you were doing *well*, you'd hear 2,500 hammers pounding on tables, and you're supposed to know that that's laughter. *Whack, whack, whack* actually means "Gee, that's funny."

Finally I did my time and walked offstage. As I passed Melissa in the wings, she said, "What'd I tell ya?"

I said, "But I'm not crying. And I did my twenty minutes."

She said, "I've been standing here ready the whole time. I didn't think you'd last this long."

Now, I'm not a drinker, but after this show, I needed alcohol. A lot of it. So I went with the band down to the bar. A few beers later, I was feeling almost okay when this big guy—checkered sports blazer, gold medallions, big cigar in his mouth—came over. He started buying drinks for the band.

"Great show, you guys. Great band." He said to one of the musicians, "What did you play? Drums? Good, good. How about you? Oh, the bass player! That was some good bass playing." Then he came to me. "And you? What did you do?"

I sucked it up and admitted, "I was the comedian."

Long pause. Deathly quiet. And then he said, "Oooooooh, boy!" He put his arm around me, very paternally, and he said, "Let me tell you something. Forgive me for saying. The problem is your material. See, your material, the problem with the material is—it's very bad. It's bad material."

I think I said, "Thank you."

He said, "Who writes your material?"

I said, "I do, actually. I write my own material."

Another pause.

"Oh. Well...It's really...It's just very bad."

And then—my favorite part—he said, "I don't mean any offense." Of course not.

I remember the next night, we went somewhere else—and I had a great show. And I thought, *Okay, that's better. I'm not entirely without skill. Last night, that was just bad. That's why they call it a bad night.*

But I did write some new material.

GIVING MY FANS AWAY

✳ Paul Rodriguez

In 1987, I did eight shows in eight days. I went to Denver, Dallas, San Antonio, and Houston, and, on the way back, Albuquerque, Phoenix, and then Los Angeles, where I played the Strand in Redondo Beach.

When I was in Albuquerque, I noticed this chick in the audience. This woman had probably been very, very attractive at one time, but was now dragging around her thirty-five years. She stuck out from the other women there for two reasons.

First, she was a blonde white woman, and back in that day, my audience was about 98 percent Mexican-American. There are some blonde Mexicans, but they're Revlon blondes, with really tan skin and blonde hair. Imagine Jennifer Lopez as a blonde.

Second, she didn't laugh. This chick had that thousand-mile stare that war veterans sometimes have. In fact, she appeared to have been in a few battles. She was just there—attentive—the way a dog focuses on a tennis ball when you're about to throw it. I tend to pace onstage, and those crazy eyes followed me like I was going to take off and fly around the room.

At the end of the show in Albuquerque, she said to me, "I'll see you in Phoenix." Suddenly, Beethoven's "Pathétique" sonata played in my head.

I said, "Oh, you know somebody in Phoenix?"

She said, "You."

The music in my head got louder and I said, "Well, am I wrong, or haven't I seen you before?"

She said, "I've been going to every show that you've done."

"Every show? Why?"

She said, "It will be revealed to us."

Spooky as she was, I figured that after a couple of shots of tequila, she wouldn't be all that bad—a quick bang-bang. On a slow night, I would definitely do her. If men are dogs, male comics are wild coyotes.

So I said, "Okay. You know it could be revealed now."

She didn't react. My little joke just bounced off her forehead, which was odd since most comic groupies laugh at anything, because they want to score a comic.

I didn't see her in the Phoenix crowd. She was there, all right; I just didn't see her. After the show, I got a note from her critiquing my show in some detail; I had flipped one routine, hadn't done another, and hadn't punched up a certain bit.

It was out of control. I had a critic stalker.

At the last show of the run, my agent booked a very funny young comic, Martin Lawrence, to open for me.

Between shows, Martin mentioned "a crazy chick who didn't laugh, just stared," sitting up front. I knew it was her.

I spent most of my show watching her watch me and trying to figure out her motive. She wasn't one of those drunken hecklers who want to be part of your act. She just sat there. It bothered me that she didn't really laugh, but if you have a choice between someone heckling or just being quiet, most comics prefer quiet. Sometimes someone even laughing in the wrong place, for no reason, can be worse than a heckle.

After the show, the limo driver (whom I didn't know) said to me, "Hey, your wife is surprising you. I'm not supposed to tell you, but she's in the limo."

I said, "My wife? What are you talking about? I'm not married."

The limo driver said, "Hey, she showed me pictures of you and her, and she talked about your life and everything."

I said, "Dude, pictures of her and me?"

I had to do something with this chick, and fast: another girl was dropping off the guy she'd come to the show with, and getting together with me. We had it all prearranged; every comic knows what I'm talking about.

I leaned into the limo and said, "Hi, excuse me. Listen, you told the limo driver you're my wife?"

She was seated comfortably, with this certain fixed expression, like her whole face was shot with Botox. She said, "Sit down, I'm gonna tell you."

I opted to stand, just outside of knifing range, and said, "Yeah? Tell me what?"

She proceeded to tell me this story about our having been married in a past life. We were very happy, I died early, and my spirit came to her and told her that in her next life she was to look for the most famous Latino comedian—that would be me—so we could resume our lives together.

I don't know where in my brain it came from, probably from the same place the jokes do, but out of nowhere, I saw a way out.

I said, "Whoa, whoa, whoa! Wait a minute. My spirit from a past life said 'the most famous Latino comedian,' right?"

She said, "Yeah."

I said, "That's why I can't remember you! The most famous Latino comedian is Cheech Marin from Cheech and Chong."

She said, "Cheech?"

I said, "Yeah, Cheech. He's Mexican, he's Latino, from Cheech and Chong. He's the most famous! Didn't you hear of the movies *Born in East L.A., Up in Smoke?*"

And an immediate realization came over her face, like it all made sense. She started repeating his name, a stalker mantra: "Cheech Marin. Cheech Marin. Cheech Marin."

This chick didn't even say good-bye, didn't even look at me.

It was as if the Paul Rodriguez switch got flipped off. She just opened her door, got out, and walked away. I never heard from her, ever again.

I've run into Cheech many times since, and each time I've expected him to say, "You put that crazy bitch on me!" My conscience sometimes makes me wonder why I passed on this potential problem to a guy who was never anything but nice to me. Thankfully, though Cheech and I have done all kinds of shows and a couple of movies together, he never mentioned the psycho.

One comforting thought: Cheech's wife, Patty, wouldn't have let this chick get near her man. Patty would have kicked her ass! Besides that, Cheech is a very faithful cat and he doesn't perform live now, so it's unlikely this woman could get near him. And he makes more money than I do, so he can afford better security.

There was a part of me that enjoyed this bizarre woman's attention. It was like I had arrived. Sort of an updated version of the old Dean Martin song, "You're Nobody Till Somebody Stalks You."

A CLINGING LOVE

✳ John Heffron

In 1991, years before I met my wife, or even dreamt there might be a woman as wonderful as her, I met this girl when I was working a Michigan bar called Mister G's. It was a Sunday-night one-nighter frequented by strippers on their off night. Every comic wanted to do the gig, because even if you had a bad set you hooked up, and the comedy bar was set mighty low at this place. The host warmed up the crowd with gems like, "Come on, throw up your condoms. Whoever has a condom gets a free blow job."

So I met this dancer. That's what she called herself, and I didn't really know enough about the Joffrey Ballet to disagree. I've since learned that even if you move in time with the music, if the White Snake song ends and you're naked, you're a stripper.

We went back to her place and she took out this big boa constrictor. I don't know if it was just a pet or a tax-deductible part of her act. She wanted me to touch it. I touched it, trying not to look afraid, figuring it might be some sort of Excalibur test: "He that toucheth my snake can enter my kingdom."

I remembered hearing something about not staring at wild animals, so I looked away and saw a picture of another girl on the nightstand.

She asked, "Do you like her?"

I forgot she was in control of a large snake and replied honestly, "Yeah, she's cute."

"Do you want me to see if she wants to join in?"

"What?"

"Hold on." She walked out of her room and returned immediately with the girl, who was her roommate.

She looked at me. "Oh, you're one of the comics?"

Clearly I was the hundredth guy to touch the snake and win the damsel's heart.

She was very considerate of our health. "Guys, I would love to, but I have a wicked cold. So you guys just have a good time."

We went at it. I was really drunk and forgot about the python still on the bed. Maybe she said the snake just liked to watch. I felt the girl's leg wrap around mine and thought she was really flexible, not unusual for a dancer. When her leg moved toward my ass, I realized that the snake was not just a watcher; it was an interspecies sexual opportunist. Sober, I probably would've turned it into a scene from a Tarzan movie, but I was drunk and deep in her kingdom.

The only question for my alcohol-soaked brain was whether it was possible for me to finish before the snake ate me.

I managed to blurt out something like, "The snake."

She never missed a beat. "No, it's fine. He's in here all the time."

Sure, the python has to eat, too.

I beat the snake; fear of death can really move things along sexually. She helped get the snake off me. I probably should have checked the closet for the personal belongings of all the comics who'd fed the snake before me, but I wanted to leave before the roommate brought in her pet wolverine.

I never saw the girl again. I imagine her now as a churchgoing soccer mom with better bedtime stories than the ones she tells her kids.

THEY WEREN'T SEDATED

✳ Ritch Shydner

In 1978, I was eager for stage time. I was living in Washington, D.C., and there were no comedy clubs there at the time, so I grubbed for audiences in bars and coffee houses, and at outdoor political rallies.

One night the owner of one of my drinking hangouts said to me, "I got this band coming down from New York and you're going to open for them."

I said, "Great."

He continued, "They're kind of a rowdy band." My attitude was, "No problem, I'm a rowdy guy."

The place was a big pub off Dupont Circle. When the room was filled with two hundred people, all smoking and spilling beer, it was possible to experience the sense of death by suffocation with a stale gym towel.

The night of the show, every glue-head in the metropolitan area jammed into the room to see the seminal punk band from New York, the Ramones.

I was waiting in the bar's kitchen when in squirted the owner from the jam-packed bar. He poured two shots of whiskey. "You ain't gonna last two seconds with this crowd. I mean, I knew that when I hired you, but by contract I had to put on an opener."

He drank both shots of whiskey and started laying lines of cocaine on the stainless-steel counter. "Fuck putting a musical act in front of these guys, 'cause I gotta shell out like five, six hundred. No sense doing that when I can get a comic for thirty dollars. Don't get me wrong. You ain't a comic. You been coming in here for two years and I ain't heard you say one funny thing, but if you're willing to go in front of this crowd for thirty dollars, you can call yourself anything you want. You're gonna be a magician."

Not seeing his joke coming, I tried to tell him I didn't do magic.

He let me have it. " 'Cuz you're going to be disappearing in about three minutes."

I was also the agent who'd negotiated my deal, so I had to remind him of all the terms. "And free beer. I get free beer."

He snorted both lines of cocaine and then handed me the rolled-up dollar bill. I looked at the empty counter. The man had cut himself free of the bounds of decency. He was flying so high, morality looked like an ant from the top of the Washington Monument. Joining the party, I slid his dollar bill into my pocket.

I was not far removed from my high school and college jock mind-set, so I tended to view each performance as an athletic event, a game to be won or lost. I told him, "You'll see. I'll do my fifteen minutes."

Suddenly he thought I was the funniest person in the world. He stopped laughing only long enough to snort another line of cocaine. "I'll go double or nothing for your pay if you make five minutes." He snorted another line and his inner drug fiend raised the bid: "Make it a hundred bucks. I'll give you a hundred if you make five minutes."

I knew who I was dealing with, so I said, "Let Leo keep the time." Leo was the bartender and my friend. The owner lit a cigarette off his dying cigarette. "Go tell Leo. I got to get the Ramones." I wanted to see if he had them stashed in the walk-in-freezer, but instead I went into the bar.

Five minutes later the owner went on the "stage," a six-inch riser. He was laughing so hard, he barely got out my introduction. "Ladies and gentlemen, please welcome comedian Ritch Shydner." He then screamed to Leo at the bar, "Start the time now!"

The audience booed so loud I didn't even hear my first joke. Seconds later, someone threw a beer in my direction. It didn't hit me, but there was no time to determine whether it was thrown as a warning or simply to gauge distance, because the next one *did* hit me. Once they saw I wouldn't move and they wouldn't get tossed, the crowd had themselves a new sport. I just plowed through my act, holding the mike stand with both hands to help brace against the beer shower. The place served beer in thick glass mugs and pitchers, so it could have been worse. Someone would run to the stage, toss a beer, and the crowd would cheer. If I ducked or the beer thrower missed, the audience booed.

Finally, Leo yelled, "Time," and rang the bar's big brass tip bell. The owner stood at the kitchen door, waving my money. "Come on, asshole. You got it, fucker. You got it." Drenched in beer, I entered the kitchen just as the Ramones, guitars and drumsticks in hand, headed for the stage. As we passed each other, one of the Ramones said, "You're good, man. Fucking good." He thought this was my act, to let people throw beer at me, the Human Beer Sponge. I didn't get a laugh onstage, but I felt pretty good. Not just because of the hundred dollars. It was that sense that I held the stage. I won the game.

Please Don't Hurt the Dummy

✳ **Jeff Dunham** I was working onstage in Jacksonville, Florida, with my dummy, Peanut, when a fight broke out. One of the guys tried to explain it. "That dummy kept poking at my wife!" Peanut yelled back, "Well, who hasn't?"

✳ **Peter Hefty** I was working Daytona Beach, Florida, during Bike Week in 1978. I'm a ventriloquist, and my main dummy is Justin. I was onstage, and this guy just kept throwing out insults back and forth with Justin. Nothing unusual there, but this guy got really pissed. He walked up to the stage. Everybody thought it was part of the act. He got right in front of the stage and said to me, "Listen, I have nothing against you, you know, it's that damn little dummy." Of course, the audience laughed. Still not getting it, the guy hit Justin, the dummy, over the head with a beer bottle.

WRONG MOVE ON THE WRONG GUY

✳ Tim Allen

I was working with the Canadian comedian Mike McDonald at Detroit's Comedy Castle. This guy was screaming during Mike's punch lines. It was the worst sort of heckling; nothing McDonald could respond to, just an unstoppable, incoherent joke killer.

Mike tried being nice, asking the guy what he wanted to say. Of course, the guy had nothing to say. He was probably just a stupid guy who got drunk, and then was freaked out by all the strange sounds and lights and laughter he didn't understand.

I remember Mike even pleaded with the heckler, "Come on, man. Let me finish this." That surprised me, because Mike wasn't known for his patience and tolerance. I wasn't surprised when the guy screamed again and McDonald said, "You do that again and I'm gonna come and punch you right in the fucking face."

Of course, the guy yelled all through Mike's last bit.

When Mike came offstage, he lost it and punched the guy right in the kisser. A little later we were backstage when a waitress said the guy Mike had punched wanted to talk. Mike came out, and the guy he'd punched said he actually wasn't the guy who'd yelled. Mike felt so bad he bought drinks for the guy and his buddies and hung out with them for an hour. Just as Mike was leaving, the guy said, "Hey, asshole, I was the guy who yelled."

I thought Mike was going to hit him again. The guy sued Mike and the club. He lost the case when it was proven he had provoked entertainers all around town in hopes of getting a lawsuit.

PAY FIGHT

✴ George Westerholm

I used to be part of a musical comedy team by the name of Al & George.

My memory is a bit hazy on this, as it happened between the years of 1984 and 1994, but if I remember correctly, Al and I got back to our hotel room one night—we often had to share—and we decided to take our gig money and pool it in a pile in the middle of the floor. We thought it might be a laugh to dive into it and grab our take for the week. I think we shouted "Go!" and just dove into the pile of cash. We grappled and knocked our heads around until there were no more bills to grab, and then we went to opposite ends of the room to see how much we'd managed to get. For some reason, we decided we should keep doing this. We learned to ask the club to pay us in smaller denominations so that one lucky bugger didn't grab all the hundreds. It was surprising how even it would come out when we did it. It was all an idiotic lark, and innocent enough, although I do remember our unique payroll exercise getting a tad more "intense" as time went on. You know how partners are.

One night we did our "money scramble" in front of the headliner, Jim MacAleese, and he told the club owner in Hamilton. A few nights later, when we went around to the office to get paid for the week, the club owner held our pay envelope and casually asked if it was true that we fought each other for the gig money. We said, "Yeah," and he thought it would be a brilliant idea if he could throw the money up in the air for us when we did it. We had no problem with that. What the hell; on the floor, in the air, who cares?

So in the dingy, shitty back hallway of the Hamilton club we fought for the money in front of a small audience of bar staff and the club owner. As usual, we tore into each other, fought and swore, madly snatched up all the cash, and scurried back into opposing corners to count up our spoils. I wasn't there the first time this club owner banged two waitresses at the same time, but the delight on his face from watching us fight for our cash couldn't have been equaled even then.

Word spread pretty quickly, and soon all the club owners wanted to see us fight each other for our money—the sick fucks. As you can imagine, our money scramble quickly lost its charm for us. We didn't want to become an amusement for our Dickensian employers; we just wanted to simply pound the crap out of each other for our own hard-earned money.

What really ended our bare-fisted paydays was when we went on our first tour of Britain and found there just wasn't any money to fight over anymore. I guess that's when the real fighting began.

COMEDY HOUSE CALLS

* Christopher Titus

Casa Carlitas was a Mexican restaurant in Hayward, California, that had a comedy night, a salsa night, a football night, and a sumo wrestling night. On this last one, people climbed into huge, padded suits soaked in the sweat of a thousand other people. They should have called the place the Anything to Sell Margaritas Bar & Grill. The stage was two boxes upside down, with a piece of plywood covered in AstroTurf on top. The microphone was plugged into the house speaker system on an eight-foot cord. This club owner had made a real financial commitment to comedy.

In 1987 I did a two-man show there with Steven Pearl, a really funny and super-loud comic. One of his bits at the time was an impression of *Scarface*'s Tony Montana doing kids' parties and being a standup comedian. The line "Here is some motherfucking goose rhymes" used to kill me. When he did the bit, Steve also stuck his head into a plastic bag of flour as if it were cocaine.

We finished the Sunday show to uproarious laughter, and no chimichangas were thrown. Steve and I were waiting to get paid when a huge man in a red velvet sweat suit (the man's size pointed to its never having seen sweat), wearing huge sunglasses from the Mocking Elvis Collection, walked up holding a brandy snifter. "Great show! Do you guys do private parties?"

As I was surviving on one piece of pizza a day, I did any show, party, leper colony, or Kiwanis picnic. "Yeah, I do private parties."

"How much?"

I figured I'd nail this rube, so I doubled what I got at the Mexican place. "One hundred and fifty bucks." I was thinking, *Man, if this goes down, I got pizza for a month!*

Steve, who was headlining, doubled his paycheck, too. "Yeah, three hundred bucks for me and we'll do your party. When is it?"

The man took another swig and said, "Tonight."

Steve and I both looked at our Swatches and noticed it was 11:14 P.M., which on a Sunday night was not the ideal time to book a second show. We said, "We have to get paid first."

I smiled, thinking that hearing the big bucks we got paid for *one* show would drive the man deep into his brandy glass and away from us.

"I gotta go to the ATM; wait here."

Twenty minutes later, Steve and I were sitting in an empty Mexican restaurant, waiting for Alan Funt to walk in. But "Not Elvis" came back with the cash.

"Where is this show?" I asked.

"At my friend's place, follow me."

Steve and I got into his car. Here's where I knew it was getting weird. As I shut my door, Steve said, "There's a knife under your seat. I'll use the gun." To which my twenty-year-old mind responded, "Why do you get the gun?"

Steve looked at me with his New York face. "It's *my* car, that's why I get the gun."

We went through the backstreets of Hayward, California, to a small tract house. I figured it must be a surprise party we were performing at, because there were no lights on. I thought, *When so-and-so gets off their shift at Denny's, we're gonna do one hell of a comedy show.* We went into the house, and sitting on the couch were three people: Velour Sweat Suit Guy and a very nice-looking husband and wife who looked oddly like hostages, and their small terrier. "Is this it?" Steve asked in a "What the fuck?" tone.

The guy raised his brandy snifter, handed us our money, and told us to start the show. But first he asked if he could tape it. He then turned on this old *Mission: Impossible*–style reel-to-reel tape recorder and sat down.

The big problem was that these people had just seen the show. I only had thirty minutes of material, total, and at this point in my career I could barely riff with a hot crowd. How was I gonna stretch with three people and a dog? Hey, one hundred fifty bucks is one hundred fifty bucks. "Good evening, and welcome to...this guy's house! How we feeling tonight?" The dog barked, the couple looked uncomfortable, and Fat Guy toasted me with a refilled brandy snifter. "Okay, well, how about that Huey Lewis...?" I did my whole act, *the one they had just seen,* as if I were playing to five hundred people and two hundred dogs. I finished and brought Steve up. "Lady and gentlemen...and dog, please welcome Steven Pearl!"

Now, you need to know something about Steven Pearl; he was schooled at comedy at the Holy City Zoo in San Francisco. The Zoo was no bigger than the living room we were currently in, so Steve was a master of it. I was watching a guy in someone's living room KILL!

But Brandy Guy was so hammered by now, he started heckling! As Steve went into his *Scarface* bit, the guy started yelling, "I love you, Tony Montana, I love you!"

Steve slammed the guy, and I laughed, but then realized that in a club slamming a guy is funny, but in his own house it just seems rude. The dog walked out and Steve was trying to do his closer. Sweat Suit was now so in the bag he got up and hugged Steve, who was by now covered in flour. "I love you, Tony Montana! I love you!"

Steve sat the guy down. "Great. I love you, too. Now sit down and shut up." The guy was quiet for about thirty seconds, but then he was up again. "I love you, Tony Montana! I LOVE YOUUUUU!" I walked between them because... well, this guy's house didn't have a bouncer.

Before I could grab the guy, Steve grabbed him and said, "If you hug me one more time, fucko, I'm gonna shoot you!" Okay, Steve doesn't need a bouncer. The husband and wife on the couch were now looking really scared. Steve was still holding the guy, and in this moment of weirdness, the guy on the couch put a protective arm around his wife and said, "Great show. You guys can go." I was thinking, *Great show? Really? Did you like the bit about...*

Steve grabbed me, and we bailed out the back with the most money I had ever made for a night's work. As we drove away, I swear I faintly heard, "I love you, Tony Montanaaaaaaaaaa!"

I don't know who books that gig.

WILLIE AND RICHARD AT THE COMEDY STORE

✳ Charlie Hill

It was a regular Tuesday night in 1978 at The Comedy Store on Sunset Boulevard. The club had just closed for the evening when there was a knock at the door. I opened it, and there was Willie Nelson. Willie had been at the club two nights earlier, and he'd had such a ball he'd decided to come back. Willie joined the group already inside: Richard Pryor, Argus Hamilton, Burt Reynolds, Sally Field, Robin Williams, and me. Everyone was drunk, high, or both.

I was sitting next to Sally, and every time Burt turned his head the other way, I said to her, "What do you say? Flap your nun wings and we'll head up to my place. I never had nun fun." She was giggling.

All of a sudden Pryor started yelling in his preacher voice, got onstage, and started healing people. Then Robin got up and the both of them started doing characters. Then Burt joined them. After Sally got up there, I had no choice but to do it, too. Everyone except Willie was onstage.

Pryor was doing characters none of us had ever seen. Robin was literally climbing the walls, balancing on the backs of chairs, anything to get a laugh. It was just one of those magical evenings, a handful of people having the time of their lives making each other laugh.

We'd started to run out of steam when Willie stood up. "I'll be right back. Don't lock me out." Three minutes later he came back in with his guitar. He said, "You guys entertained me for an hour, and now I'm going to do it for you." Everyone got offstage except Pryor, who introduced Willie in his Mudbone voice. Willie took the stage and sang everything for us, every song you could imagine him singing. And just the six of us got to hear it.

Funny has gotten me into a lot of cool places.

A SHINING STAR

✴ Shelley Berman

One night in 1960, I was a young comedian working at Mr. Kelly's in Chicago. I was rather new and gaining some heat. But I had a heckler, a guy who just kept after me incessantly. I can't remember exactly what I said to him; all I know is that I killed him and the audience went wild. The guy then stood up and said, "Come on outside and say that."

Milton Berle, an easily recognizable star whom I didn't know and had never met until that moment, was in the audience that night. He stood up and said, "Shelley's busy, but I'll go outside with you." The audience went to pieces.

RODNEY AND ME

✳ Jackie Martling

Back in 1980, my friend the comedian Richie Minervini walked into my house (actually it was my grandmother's house, where my girlfriend and I had been squatting since she had passed away) and told me he had gone on at Dangerfield's the night before. Richie said he'd not only killed, but that Rodney had seen him and had spoken to him about using him on a TV show. I was so jealous I could have exploded.

Becoming Jackie the Hustler, I immediately sat down at the typewriter, stuck in two sheets of paper and a carbon, and methodically went through every joke I knew, choosing and molding bits that I thought would work for Rodney and his "I don't get no respect" persona.

A few weeks earlier I'd been awakened at about five in the morning by a close friend who was calling from, of all places, Peru. He was there either doing or buying cocaine and had met some wild guy from the South who'd told him something he thought was really funny: "This girl was so ugly she was known as a Tennessee Two-Bagger. That's a girl who's so ugly you not only have to put a bag over her head, but you have to put a bag over *your* head, in case her bag rips."

Of course, I typed "The Tennessee Two-Bagger" into those six delightful pages to Rodney that would be my entry to Real Show Business.

The next time I saw Richie, I handed the pages to him in one of my Off Hour Rockers envelopes—even when I couldn't afford to eat, I had company stationery—and said, "Do me a favor and hand this to your new pal Rodney Dangerfield."

Richie looked at me sheepishly and said, "Oh, man, I was lying. I didn't even get onstage there the other night...Rodney wasn't even there."

"So I guess your spot on his TV show is on the back burner."

"I'm sorry, man."

"You weren't even there, were you?"

"Yeah, I was. They told me to come back, that I'd get on next time. Look..."

He reached in his pocket and pulled out a matchbook. It read, DANGERFIELD'S, 1002 FIRST AVENUE, NEW YORK, NEW YORK. It had the phone number and the caricature of Rodney sweating and pulling at his tie. It was authentic. He had at least been there.

This makes Richie sound like an incredible bullshit artist (which he is, but that is strictly a coincidence). But in Richie's defense, all starting comics—let's change that to *all* comics—lie about their shows and how their careers are going. There's even a classic joke— I call jokes "classic" because it has a nicer ring to it than "old"— about two Catskill comics who live together. One guy goes out to work, and when he gets back that night, his roommate says, "So how'd it go?"

He says, "You wouldn't believe it. The best show I ever had. The laughs were fast and loud and powerful and crisp. They bought every premise. Joke after joke, I had to wait for the room to die down. I got a standing ovation, two encores. It was unbelievable."

"I was there. You weren't so hot."

"The band fucked me up."

Anyway, not wanting to give up after having taken the trouble to put all these jokes together, I ended up mailing the six pages to Rodney, at the Dangerfield's address on the matchbook.

Two days later my girlfriend and I were sitting in Grandma's kitchen when the phone rang.

"Hello, Jackie, this is Rodney."

"Rodney who?"

"See that? You're funny. You're fucking funny. I knew that..."

Meanwhile, I was cupping the phone and telling my girlfriend, "It's Rodney Dangerfield!" I was about as excited as I've ever been. I was talking to not just a celebrity, but my hero, my idol, one of the funniest guys ever. He went on.

"I got the jokes. Some really funny stuff here. I'm gonna send you a check for five of these. Want to come meet me? I'm playing the Westbury Music Fair Friday night."

"I'll be there."

"That 'Two-Bagger,' that's a funny fucking joke. See you Friday. Just tell them you're with me."

At the Westbury show, "Two-Bagger" brought the house down. After the show, Rodney almost shit when he saw I had a ponytail down my back and was in ragged blue jeans. But he couldn't have been nicer.

"Look at your fucking hair. And the jeans. Jesus Christ. Have a piece of fruit. Want a piece of fruit? Some funny stuff. Send more, send it to my house. I'll put my home address in the letter with the check. You want something to drink? I like that fucking 'Two-Bagger.' Yeah. Send more."

A few days later I got a letter explaining which jokes he was buying, and a check for $200, signed by Rodney Dangerfield. And suddenly we were pals. Not bosom buddies by any stretch, but, in some sense of the word, pals.

I kept sending jokes, and each time I'd include a note with them, usually asking Rodney to take me on the road sometime, that we'd have a good time, we could write, whatever.

A few months after that first meeting, Rodney called again.

"Come to Vegas; it's on me. We'll have a good time. I'll fly you first class, the whole thing. I gotta go to Fort Lauderdale first. I'm taking my daughter and her friend to Fort Lauderdale. Sure, come to Lauderdale. The whole two weeks, see what happens."

Of course, I accepted the invitation. Soon we were in Vegas, and one night, after both of Rodney's shows at the Aladdin, a bit of craps, and a lot of drinking and whatever, he said, "Let's take a walk over to the MGM." (The MGM Grand Hotel used to be next to the Aladdin on the Vegas Strip.)

It was the week after Easter in 1980, at the height of the gasoline shortage, so Vegas business was way off, not to mention it was very, very late. When we found the MGM hotel, it was close to barren, so we turned around and left. As we walked back along the Strip, the sun was just starting to peek out at us.

We were almost to the Aladdin when Rodney said, "You gotta take a leak? I gotta take a leak."

I'm a beer drinker. I said, "Sure, I can always piss."

Instead of waiting a few short minutes until we were in the lobby, we walked around to the back of the hotel. Soon we were standing next to two of the most gigantic Dumpsters I had ever seen. They were literally the size of a small McDonald's. Rodney unzipped and started peeing on one of them, and at ninety degrees to him, about twenty feet away, I started peeing on the other.

As our streams doused the bottoms of these huge bins, Rodney turned his head to me, cock in hand, and said, "Welcome to the big time."

I shook my head (actually, I shook both my heads) and said, "Do you know how many people I'm gonna tell this story to?"

He said, "Go ahead, have a party."

BAD TIMING

✳ Colin Quinn

This story is about the first time I attempted to do standup. The key word here is "attempted."

One Sunday morning in 1983, I awoke in a Brooklyn gutter. A drunk in a gutter is a cliché, I know, but it's a cliché for a reason: drunks tend to fall down and roll, and gutters are designed to catch all the things that roll in a street. Luckily I was still wearing my clothes and miraculously had money left in my wallet, in violation of Galileo's Fifth Principle of Physics: Gutter sleep equals no money.

This hangover was different from most. Usually I awoke in my drunken, pathetic condition and swore never to do it again. This time my first thought was, *I'm gonna go to the Improvisation tonight and start my career as a comedy star.* It wasn't dedicating my life to serving the poor, but it was a step up from heading back to the bar for a little hair of the dog.

I'd thought of trying to do standup for a few years. What Irish drunk didn't think he was funny at the bar at one in the morning? But it was the thought of doing it sober, in front of a crowd not composed of other drunks from my neighborhood, that kept me from going to an audition night for two years.

Even though I felt like shit, I pulled myself from the gutter and went to Manhattan. Of course, my careful planning didn't reveal that the Improv was not open at noon on a Sunday. A bum on the street told me the club started handing out numbers for the open mike at three-thirty. I thought if I was lucky I'd follow this guy, so that the crowd might think the odor was still from him and not me.

I had three hours to kill. Since I was already physically and mentally burned out, I did what any drunk would do, and went to a bar. A few drinks made me more tired, so I reached into my bottomless bag of Bad Ideas and pulled out a gem: Go to the porno theater across the street and find somebody with drugs.

I bought a ticket and took a seat in the porno theater, the perfect place to prepare for your comedy debut. Two hours later I returned to the Improv with no drugs and stained underwear.

Meanwhile, I was operating under the delusion that any comic at the audition automatically got a number and got onstage. I never imagined for a second that there was a chance I would not get onstage. Of course, the Improv handed out numbers to five guys out of the thirty who were there, and I didn't get one. Naturally my first thought was, *Shit, I really do need some drugs.*

I headed to 42nd Street to troll for speed, which, of course, they never had there. Even the drug dealers didn't want the street junkies moving faster than they did. I was such a garbage-pail head that, although I was hoping for speed, I gladly made a deal for procaine instead. It could have been propane and I'd have been doing it anyway.

The dealer took me into his office/hallway, but before we were able to complete our transaction, the door was kicked open and four fucking plainclothes cops crashed in, shoving us against the wall and handcuffing us. I found out later that the cops always do a big sweep during the Sunday matinee shows. Apparently every guy dragged in from the suburbs by his wife has to score some dope to make it through a Broadway show.

We were marched down 42nd Street to a little ratty substation on Times Square.

I was raving, "I am a comedian! I have to go on at the Improvisation! Let me go! Let me go! I have a show to do!" Despite the fact that I'd never done comedy, I was ranting like I had to do a command performance for the president, whom I probably couldn't even name at that moment.

I kept this up until one cop said, "You're a comedian? All right, let's see your act."

I swear to you, the cops removed my shackles and told me to start. My first audience was arrested guys and cops. My stage was a milk crate or something similar. I did maybe three minutes of excruciatingly corny jokes, really bad jokes, but not "joke jokes." I was doing the act I'd intended to do that night at the Improv. "Hey, you guys. I grew up in Brooklyn. In Brooklyn, I'll tell you, everyone thinks it's all guys with gold chains—Italian guys. That's a stereotype. That's Staten Island."

I was just bombing brutally. It was a *looooong* two minutes. People don't realize how terrible jokes can stretch out time. The cops were just glaring at me. Even in my drunken stupor, I was totally ashamed.

Then one of the cops ended it by saying, "Okay, we were gonna let you go 'cause you said you were a comedian, but now we know you're lying." And they just kept me there.

My first appearance as a standup, I bombed so badly I got booked into a jail cell.

A LARRY DAVID CROWD

✳ Chris Albrecht

Back in 1978, everybody in the business was familiar with the Larry David Throw-Down. Larry was a comic's comic, and he never really got the response onstage that all the comedians thought he deserved. Somehow he wasn't really connecting with the audience on a regular basis. I always tried to keep the crowd in the club as long as possible, so I generally put him on late at night so as not to shorten the evening unintentionally.

One of the things that always happened with Larry was he would go onstage and start his act and eventually get frustrated and just walk off. This would psych him out, and eventually it snowballed to the point where it took less and less time onstage before he got frustrated enough to end his act early.

So I was talking to him and we decided that what he really needed was a good, fresh crowd to kind of break him of this and get his confidence back. So we put him on Saturday night, the 10:20 P.M. spot, first show—a guaranteed kill spot.

Larry came into the club, looked at the audience, and began psyching himself out. He already knew who in the audience was not going to laugh and which ones were going to outright hate him.

Bob Shaw, the emcee, introduced Larry to a full house, a hot crowd. Larry went onstage, grabbed the mike, looked at the audience, and said, "Forget it." He didn't do a single joke, just dropped the mike and left the stage. Shaw ran to the stage and saved the evening by doing another version of a story he'd already told.

MOVING ON BLACK TIME

✳ Lisa Lampanelli

I've banged a black guy for two years now, which is nine and a half years in black. I figure I've done my time, so I can do all the nigger jokes I want. Also, black people usually love me. I did *BET Comic View* and the blacks stood up. I'm like a white bitch, so I figure, okay, I can say what I want.

I was at Stand-Up New York back in 2004 when I had this incident with a black guy. That fuckin' club attracts all the idiots. I was doing my stuff, starting off with Italian, then gay, then spic, and whatever's left. A middle-aged black guy sitting with a black woman yelled, "You're a racist!"

The audience started booing and vibrating nervously, afraid that things might get violent.

I said, "A racist thinks that one race is better than another. I think we're all fucked." This got a laugh from the three people who were running for the exits, or diving under their tables.

This prick still wanted to dance and said, "All you do is do black jokes."

I was like, "Didn't you hear me rip the Itals, the gays and spics and everyone?"

He yelled, "We just got here!" He was pissed, like that was my fault. His woman was yelling, "That's right," at anybody near them.

Nobody was listening. I was really just talking to myself when I said, "If you weren't on black-people time, maybe you'd have seen the other fuckin' jokes."

So the lesson in that is, "Be on time, black people."

That's if you get any black readers, which I doubt.

THE WILE E. COYOTE OF COMEDY

* Paul Kozak

When I started out, I worked some gigs with a guy who was so bad at improv that he refused to go one inch off his act. This was really tough, because the guy attracted more accidents and mishaps than a Roadrunner cartoon.

One night Dennis Miller, Wile E. Jokie, and I were working a club in Pittsburgh called the Dubbing Rabbit. A guy heckled Wile E., who took the microphone and charged offstage like Phil Donahue used to before Oprah knocked him into retirement.

Wile E. put the mike in the guy's face and asked, "What did you say again?" The guy then coldcocked Wile E., who just turned around, got back up onstage, and continued with the act as if nothing had happened.

Another time this same hard-luck comedian was working the Holiday House in Pittsburgh. It had a short ceiling and a tall stage. When he got introduced and hopped onstage with his usual over-exuberance, he hit his head on a ceiling fire sprinkler. But he went right into his show as if nothing had happened.

As the show continued, he thought he was sweating, but it was blood from his head wound. He kept wiping his forehead and smearing the blood all over his face.

The audience was dying, and he thought he was killing. He finally realized it was his blood that was cracking them up, but he never called attention to it. He never asked for a towel, never said a word. He just finished his set, said "Thank you," and, still bleeding, walked offstage. That was the thing with this guy; he never acknowledged a real moment. He would continue with his material if a space alien walked into the room.

He also used to do this Tom Snyder–*Mission: Impossible* impression, and one time he decided to try to get a tape recorder to self-destruct as it did on the TV show. So I gave him some flash paper and flash powder to put in this old reel-to-reel tape player he brought onstage. He had the lit cigarette going already for the Tom Snyder impression, so I told him to just touch the cigarette to the flash stuff.

Instead of practicing or rehearsing in any way, he loaded up the tape player with flash powder and tried the bit for the first time in front of a full crowd. He sat in the chair doing Tom Snyder, and then leaned down with his face right over the tape player, and touched off this huge explosion. His face was all black. His hair was smoking. But he never said a word. He just continued with the bit as if nothing had happened.

PRYOR AND THE FIRE

✳ Harris Peet

Sometime around 1981, I was a standup comic/doorman at The Comedy Store in Los Angeles. One night when I was working, the building next door to the club caught on fire. Coincidentally, this was Richard Pryor's first night performing since he'd accidentally set himself on fire and nearly died. He was up onstage when all of a sudden, out the window, smoke started billowing by, heading east on Sunset. A fireman came in, got onstage, and whispered to Richard that the building next door was on fire and The Comedy Store had to be evacuated. Everyone was aware of Richard's bout with fire, so they thought the fireman was a fake, a bit.

Richard said, "Ah, ladies and gentlemen, I don't want anybody to panic, but you know the building next door is on fire. There's no danger; they want us to evacuate the building, so we're gonna do it very calmly. You know, there's no danger of being on fire, because if there was, I'd be the first motherfucker out of here. I mean, I would eat my way through someone's ass not to catch on fire again." He made up that bit that night, and it became a big part of his next concert film, *Live on Sunset Strip*.

So everybody began to evacuate The Comedy Store. The piano player was playing a slow melody while Richard stayed onstage and improvised a funny song. The last two people to leave the building were Richard and the fireman. Later I saw Richard smoking a cigarette while watching the building burn down.

DON ADAMS HATED STANDUP

✳ Ron Zimmerman

My second job in show business was rewriting the movie *Back to the Beach*. Don Adams showed up one night to do a scene that I had to write for him on the spot. Writing it didn't take much time, and once I was done they sort of asked me to sit and hang out with him, because he was going to have to be there all night to shoot his scene at sunrise.

We sat in Don's trailer. He was really nice, full of stories, and he told me that he'd started as a club comic, working with Lenny Bruce, Buddy Hackett, and those guys. But he fucking hated it. Even the thing that every standup loves, the laughter, was a pain to him. After he became a huge star as Maxwell Smart on the sixties spy spoof sitcom *Get Smart,* he was getting paid $50,000 a night to do ten minutes in Las Vegas. He'd go on, and no matter what he said, the audience just cracked up laughing, and still he hated every second of it. He called it "the most awful, humiliating way for a human being to collect money."

He told me a story about how in the fifties he was working at some club where Lenny Bruce, Buddy Hackett, and Jan Murray played. A guy came around saying he needed somebody to open for Mae West. He was paying fifty dollars, great money at the time. Don was the one who had the most kids and needed the money the worst, and everybody else there was a little bit more successful than he was, so the other standups gave him the gig. He did have to drive from New York City to the show in Boston, but fifty dollars is fifty dollars.

The venue in Boston was a burlesque theater, and Don had no dressing room, so he was hanging around backstage when Mae West's manager found him and said, "You must be Don Adams, the comedian. Mae is very excited. She's heard all about you."

Don was surprised. "How? I'm totally unknown."

The manager was slick. "Oh, Mae uses opening comics all the time, so she keeps her eye on that world. She knows all about you guys. One thing that you have to do that Mae likes. You have to come with me into her dressing room before the show and just do your act for her first."

Don said, "I can't do my act for one person in a dressing room. The material is geared for an audience. It's not for one person. That's impossible. It's not going to be funny at all."

"Don't worry about it. Mae thinks you're a riot. She just wants to hear the material and know what you're going to say before you go out there. She's not judging you that way. And come on, it's Mae West. She's a *legend*."

So they went back into the dressing room, which was nothing but wardrobe carts. Mae West had twenty costume changes. Don called it "this mausoleum of clothing."

The manager was calling out, "Mae, Mae. The comedian is here. He's going to do his act for you." Then Don heard a tiny voice way in the back of the room, behind all these clothes. The manager pulled the rack out and there was the real Mae West, without the wigs, makeup, or heels. This old, wrinkled little woman in a worn robe, with a cigarette hanging out of her mouth, looked Don up and down and said, "Okay, kid, let's see what you can do."

Don wanted to vomit just looking at her, yet he had to do his act. So he ran through it, and as soon as he'd finished, Mae called her manager over and they talked quietly for a minute while Don just stood there.

With Mae still standing ten feet away, the manager walked to Don and said, "Mae thinks you're brilliant. Don't change a word. She was hysterical, cracking up. You're going to be great. You might get some more jobs out of this. She loves you."

All of a sudden, Don was Mae's biggest fan.

He went back to waiting in the hall. The manager came out and said, "Listen, I told you Mae loves it, right? She thinks you're just fantastic and the best comic she's ever seen."

Then the manager said, "Mae asked me to ask you for one little favor. She thinks all your jokes are hilarious, there's not a loser in the bunch. But when you get to the end of the joke, like the last couple of lines, don't do those. Do the whole thing, 'your mother-in-law comes to stay with you,' and all that stuff, but then the part about how she breaks her hip, don't do that part."

Don said, "Oh, okay. That joke."

The manager said, "No, on all of them. Everything. Just get up to the last part and then stop."

Don was shocked. "Those are my punch lines. Those *are* the jokes. *Everything* is leading up to the last part. They're not jokes if I don't say the last couple of lines."

"Yeah, that's the part that Mae is not crazy about. She wants to take you on the road with her, but she says, 'He's just got to learn that less is more and that these stories are so funny that you don't need to tell the end.'"

"You want me to go out there for a half an hour and tell jokes with no punch line?"

The manager said, "It's not me, it's Mae. And she is Mae West. I think she knows a little bit about comedy. If she says this is the way to go, I think you can trust her on this."

Don panicked. "Jesus, I really don't think I can do this. Maybe I should just go home."

"Oh, do it, come on. It's not a big deal. Don't be a pussy."

The problem was, Don didn't even have enough money to get home from Boston unless he did the job. So he had no choice. He went in front of this packed audience of four hundred people and told all his setups, with no punch lines.

There was no sound. People didn't heckle. Back then people were very reluctant to heckle—or maybe the crowd was too stunned by what he was doing to react. It was beyond bombing. It was total silence, and silence where there should be laughter is the most painful sort of silence.

When Don came off the stage, the manager told him Ms. West still thought he was brilliant and hilarious, but he'd been better in the dressing room.

YOU HECKLE ME, YOU HECKLE DEAN

✳ Bill Maher

I remember a lot of heckling when I first started out, but most of it was brought on by me. I don't think hecklers are a very common phenomenon, I really don't. I just don't think most people have the balls to do that. I think there's a common idea that heckling is rampant, but it's very rare.

I mean, in the thirteen years since I started *Politically Incorrect* until now, I've said a lot of controversial things, never shying away from the stuff that really pushed people's buttons. But the number of times somebody has come up to me in those thirteen years and said "I have an issue" is maybe twice, including after September 11, when it was front-page news that I was evil.

I'm not saying that people don't hate me. They do. I'm just saying it takes a lot to express that, and I think it's the same thing in a heckler situation. You may think the guy onstage stinks, but it takes a lot to lob that out at them. I think anytime I was heckled it came from me, the sort of crowd interplay we've all used a lot because it helps your material. Also, a lot of the time if the joke didn't work, I would insult the audience, and of course if you insult them enough they'll come back at you with something. I think I almost always brought it on myself, though.

It's funny, because when I started out I did so much preparation for hecklers. I had so many little retorts written on cards. I *wanted* people to heckle me because I didn't have an act back then. I had a list of a hundred things that I had written down as a kid watching the Dean Martin roasts on TV. I had all these insults stored up as a twelve-year-old, but you can't use them on your mother when she's making you breakfast: "Hey, Mom. When your IQ reaches six, sell," or "We had a prize for you, but the Wizard already gave the brain to the scarecrow."

Just after I did *The Tonight Show* for the first time, I was on stage in Columbia, South Carolina. When one of my jokes didn't get the response I expected, I said, "Johnny Carson loved that joke last night." A deep voice in a Southern accent boomed, "Well, Johnny ain't here tonight."

Getting Lucky

✳ **Jim Edwards** My first time onstage, I went in front of maybe eight people and bombed for five minutes. But after the show, this woman came over to me and said, "You're very funny and I think you're very cute." That night I had sex with her. The next day I said to myself, "This is a great business," and because of that five minutes onstage and five minutes with her, I've stayed in it ever since.

✳ **John Bizarre** I was in Bethlehem, Pennsylvania, working at the Holiday Inn. After the show this beefy woman approached me at the bar. She said she was a guard at a nearby prison. She came to my room, where we sat on my bed for an awkward moment, until she blurted out, "Okay, let's get to it." She pushed me back, and she just completely took control, taking off my clothes and tossing me from one side to the other. Then she got up on top, and finally, in a move that I've never seen before or since, she flipped me from under her up into the air, then scooted under so that I landed on top of her. She then whipped my butt like a jockey taking a horse to the finish line, yelling, "Now, now, now, now!" After I did what she commanded, she immediately jumped out of bed and began dressing, while I lay there, a quivering little lump. While dressing, she said, "Hey, I just wanna tell you, you were really funny tonight. But I gotta get outta here 'cause I'm the designated driver." She blew me a kiss and walked out. I passed out. The next morning I checked to see if she'd left me any money on the dresser.

✳ **Joe Mulligan** I met a woman at one of my shows and wound up back at her place. She told me she was born again and read a chapter from the Bible to me. She asked me if that revealed anything to me, and I said no. We talked a bit more, and wound up in her bed, where, immediately after sex, she prayed and asked God to forgive us for having sex while not married. When I told the story to my friends, they asked why I'd even stayed there after she broke the Bible out. I truthfully answered that it was worth sitting through the sermon to get to Communion.

✳ **T. Sean Shannon** This one was told to me by my friend Jim Patterson, who passed away. He was in Dallas doing The Improv as the opening act. After his show he met this chick, who offered him a ride home. She took shortcuts to the comedy condo he never even knew. They went into the condo and she said, "You know, I've never done this before." He asked, "What, a one-night stand?" She said, "No. Go home with the opener."

A LOST TOY

✳ The Amazing Jonathan

If you don't want everybody in the standup community to know your business, don't do anything worth talking about. If you do, never ask Roseanne for help.

Here's a story that has made it around the circuit for the last fifteen or so years. Nobody is sure who it happened to, because I'm discreet and I don't name names. Not because I care about reputations, but I find it helps get me laid a second time.

This woman, whom we'll call "Red," was my opening act at a club, and of course I liked to get to know my coworkers. She had a vibrator, which I inserted up her ass one night while I was fucking her.

Afterward, I went to take the vibrator out of her ass and it wasn't there. I figured it must have fallen out. Red was lying on her back, catching her breath, and I put my hand on her stomach and felt it vibrating. Ahhh, okay, she was lying on it. Then she rolled over and it wasn't there. It must be under the sheets, right? Wrong. I felt her stomach again and it dawned on me that the vibrator was inside her!

It had worked its way up inside her so deep my fingers couldn't even touch it. I panicked, thinking it would eventually touch something in her that would kill her like a hidden "off" button. Red remained calm, though, and was even joking about it.

We had to get to the hospital, but didn't have a car handy. I called Roseanne, who lived close by, and asked to borrow her car.

"What for?"

I told her I needed to take someone to the hospital.

"Why?"

I told her it didn't matter. She was Roseanne: "Tell me or you can't use the car!" Finally I told her and listened to her laugh for what seemed to be a half hour. But she did let me borrow the car.

When we got to the hospital, I explained what had happened and they said to relax, they saw this kind of thing every week. I felt better not to be the only incompetent pervert in the area. My playmate told the nurse that she just wanted to have the batteries changed, and everyone lightened up. Away went Red, and I sat waiting like an expectant father.

When Red returned she was fine, but when we went to collect the vibrator, they refused to give it to us. Supposedly they had to "run tests on it." What they were really telling us was, "If you don't know how to play with the toy, you can't have one." Fair enough.

By the time the story had made it around the standup community and back to me, the vibrator had to be removed from *my* ass, along with two strippers and a tuning fork.

THE STAR RETURNS

✳ Jonathan Winters

Here's something everybody can identify with: going home. It's about what happens when you go home after a long time, especially if you've attained some fortune of some kind. What you find are lots of guys, your buddies, who never left.

Several years ago I went back to Springfield [Ohio] and I called up my friends Fred Ray and Eldon "Howdy" Ray. They were in the nursery business with their dad. Ray and Howdy were tough little guys. They had to be tough. They were in the nursery business.

We all went out fishing at a big place called Muzzy's Lake, run by a guy named Wally, who was at least three hundred pounds, wearing bib overalls, chewing, spitting. We walked into the store to get some nightcrawlers, and rented one of those orange boats with the numbers on them.

I said, "Wally, I know you remember Howdy and Fred. Do you remember me, Johnny Winters?"

"I sure do, you son of a bitch. Was you in the war?"

"I was in the marines."

"Goddamn jarheads. I hate marines. Why did you go into the marines?"

"'Cause I hated the navy. I wanted to kill people. I just didn't want to stand behind a cannon and hope I hit a beach. I wanted to see the guy."

"Did you kill people?"

"I killed a lot of people in the South. No. I'm kidding." I had to say that a lot when I went home: "No. I'm kidding."

Wally said, "Do you remember Marybeth Lionheart?"

"Oh God, she was almost homecoming queen."

"She's a pig now."

"What do you mean?"

"I married her. Remember how pretty she was? Shit, she's as big as I am now. She sits up on the fridge and sucks on Coors and watches *The Young and the Restless*."

All I could say was, "I see."

"We've got seven kids between the two of us. Her first husband was Elmer Denton. Remember him? He was the basketball team's tallest guy on the court. He was six-one. He went to Miami and failed. He's dead now; he was killed out at IH, International Harvester."

Then he asked, "Johnny, what do you do?"

"What do I do?" I had attained some fame by this time, so I kind of thought for a few seconds this guy was kidding or putting me on, but he wasn't. Howdy and Fred both looked at me, thinking, *Jesus, the guy doesn't know.*

I said, "Oh, I married a gal from Dayton."

"You was always going over there looking for a woman. Just as many good-looking women here. Who'd you marry over there?"

"A married a gal named Eileen, very pretty lady. We've got two kids. They're pretty well along now."

"Well, where are you in the country?"

"Well, I'm out in California."

"Lot of queers out there, and communists."

"Oh, I suppose there's pockets probably everywhere, you know, but no problem where we are. I haven't seen a hammer and sickle in a long time, and I see a gay guy, you know, once in a while, maybe on Halloween."

So Wally said, "What kind of business you in? Are you in the aviation out there, Lockheed or one of them people?"

"No, I'm in television."

I never got a chance to go any further with it; the guy just went on, "You know Marybeth, my sister, she's got an RCA Victor. I wonder, I think the picture's gone. Would you take a look at it?"

I just said, "Of course. I don't think it's the picture tube. I've got some stuff in the pickup. Fred, let's forget about fishing for a few minutes. Is she home now?"

"Well, you can go over there after you fish."

You suddenly realize where you are, and who this is, and that not everybody watches television.

UPSTAGING RICH LITTLE

✳ Kevin Pollack

I started performing at the age of ten. My act was lip-synching Bill Cosby's first album, the "Noah and the Ark" bit. The sight of a precocious ten-year-old Jewish kid lip-synching was an instant hit. I did this from grade school through high school, when I added impressions. One of my favorites was Colombo, Peter Falk's character from the TV show.

In my senior year of high school, Rich Little was to perform at a local place called the Circle Star Theater, which seated about 2,500 in the round. I became convinced that upon seeing my Colombo,

Rich Little would knight me. I bought two tickets, including one for my friend so he could witness this great moment in showbiz history. Actually, I needed his father's beige overcoat for the impression, so his ticket was payment for his contribution to the new star's wardrobe. I added the dark pants, white shirt with a thin black tie, and a little half-cigar. I mussed my hair and was ready.

I was in my seat, watching Rich Little kill. I wasn't really enjoying the show, just looking for the right moment to leap into a little Colombo. I needed Little to see me because he was the best impressionist working at that time. There were David Frye, Frank Gorshin, and George Kirby, but Rich Little was the king.

He finished a long bit involving many voices, and the audience was roaring. He walked over to grab a little towel and water, to reload.

I tried to get up, but the trench coat's belt snagged on the seat and pulled me back down, as if God was saying, "You're sure you want to do this?" But I hadn't been listening to God up to that point, so why start then? I ripped that belt out and bolted for the stage. The audience was ending the applause, and Little was acknowledging it as he took a sip of water, when I yelled out, as Colombo, "Mr. Little, excuse me, sir. Geez, I hate to bother you. I don't mean to be a pest. Sorry, sir, if I could just have a second."

He saw me and moved to my side of the stage and said, "Look at this, ladies and gentlemen, Lieutenant Colombo is here. How are you, Lieutenant?" He placed the mike in front of my face. I stayed in character: "Oh, Mr. Little, this is such a thrill. The show has been incredible. I hate to interrupt, I honestly do." He then took the microphone back and started doing Lieutenant Colombo himself. Now, Colombo was not in his repertoire, and Rich Little was not an improviser. His Colombo was terrible and this was apparent to him in three seconds, so he shoved the mike back to me. Not only had my hero failed, but I'd set him up to crash. I was behind the looking glass, and suddenly my Colombo wavered. I flailed about, and like the great pro that he was, he regrouped. He took the mike back and said, "I tell you what, Lieutenant. Why don't you come up onstage and tell me what I can do for you."

I figured I'd get tossed, not asked onstage. For the first and only time in my life, I had tunnel vision. I saw only Rich Little, actually just his face. I can't imagine what was going through his mind as this kid with the look of a juvenile serial killer approached.

I got onstage and he prompted me again, "What can I do for you, Lieutenant?"

Now I caught my balance and went into my prepared bit. "Well, here's the thing. Me and the missus see in the newspaper about six months ago you're coming to town. I get tickets. We've been planning on this evening for six months, Mr. Little. At the last second, Mrs. Colombo falls ill. She's home in bed. She can't come to the show and insists that I come anyways. And she told me that if I don't get your autograph, she's not letting me back in the house. I don't know how this works, sir, but I need to get something on paper." And I handed him a piece of paper and a pen. He took the piece of paper and the pen, looked at the audience, and rattled off Heckler Comeback Stock Line #17 from 1959. He said, "This guy better watch out or I'll do Rin-Tin-Tin and he'll be the tree." He was referencing Rin-Tin-Tin, and it was 1975.

The audience was laughing, and while they were laughing I was still in character. "Geez, that's funny. That was terrific." Meanwhile, Little unscrewed the pen in the middle. While he was fumbling with the copper ink cartridge, he turned to the audience. "Lieutenant Colombo gave me a broken pen."

I stayed in character. "Oh, Jesus, is that busted? I had no idea. I feel terrible. I don't know what to do here. I got to get the autograph."

He eased me off the stage. "I tell you what, Lieutenant, why don't you come backstage after the show and I'll be happy to sign an autograph for your wife. Ladies and gentlemen, Lieutenant Colombo."

I took my bow, returned to my seat, and for the next fifty-three minutes he was a god. I was screaming at everything he said. I just knew that at the end of the show I was going backstage. Rich Little was taking me to his jet and off into show business. I got laughs onstage with Rich Fucking Little. It was a done deal. I was in. I was just waiting—waiting and laughing.

After the show, I went backstage and there were thirty-seven people in line. I took my place at the end of the line. The same putz who'd interrupted a man in the middle of a show now got in line.

By the way, if someone did that to me today, I'd have them tossed. I still can't believe to this day he brought me onstage.

So the young showbiz psycho with that kind of nutty chutzpah now got in line with the rest of the citizens. I didn't say, "Excuse me. I hate to bother you." No, I got in line.

I finally got to the front of what was basically an assembly line. The fan handed Rich Little a piece of paper; he asked their name, signed it, thanked them, handed them the signed autograph, and turned to the next fan.

My turn came, and of course he recognized me. "Hey, there he is. Okay, so what's the name?"

"Kevin."

He said, "All right, Kevin."

Suddenly he's signed the piece of paper, shoveled it back to me, and turned to the next person: "What's your name, darling?"

It was over in a heartbeat. I was standing there in my little Colombo suit, holding a piece of paper and feeling crushed like a walnut.

I prayed for Rich Little's death for the next seventeen years. I didn't know it at the time, but that kind of reaction meant I was already in show business.

THE VANISHING GIG

✳ Vince Moranto

I was living in Chicago and was booked for a one-nighter in Michigan. It was stupid because it was too far away and the money was shit, but I ended up taking the deal anyway because some money is better than no money.

I was watching The Weather Channel and saw that a big storm was coming, so I decided to get up at four in the morning to beat the storm. Of course, The Weather Channel was wrong and I ended up following the storm the entire way to Michigan. What should have been a five-hour drive turned into a twelve-hour drive. On the way, cars were going off the road. The cabs of overturned trucks dangled off overpasses. I saw people spinning off the road like in *The Road Warrior.* I wanted to help, but I had $175 waiting for me in Michigan, so I drove on.

It was dark by the time I got to where this one-nighter was supposed to be, and I couldn't find it. I drove back and forth, back and forth. Finally I pulled to the side of the road, trying to figure it out. I was sitting there looking at my map and the directions when I smelled the smoke.

I got out of my car and looked around. I was exactly where I was supposed to be, but instead of a building, there was a smoldering husk. The club had burned down earlier that day.

I certainly enjoyed my twelve-hour drive back, without the money.

Everybody's a Comedian

✳ **Orny Adams** One night at one of New York City's seedier comedy clubs, The Boston, a female comedian was a few minutes into her set and focusing on a table of four unsatisfied women in the front row. She asked them, "What the hell's your problem?" The heckler said, "We were here last week and you're doing the same jokes. How about something new?" The comedian said, "How about fuck you." The audience laughed.

The poised heckler didn't miss a beat and shot back, "That's new."

✳ **Tom Dreesen** It was 1:00 A.M. at the Improv and I was trying out new material. There was a guy way in the back, in the dark. Every time I got a laugh, he would say something for a bigger laugh. I would say something back to him and get a laugh; he would respond and get a bigger laugh. So after about ten minutes of this I said to him, "Just between you and me, I won that one." There was a pause and he said, "Just between you and me, you needed it." Again he got the biggest laugh.

✳ **Kerry Awn** I was in Houston, Texas, at the Comedy Showcase, doing a bit about tattoos, when this woman said she had a Tweety Bird tattooed on her thigh. She came on the stage, put her foot up on the stool, and lifted her skirt up to show me her thigh. There was no tattoo. So I said, "There's no Tweety Bird on your thigh." And with perfect timing she said, "Oh, I guess my pussy ate it." She left the stage to a huge laugh.

＊**Jamie Kennedy** One night this guy yelled, "Hey, Jamie, how soon is it before you start doing infomercials?"

＊**Mike Langworthy** I was an emcee and I asked some guy in the audience how he was doing. He looked at me and he said, "I'm all right, just waiting for the comics to show up." It wasn't even a heckle. It was just so dismissive that I laughed right along with everybody else. I said, "You know what? Me too."

＊**Clay Heery** At a show in Philly, I was ragging on the local TV station, and this cute cohost of the evening magazine show was in the audience. She'd had a few drinks and started heckling me. I said, "Next time she opens her mouth, somebody stick a dick in it." She jumped out of her seat, waving her arms and shouting, "I'm over here."

DRIVING MISS STRIPPER

＊**Kelly Monteith**

I was working the Way Out Lounge in Dayton, Ohio, around 1968. One night, two of the dancers from the club asked me for a ride home. They lived in Middletown, between Dayton and Cincinnati. I said, "Yeah, sure."

It was four in the morning and raining. One girl was in the

front, and one in the back. A few minutes into the ride, one said, "What did you say that to him for? You got us fired, you fucking bitch! He wanted to fuck you, you should've fucked him."

The second dancer shot back. "Oh, fuck you. You're the one that started arguing."

They were getting heated, so I asked them to calm down. They stopped for a minute and then jumped right into "Yeah, you fucking bitch." "You cunt." "You fucking bitch, you." "You fucked up this whole job." "Fuck you—I don't have to take that shit." Next thing I knew, the one in the back threw a punch at the one in the front. Soon I was driving down whatever interstate it was with two women pulling hair and punching the shit out of each other next to me.

I yelled until I finally got so mad I pulled over and said, "Get the fuck out!" I went around and opened the passenger door, and this girl fell on her back in the mud.

Now they'd stopped fighting and she was a bloody, muddy mess, so I felt bad and said, "All right. Get back in the car."

She said, "No, fuck you. Bullshit." She slammed the door and walked across the six-lane highway to a gas station.

The other girl was cowering in the backseat when I got back in the car and announced we had to go make sure her "friend" got home.

I went to the gas station, where the dancer, muddy from head to toe, hair and clothes a mess from the fight, was hobbling around because she'd also broken a high-heeled shoe.

This was back in the day when gas stations had an attendant. So this seventeen-year-old kid working there was wide-eyed, staring at these two wild women and me.

I was looking in the phone book for a cab company when suddenly I was hurled against the wall. The ex-husband of the bloody, muddy dancer had been driving past and had seen her. He thought I'd beaten her up, so he pulled over and got me by the throat. He looked to be straight out of prison, with this maniacal gleam in his eyes.

The other girl pulled a knife from her purse and threatened him with it. "Get back, it wasn't him. He didn't do anything, it was me. I had a fight with her because she got us fired." She went into detail, and I don't think she left out one "fuck you" of their exchange. Now the guy had become a confused wild animal. He looked at his wife and he looked at me and said, "Is that right?"

She said, "Yeah."

He said, "All right, all right." He let me go and took his wife out into the bay and beat the shit out of her. "You fucking cunt"— BLAM. I grabbed the other chick and got the fuck out of there.

I didn't learn a thing. I still hung out with strippers for a few more years. I kind of hoped that gas station kid learned a lesson, but thinking back to myself as a teenager, he probably saw me with those two wild women and thought, "Wow. How can I get that job?"

THE DREAM OF DOING STANDUP

✳ Larry David

When I was doing standup and bombing more often than not, I once had a dream that I was sleeping upstairs in a mansion. In the dream, I was awakened by sounds of gunfire and cannons that seemed to be coming from downstairs. I got out of bed and, in my pajamas, walked downstairs, where there were soldiers in uniform, firing at each other in my living room. I also noticed there was a small, elevated stage area off to the side, with a microphone and a piano. I scampered across the room, dodging bullets, and took cover behind a couch next to a soldier. I asked him why there was a war going on in my living room. Before he could answer, another soldier walked up and, standing over me, put a gun to my head, motioned toward the stage, and said, "Get up and do a set." I said, "Get up and do a set? Are you crazy?" "Do it!" he barked. "But how can I do a set? There's a war going on here. No one will listen. I'll get killed." That didn't seem to dissuade him. He cocked the hammer. "Do a set or I'll blow your brains out."

So I started crawling toward the stage area, as bullets whizzed over my head. When I finally got there, I stood up, took the microphone, and said, "Good evening, ladies and gentlemen. How's everybody doing…?"

EIGHTY-PROOF REVIEW

✳ Ron White

Twice a year, Howard Trustman, who booked the Laff Stop Comedy Club chain, came to Austin, Texas, to scout new talent. In 1989 he saw me do a ten-minute set, and I killed—killed like you wouldn't believe. I beat them up, just beat them bad in ten minutes. Like a pie at a fat-man convention, there was nothing left.

Howard came up to me and said, "Man, you are the next big thing. You are something else."

Of course, I believed every word of it, too. "Yeah, yeah, I'm amazing as I can be."

He said, "I want to book you as a headliner."

I immediately backed off a bit. "Oh, wait a minute." I'd only headlined one room ever, and that was some little shithole in Arkansas. But he was certain.

"No, man, I know what I'm talking about. I book these rooms." He sold me on it, and I agreed to celebrate my third anniversary in standup by headlining the Laugh Stop in Irvine, California.

The day came around and I was nervous. I looked at the club's flyer and saw that the two guys who had headlined the two weeks before me were Bobby Slayton and Jerry Seinfeld. Now it's Ron White and his little cavalcade of fucking jokes. I hadn't told a joke within 1,200 miles of Los Angeles. Not one fucking joke. Then, just before I went onstage, a waitress pointed to a guy in the audience. "That's the reviewer for the Orange County edition of the *L.A. Times.*" I'm sure her intent was good, but she might as well have set my hair on fire.

I got onstage and my hands were shaking so bad that I had to grab my pants just to keep them still. My first joke got a laugh and I thought, "Well, that ain't so bad." I did the next one, "That ain't so bad." I finished the set and thought it went pretty well. I didn't quite get to the forty-five-minute headliner minimum watermark, but it was an okay forty-one.

Well, the next night, I walked in with confidence. There was a middle act from Texas, Michael Epstein, doing a guest set, so I felt a lot more at home. Plus, it was an open-mike night, so there were a couple of really green comics. I went up and just killed. And afterward my ego was just flaring; I was giving better comics advice on delivery and writing. I just had it in my mind that I was about to meet the girl on the Tecate beer poster and settle into a life of fame and fortune. I was real proud of myself. And that night the liquor *flowed,* baby. The liquor did flow.

I got up the next morning, thinking that the review of my set was going to come out. I couldn't wait to read it. There were no papers in the hotel lobby, so I walked down to the club and into the back office, and the girls went, "Don't read it, Ron."

I said, "What?"

"Ron, it's not true. He's a hatchet man. He doesn't like anybody. He's a sour fucking old critic."

I read it.

First of all, the picture, a big five-by-seven one, was of me making a face that, I swear to God, I never made before in my life. I didn't even know I was being photographed, but there I was mugging it up, caught in some kind of contorted laugh face.

The big print right above the picture said, EVEN WHEN WHITE'S NOT BLUE, HE'S NOT FUNNY. The rest of the article said, "Watching White's 45-minute," and it crossed that out and put, "41-minute show was like watching a polar bear lumber around onstage: uneventful, with something comical or interesting happening only occasionally." I was only able to read about three words at a time before dropping the paper, hyperventilating, and then reading another three words.

I bought a bottle of tequila and a pack of razor blades. I mailed the razor blades to the reviewer with a note that said, "Just in case you're ever in the mood. Love, Ron White."

The highs and lows that we experience in standup are so extreme and so fast to come: you're great one minute, you're shit the next. The problem is, the shit-stink hangs around longer than the great feeling. I truly believed I had been found out. I believed that this guy was right. It was all over. I was pretty naïve at this point, three years in the biz, so I was wondering if they had to pay me for the last two nights. I didn't have a ticket home, or money to pay for the hotel. Thank God I had tequila and pot money. I was just wasted on top of my showbiz ignorance. Nothing good was going to come out of this.

After reading the review, I went back to my hotel room and burned the words into my brain with massive amounts of pot and tequila. And literally I passed out and created a drool stain on the article. I came to thirty minutes before show time, but that didn't bother me since I was sure nobody was going to be at the club. My plan was to stagger down to the club, accept whatever scraps they paid me, and wander off into the showbiz sunset. The day before, I'd been leaving my wife for the girl in the Tecate beer poster; now I called her with a different attitude: "I just love you so much. I don't know about all this traveling. I just want to stay home with you."

Of course, I got to the club to find the parking lot packed. This was 1989—every ticket to every comedy show in America was sold. It was the peak of the standup boom. It didn't matter who the fuck was performing.

I was in no shape to get in front of people, unless it was in a police lineup. I was unshaven, unshowered, and dressed for a night in a storm drain. I was fighting a fresh hangover at seven in the evening. There was only one thing to do: start pounding it again.

I went on and did the worst set of my life, drunkenly prepping each bit with something like, "Here's the next thing I wrote and it's not even mildly fucking amusing." It was a real sad story taking place onstage.

Howard Trustman, the genius who'd booked me into this room, called between shows while I was sitting at the bar, getting ready to destroy my second show. They put me on the phone with him and he tried to talk me down. I came back with a series of fuck-you's. He stayed on me, though: "Ron, you're a good comedian. You're young; the guy took a fucking sledgehammer to your head. It would have crushed anybody, especially someone as new in the business as you are."

All I can say about my second show that night was no one tried to lynch me.

But that review was the best thing that could've happened to me. I needed to be slapped down because I thought I was better than I was—whether I needed to be slapped that *hard* was up for debate.

I wouldn't go out to L.A. again for years, which was probably good for my career, too, because it kept me performing for people who "got" me, which allowed me to keep being me. When I finally got to L.A., I was really a comic, a fresh face with fifteen years of road gigs under my belt. They were like, "Where the fuck did this guy come from?"

He came from towns where they don't read newspapers.

SUNDAY NIGHT IS BLOW-JOB NIGHT

* Clay Heery

In 1979 I was fresh to comedy and paying my dues at a real shithole in West Philadelphia called the Jail House. It was shaped like a subway car. We performed in the middle of the room, so nobody was seated in front of you, just a hundred people stacked on each side of the stage. It was a bad variation of theater-in-the-round: standup-between-two-bleachers. While you turned to work one set of bleachers, drunks in the other one tried to hit the back of your head with beer-soaked bar napkins. Oh, and we performed for free.

One night a guy came in and said to fellow standup Grover Silcox and me, "I'll pay you guys to work at my place." I didn't even ask how much or where. Never before had someone offered me money to do standup. So it didn't matter if his "place" was a five-dollar naked prison show; I was getting a butt plug and showing up.

The name of the place was the Airport Tavern, so we had visions of performing for pilots, flight attendants, and international travelers. That dream slowly died as Grover and I got off the Pennsylvania Turnpike and drove for over an hour on dark country roads. It was easy to find the bar; it was the only lighted object for miles. It seemed that the name was an example of local humor; someone, at some time long ago, had planned to put an airport out there, but never had.

The parking lot was filled with pickups and motorcycles. They had a cheap flashing sign on the back of a trailer announcing COMEDY NIGHT, CLAY HAIRY AND GROVER SILCOCKS. The guy who'd hired us greeted us outside the tavern with a smile. "If you fellas get lost or in trouble or anything, remember to say you're with the Wolf."

He was missing a few teeth, something that I didn't remember noticing when we'd met in the city. His outfit was steel-toed biker boots, leather chaps over jeans, an open vest over a bare chest, and a western-style gun holster, topped off with a real, loaded pistol. He noticed me staring at his gun and explained that just the sight of it "keeps most of the assholes in line."

Grover had bigger things on his mind, like questioning our host about the misspelling of our names on the sign. He was worried that our nonexistent fans might get confused and drive away. The Wolf explained that he knew the proper spelling of both our names, but thought these were funnier. The *Deliverance* banjo riff played in my head.

Once we got inside, we realized it was *Road Warrior* theme night. Everyone was dressed like their favorite murderous biker from the postindustrial apocalypse, except Grover and me, who were dressed like freshman fraternity pledges.

The Wolf seated us at a table located between the men's room and the ladies' room. This was prime real estate, according to our host: "You'll see some shit happen here." Right on cue, a woman entered the ladies' room and three guys followed her in, saying, "Honey, we wanna look at your pussy." We didn't hear any objections from the lady.

We flipped a coin to determine who went first. Grover won and sent me up first, probably figuring they might be sated after torturing and killing me and might let the second comic live. At ten o'clock I took the stage, which was just a three-foot-by-three-foot piece of plywood loosely sitting on concrete blocks. When I shifted my weight, the whole stage moved. I was performing on an oversized skateboard. The lighting was a couple of old Hi-C cans with high-intensity lightbulbs inside, throwing off a tremendous amount of heat and light. I alternated between feeling like a moth and like a McDonald's french fry.

Wolf introduced me: "This guy is funny as shit, and you fuckers better listen up." I took the stage and I swear I heard guns cocking amid the scattered applause. People did stop talking, but the TV was still blaring out a Flyers game, and the noise from the electric bowling game and the pool tables was even louder. I was squinting through the blinding lights and hunched down in a futile effort to avoid the scorching heat. Soon I realized that even if they could hear my material, it didn't fit this new Quasimodo character I was affecting.

Finally I just said to this guy in front, whom everybody seemed to be pointing to and laughing at, "So, where are you from?" The guy said, in a voice loud enough to be heard on Martin Luther King Boulevard in Atlanta, "I live in nigger town." I said, "Oh, I bet they like having you there; it gives them somebody to look down on." The whole place just erupted in laughter. I could see this guy was thinking of a good place to dispose of my body, so I went to someone else.

That was it for my set—hit-and-run put-downs of the audience. It was pure primitive comedy: everyone loved seeing someone else squashed. My ego was sick to be resorting to this, but my body didn't care because it was the one that would be suffering any bone breaks, facial contusions, and internal injuries if this mob got bored and decided it needed a new source of entertainment.

After I finished, I talked with Grover about what he might do for his midnight set. Messing with the audience was not Grover's shtick, so the gladiator style I'd used to survive wasn't going to work for him. As we were talking, this six-foot-eight, three-hundred-pound guy exited the bathroom, pulling up his zipper. He spotted us and laughed to himself before introducing himself as "Bulldog." Apparently everyone used aliases in a joint like this.

Bulldog said, "I'm gonna teach you boys how to be co-medians." I don't remember if either of us said anything more than "Sure. Okay."

Bulldog looked at Grover. "Sil-cocks. You going up there?" I thought he was going to break into a version of Robert Shaw's speech from *Jaws:* "You going onstage dressed like that? Those people going to see you dressed like that? Farewell..."

But Bulldog was serious: "Sil-cocks, if you wanna get the attention of these people, you gotta piss on 'em. You gotta take your dick out and piss on 'em."

Grover acted like he was getting advice from Bill Cosby. "Okay, that's a good idea, Bulldog. Thank you, it's really good."

Then this gorgeous girl, a young Valerie Bertinelli type, walked out of the ladies' room. Bulldog pulled her onto his lap and said, "Honey, did you ever blow a co-median?" She thought for a moment and said, "I don't think so."

Bulldog was right on it. "Well, how'd you like to blow three comedians tonight?" It made me angry that Bulldog had elevated himself to comic status without even going onstage, but being a guest, I did the polite thing and bit my tongue, hard.

I was brought back to the unreal reality when the girl said, "Well, I'll blow one of youse, but I won't blow all three of youse." She was probably superstitious and applied the three-on-a-match prohibition to blow jobs. Bulldog, without consulting Grover and me, or even offering to draw straws, tossed her three feet in the air. "You ain't blowin' all three of us, you ain't blowin' *none* of us." Bulldog was obviously not the type to negotiate. If you didn't take his first offer, you were likely to miss the opportunity. Actually, I really admired the fact that Bulldog had only been a comedian for thirty seconds but already had a strong sense of comic solidarity.

For her part, the woman stuck a nice clean landing and strutted away. The women in this area were probably accustomed to hitting the ground after long free falls.

Twelve o'clock rolled around. Same crowd, just two hours drunker. The only difference was that the TV blared *The Tonight Show*, a further reminder of how far we were from the Center of Showbiz.

Wolf started the introduction, and I told Grover if anything went wrong I'd be in the car with the motor running.

Grover got up and tried to do material, but they didn't want to hear it. Bulldog was furious. "Sil-cocks! Sil-cocks! What'd I tell you, boy?" He flipped our table. "Boy, you wanna get the attention of these people, you gotta piss on 'em! You gotta take your dick out and you gotta piss on 'em!" Then Bulldog took his dick out and pissed on the second-biggest guy in the place. I edged toward the door and showed Grover the car keys in my hand. Meanwhile, Bulldog was pissing on this guy and the man didn't move. I figured either this was already an established part of their relationship or the man knew how Bulldog might react if made to miss.

If you think people laugh from the relief that it's not them being verbally abused by a comedian, it's nothing compared to how hard they laugh from the relief of not being made a human urinal. People were howling, throwing glasses, and falling on the floor. Bulldog finished pissing and, over this riotous laughter, screamed to Grover, "See? That's what you gotta do to be a co-median in this place."

Grover said, "You know, Bulldog, when you're right, you're right."

Part of me wanted to see what Bulldog did for an encore, but a much bigger and louder part of me was screaming, *Run!*

I went over and toasted Bulldog for the biggest laugh of the night, then added, with the proper amount of regret in my voice, "Well, you know, we better go get paid." Grover was right on time: "Yeah, I gotta get back to my wife. She's due anytime." Many a married man has been saved from doing something stupid by using the wife excuse.

We went into the kitchen, where Wolf was drinking shots with the now-topless local Valerie Bertinelli. Wolf counted out our cash and said these exact words: "Well, what do you think? You think comedy's gonna go over here?"

I said, as a joke, "No. I think they really would rather watch porno and get blow jobs."

Wolf drank a shot. "Nah, we already got that on Sunday. We don't got a Sunday liquor license, so we make 'em park around back in the woods. Blow-job night sure packs 'em in, but I need something for the weekdays."

We got into the car, lost a hubcap when we drove over the curb at fifty miles an hour, and didn't slow down or look back until we smelled the cheese steaks of South Street.

LATE-NIGHT DINING

✳ Mark Russell

One of the big problems on the road is getting food after ten o'clock at night, when you're done with the show. There are many good-size cities where, if you haven't eaten by 10:00 P.M., it's either Domino's pizza or the candy machine.

So a couple of years ago I was playing a little theater in the middle of Kansas, and they put me in this motel right where every interstate in the Midwest crossed. I got back to the motel after the show and I hadn't eaten. There was no food anywhere, not even a candy machine at the motel. But on the horizon, across all the interstates, I saw the Golden Arches. I ran across twenty-two lanes of heavy traffic, only to find the door locked. A kid inside motioned for me to come around the side and stand in the drive-thru line.

I got on the line and inched my way up on foot, between a car and a pickup truck. People started rolling down the windows, honking their horns and yelling at me, "Hey, great show tonight."

A half hour earlier I'd been getting a standing ovation, and now I was standing in the drive-thru line. I ordered two burgers and a humble pie.

THE FUNNY SIDE OF TYPING

✳ Jay Thomas

When I was a kid, I lived in New Orleans. I would get records of Bill Cosby, Woody Allen, and all sorts of Southern comics. I would imitate them in my room, by myself. Then I'd write my own material and tell it at school and fuck around with my friends.

My dad, the Van Cliburn of typists, told me that I had to learn how to type. He said it would open doors for me. So in 1970, when I was sixteen, he enrolled me in the YMCA typing class located at the edge of the French Quarter. Twice a week I'd drive over and sit through the class, but I hated it. One night I left the class and walked around the French Quarter. A place called the Bayou Room was having open-mike night, but it was for singers and strippers. It was a strip club with folk music, a naked hootenanny kind of thing. I asked if I could tell jokes.

I was a kid, but they let me get on the stage, where I did Bill Cosby and Woody Allen's stuff and my own stuff. They laughed and the guy said, "You know, that was pretty fucking funny. Will you come back again?" I said, "I can be here every Tuesday and Thursday." So, on Thursday night, I drove to the YMCA and touched the brick building, so I could tell my dad that I'd gone there. I was a Catholic and didn't want to lie to my parents.

Over the next weeks my father was bragging to everybody that I was typing, and meanwhile I was getting funnier and funnier. My dad was always trying to get me to type something, so I began to bandage my hand, claiming an injured thumb or finger. Somehow I viewed this as part of my new profession of performing, rather than outright lying.

One night onstage I said, "You know, my parents think I'm at the YMCA, taking a typing course. I had a real problem last night. I got home and my dad said, 'Can you type something for me, and what's that stain on your pants?'" The place fell apart, because I'd said something that was true and funny.

For a long time, I went on avoiding typing in front of my dad. I'd pay people to type for me, and then he'd correct the typing.

My dad told me that if I went to typing class it would change my life. He was right—he just shouldn't have sent me to one that was two blocks from a strip club.

Reality Checks

✳ **Brian Kiley** In 1993 I had a great show, opening for Seinfeld in front of 4,000 people. The next morning my wife and I wake up and there's a message on our answering machine: "Brian, this is ABC TV calling." I'm thinking, *Oh my God, finally my big break.* I call back and get ABC TV, which was the name of the place where we'd taken our VCR to be fixed. I brought the VCR home and watched Seinfeld on it.

✳ **Rich Vos** One night I was onstage at Stand-Up New York with twelve people in the audience. I had a horrible attitude, because after twenty-one years in the business I'd finally just received a little notoriety from *Last Comic Standing.* They gave me the light to get off the stage and I started yelling at them, "How dare you give me the light! You know who I am? I am the biggest act onstage tonight!" When I stomped off the stage, the emcee took the microphone and said, "And now our next act, Jerry Seinfeld."

PROMO AT A FUNERAL

✳ Dante Garza

Sam Kinison was a big influence on me. He was really the first comedian to achieve rock-star status. So when I got to get to know him at The Comedy Store in the early nineties, I felt very lucky.

Within a year of our getting to know each other, Sam died. When Carl Labove (Sam's best friend) called The Comedy Store, just hours after Sam had died in the car accident, I was the guy who answered the phone. It was terrible. That week I went with my girlfriend, now my wife, Margo, to Forest Lawn in Burbank, California, for Sam's funeral. The chapel was packed wall-to-wall with comedians and celebrities. Richard Belzer emceed the ceremony. Many of Kinison's friends and family spoke. Pauly Shore talked about Sam's being like his brother and how Sam used to babysit him.

When Carl Labove was asked to speak, the place went silent. We all knew Carl had been with Sam when he died. Carl spoke for a while and then began to cry, so upset he couldn't speak. Richard Belzer finally came up to the podium to help Carl down. The whole place was a mess, everyone sobbing. Then, just as Carl was almost back to his seat, he broke free from Richard and ran back to the microphone. He'd stopped crying, and with a big smile on his face he said, "By the way, I'll be at Igby's all week! Two shows Friday, three Saturday." It was hilarious, and a nice ending to Sam's funeral.

THE *N* WORD WINS

✳ Heath Hyche

Back in 1994, I did this one-nighter in Birmingham, Alabama, working one of those clubs with a pallet from a grocery store for the stage. You had to be careful your foot didn't slip into one of the cracks while you were performing.

I had five minutes' worth of jokes, so I was the opener that night for a black comic, Henry Welch. This guy was performing for two hundred white people, not another black face in the club. I can't imagine how hard it must be to perform for an entire crowd of the opposite color. He started smart, letting them know he knew the deal. "You want to find me after the show? You'll probably find me hanging around...in a tree out back." They loved him.

Then this huge redneck lady in the front row started heckling. Henry'd come up through some tough clubs and had that stay-out-of-my-show attitude, so he started cutting her down hard. "Hey, big girl, why don't you be quiet? I think I have a Twinkie in my pocket I'll give you if you shut up."

She started crying, but he didn't let up. "Stop crying. I'll buy you a big bowl of grits after the show."

The crowd had turned. He'd made Charlotte cry.

She came back with, "What if I said you had a little dick?" To a black man. She might as well have handed him a baseball bat.

He laughed and said, "I'm sure with that big fat ass you want a big dick. But you got a big fat mouth that won't shut up, so you're never gonna get what you want."

The club owner and I were in the back, cracking up. Finally the girl stopped crying, and the crowd loved the funny black man again.

After the professional show, they did an amateur contest. This drunk redneck guy came onstage and sort of just kept repeating, "My wife's a bitch." Everyone got the idea, but he didn't have any jokes to go with that thought, so people stopped listening. Finally he said, "'Scuse me," and whistled loud, like a lunch-hour whistle. The whole crowd went silent and looked at him. He said "Thank you kindly," and called his wife a bitch. The crowd went right back to talking to each other and ignoring him. The club owner, the black comic, and I were in the back, laughing.

The club owner finally had to do a mercy killing. He walked onstage, took the mike from the drunk, and said, "Thanks, Earl. Sorry your wife is a bitch and you can't get a laugh off it." The drunk got angry and was cussing as he took his seat in the front row, right next to what looked like his wife.

Now the heavy girl who'd heckled the black guy came onstage. She said, "I'm gonna tell a joke, but I have to use the *n* word."

The whole bar froze. Everybody turned around and looked at the black comic. It was deathly quiet, and he said, "I don't care."

She told her joke and got a big laugh.

The drunken redneck slammed his fist on the table, jumped up, and yelled to the club owner, "I didn't know we could say 'nigger'!"

The Last Word: Part One

✳ **Bobby Slayton** I was onstage talking about how all guys jerk off. This guy in the front row shook his head "no." His wife said, "I know my husband doesn't masturbate." Now, with perfect timing, she held up both his arms and he had hooks for hands. I said, "Well, at least he can open a can of tuna."

✳ **Brother Wease** One night at a club in Rochester, New York, Bobby Slayton was being heckled by some guy in the front row who told Slayton he was blind. So Slayton pulled his dick out and said, "How many inches am I holding up?"

✳ **Natasha Leggero** Someone in the audience said to me, "Uh, don't you think you're a little attractive to be a comedian?" And I said, "Don't you think you're a little ugly to be talking to me?"

✳ **Peter J. Fogel** In 1985, a rowdy table of men are interrupting my set. Like dominoes, one guy heckles me . . . then another . . . and another . . . and another. I start to lose control of my set, because of this gang heckle. Finally I announce to the heathens, "Enough! Why don't you guys all huddle and come up with one thought!"

✳ **Jon Manfrellotti** I was onstage and all of a sudden this huge guy, wearing a turban and a big, white, puffy shirt, with a beard that literally came out to a point, walked past the stage. I said, "What, did somebody rub a lamp?"

✻ **Jonathan Katz** I used to do a bit where I'd ask the audience to heckle me, knowing that somebody was going to make a bald joke. I'd come back with, "Maybe you would like to explain to your friends what you find so comical about chemotherapy, Mister Smarty-pants, Mister Clever Trousers, Mister Adroit Slacks." One night in Florida, the club owner hadn't heard me ask the crowd to heckle me, so he started throwing these nice people onto the street.

✻ **Larry Reeb** One audience member I was talking to about sex said, "I'll screw anything with a hole," and I said, "I'd hate to go to Dunkin' Donuts with you."

ROSEANNE, RODNEY, AND PRITIKIN

✻ Louie Anderson

Back in the late eighties or early nineties, I toured twenty-five cities with Roseanne. If you didn't know this about us already, I should tell you that we *loved* to eat. Robin Tate came with us and was our tour guide, and in every city we'd say to Robin, "Find us the best restaurant and ask if they'll stay open for us. We'll go eat there after the show." So after every show we'd go and eat the best stuff the town had to offer. On that tour, Robin gained forty-five pounds.

After the tour, Roseanne and I went to the Pritikin Center to diet. We checked into the center in Santa Monica, then walked right out the front door and straight to this great bread place. After having our fill, we came back and told our counselor, "We needed some exercise." Our counselor said we were off to a great start on a new life.

We weren't the first show folk to abuse the Pritikin Center. When Buddy Hackett was at Pritikin, the first night there he had pizzas delivered for everybody, and they kicked him out in about ten seconds.

I was also there with Rodney Dangerfield, who brought empty containers and filled them with the center's food. I'd sit outside with him and have a cigarette, and he would smoke a joint. After the joint he'd eat like five containers of their food, then go get some more. Rodney thought that just being on the grounds of the Pritikin Center gave him a magical immunity from gaining weight, no matter how much he ate.

Rodney and I were having dinner there one night. Now, you have to understand that almost everyone at the center is rich, so it wasn't unusual that we were eating that night with nine millionaires and two billionaires. The real-life Rodney, like his character in *Caddyshack*, loved tweaking wealthy snobs. Naturally, as we ate this impossibly healthy meal, someone started fantasizing, "You know what I like? I like pork chops with gravy." The guy next to him then says, "You know what I like? I like vanilla fudge cake." Rodney jumped in, "You know what I like? I like cock." No one laughed. Maybe they were waiting for Rodney to tell them how he liked it prepared, maybe "blackened cock," or "cock covered with a mango chutney sauce." The point is, not one of those people laughed, and for Rodney a wasted joke was the greatest sin. He turned to me and said, "Let's get away from these squares."

LIVE NUDE COMEDY

✳ Marcie Smolin

So the booker calls and tells me that he has a gig for me at a gorgeous resort in the mountains just an hour's drive away, and the money is great. I should have been suspicious right there. I pull up to the gates of this beautiful resort and tell the guard that I'm the comic here to do a show. He walks out of the guard gate and I see he's completely nude from the waist down. He is wearing a shirt, badge, hat, black socks and shoes, and nothing in between. He tells me to park and they'll send a golf cart for me.

The golf cart pulls up and two very friendly people get out, wearing hats. Just hats. Nothing else. Almost as important as their nudity is that neither of them's the kind of person you *want* to picture nude.

At this point it dawns on me that the booker has forgotten to mention this was a nudist resort.

We get to the rec room where the show is going to be. The opening act is looking a bit green around the gills because they've just mentioned to him that they'd prefer he perform naked. We both immediately veto that plan.

The activities director tells us they have two rules for the comics: absolutely no profanity, and you absolutely cannot mention that the crowd is naked. Maybe they didn't know they were naked.

Soon the rec room fills with unattractive naked people sitting on metal folding chairs. To make it even worse, they are the worst, most uptight audience I have ever had the pain of performing for. They sit naked, arms crossed, looking very uncomfortable. To be fair, it might be an expected reaction for a nude audience when faced with fully clothed performers.

After ten minutes the opener flees the stage. I go on to equally hostile silence. At the very end of the personal suffering formerly known as my act, I point to Bob, the activities director, and say, "Bob told me I wasn't allowed to mention that any of you are naked, and looking at Bob I can understand why. A comic should never point out an audience member's shortcomings." That they found funny.

Just goes to show you that a small-dick joke always works—especially when everyone can actually see the small dick.

I SAID WHAT?

✳ Henry Cho

One of my first corporate gigs was in Oak Ridge, Tennessee, in 1992. Minutes before I was supposed to go onstage, the guy who hired me said, "You do speak Korean, right?" Both my parents are Korean, but I was born in the United States and don't speak any Korean. After hearing this, the guy stared blankly for a moment and then informed me that the audience was all Koreans and none of them spoke English.

I came out and was introduced in Korean by the lone translator. I did the show like I was talking to slow kids in math class. The audience was dumbfounded. I kept thinking, *Surely some of them speak some English,* but no, not a one.

After a few minutes I called the translator onstage and had him interpret. He killed. It was very surreal to tell my joke, wait to hear it translated, and then hear the laughs. Instead of doing the full forty-five minutes, I (we) did about half an hour, but the guy who hired me was ecstatic. I told the interpreter I owed him some money, but he refused. He'd never done standup before, and had had a blast.

OPENING FOR PRINCE

✳ Judy Carter

I got this gig opening for Prince. (This was before he was "The Artist Formerly Known as Prince"—*and* before white people got wind of his brilliance.) I was exhilarated—on top of getting to meet the wonder kid, I was going to be performing standup at the hottest club on the Sunset Strip, the Roxy.

My friend Ed Bluestone, a great comic, didn't think having a little Jewish woman doing standup before a black rock concert was such a good idea. "Judy, his audience comes down from coke by *eating* little girls like you. Don't do it!"

I figure if I'm crazy enough to actually go through with this, I have to figure out a way to get the audience on my side.

I got to the club early, while people were lining up outside. I was the only white person there. So I launched my plan. I stood there with dark glasses on, pretending to be blind, while playing the same song on my accordion—*over* and *over* and *over*. People in line were forced, for an hour, to listen to my playing "Lady of Spain."

Some people were putting quarters in my tin cup, saying, "Oh, I feel sorry for her." But mostly they were cursing at the agony of having to listen to me. When the line finally started to move, they cheered. "At least we don't have to listen to any more of that crap!"

They got seated and the announcer came on over the sound

system: "Playing tonight is Prince!" The audience started screaming, "Prince! Wooooo! Wooooooo!" The announcer continued, "And opening the show is Judy Carter." Dead silence.

I came out with the accordion and started playing "Lady of Spain"—and the audience laughed their asses off. They realized they'd been had.

I had them in the palm of my hand. My set killed—and I got such good word of mouth I became the opening act for every black act that came through town.

I thought to myself, *Wow, playing the accordion is a really good gimmick.* (This was way before Judy Tenuta made it a part of her persona, by the way; I was just breaking it out in case of emergencies.)

A few months later I opened for Loggins and Messina's farewell tour at Sahara Tahoe. They weren't exactly hell-raising rockers or anything, but what a lot of concertgoers do when they come to *any* rock concert is time their drugs so that they kick in just as the main act hits the stage. Unfortunately for me, the hotel delayed the show for forty minutes because the place was packed way over capacity. Soon people were peaking and they were *pissed.*

And when I came out playing the accordion, these people were way too high and angry to see the irony. All *they* saw was a bitch with an accordion—and she had to be killed.

They tried to kill me. They started by throwing shot glasses. When that didn't work, a guy grabbed a tablecloth, charged onstage, threw it over me—and lit me on *fire.* Next thing I knew, a security guard dove onstage and started spraying me with a fire extinguisher. He was screaming, "Come on, let's go, let's go!" and desperately trying to get me offstage—and I was fighting him like a tiger and screaming back, "Let me go! I *know* I can get 'em!"

So he lifted me up, accordion and all, over his shoulder, and carried me kicking and screaming offstage.

It's so surreal when I think back on it, because I remember another security guard who locked me in a bathroom and said, "Look, *chill*," and then took out a joint, handed it to me, and said, "Just smoke this."

Don't you just love the eighties?

A SPECIAL NIGHT

✳ Jonathan Solomon

In 1978 I was a year out of high school, still living with my parents in New Jersey. I had my first serious girlfriend, Janey, who had just graduated from high school, and we'd had sex a bunch of times, always at my house when my parents were out. She was too afraid of her folks to do anything at her house.

The night I finally did comedy for the first time, I kept it a secret from everyone. I drove into New York in my parents' car and performed at a place I can't remember the name of anymore. I was terrible, but I felt like I killed. I got in the car and drove home just completely buzzed.

I went straight to Janey's house. She snuck me into her room. I told her I'd finally performed, and she got totally buzzed that I'd finally done it. We stayed up talking about it, one thing led to another, and we ended up naked, starting to have sex.

Then the door to her room opened, and her father was standing there with this murderous look on his face. Janey looked at him and said, "But you don't understand, Dad. Jonathan did comedy tonight!"

THE IRISH TENOR

✳ Kevin Nealon

In 2003 I did a corporate gig in Palm Springs, along with one of the Irish Tenors and some improv group. I flew in from Los Angeles and this driver picked me up, an old Italian guy.

I got into the car and he said, "Mr. Nealon, I'm a big fan. I'm a big fan." We were driving around a little bit longer and he said, "Yeah, I like all the classics. Love the classics."

I was thinking, "Okay, he watches the *SNL* reruns on Comedy Central."

Then he said, "Are the other guys at the show already?"

I thought he was referring to the improv players, so I said, "Yeah, yeah, they're all there. Everyone's there."

He said, "Geez. Are you from Ireland?"

I said, "No, but my grandfather's from Ireland." Then I realized that he thought I was one of the Irish Tenors. There was about thirty seconds of no talking and just me in the backseat, so I just started singing "Danny Boy." I didn't even know the words. That was purely for my own entertainment.

DRIVING JOHNNY HOME

✳ Bruce Smirnoff

It was 1983. The comedy boom was on, and there was plenty of work for easygoing guys like me, funny enough to get the necessary laughs, but not so funny that I ever asked for a raise. I did think myself funny enough to do *The Tonight Show*, which at the time was hosted by Johnny Carson, probably the greatest talk-show host in the history of television, the undisputed King of Late Night.

My agent was Irvin Arthur, a cigar-chomping agent from the Sheckyolithic Period. Irvin's entire family worked in his office—his wife did the books, his daughter answered the phones, and his son Adam, a cigar chomper in training, schmoozed comics till four in the morning.

One Saturday night I was waiting to go on at the world-famous Improv on Melrose Avenue, the starting ground for some of the biggest names in entertainment—Andy Kaufman, Bette Midler, Jay Leno, Robin Williams, and, surely one day, Bruce Smirnoff.

A black car pulled up in front, and out stepped Johnny Carson, who had never been to the Improv since it opened in 1977. When Carson entered, these blasé Hollywood creatures went nuts. He got a standing ovation just entering the club.

Johnny didn't disappoint. With all eyes on him, he went straight for the bar and ordered a tall glass of something that looked dark and strong. He stood tall, drank the glass of booze right down, and headed straight for the show room. The entire bar and restaurant followed him. The show room became an instant fire violation, but also a jammed, electrified comedy room.

I thought to myself, *Wow! Whoever is onstage right now is going to be seen by JOHNNY CARSON! What a lucky stiff!* Then, as any unselfish comic would, I thought, *How come it's not* me? *It should be me. I'm ready—I've got my six minutes all set! How come it's NEVER ME?* I started to pray to go on while Johnny was still there, but there's an old saying I should've remembered: "Love like a poet and pray like a lawyer." I should have prayed to be on stage, *and do well*, in front of Johnny Carson.

The Improv's owner, Budd Friedman, ran to me: "Brucie, Maher's not here yet; Belzer's running late. You're on next."

The next thing I remember was Budd introducing me: "Let's welcome a young man who will steal your hearts with laughter. From my home state of Connecticut... Bruce Smirnoff!"

The audience gave me a hearty welcome. They probably assumed they were going to help Carson discover a new star.

I did my first joke. It got a tremendous response, more than it should have, but I accepted the laughs. I did my next joke. The crowd laughed harder than at the first joke. I did the third joke; they laughed even harder.

I was on a roll! I imagined myself walking to *The Tonight Show* couch for a chat with Johnny, when someone in the audience shouted, "You stink! Get off!"

The room went silent. I sent in my next joke, which fell dead on the floor. It was as if the heckler had awakened the audience from a magic spell and with one mind they suddenly thought, "Hey, you're right. He does stink."

I got halfway through the setup of my next joke when the heckler hit me again with the same line, but with more conviction: "You stiiiiiiink!"

This time he said it loud enough and long enough that I could see who was yelling: my agent's son.

I should have reduced this kid to a pile of dust, but instead I froze, paralyzed by this betrayal.

I took the worst possible route for a comic: I asked for mercy. I sought compassion in an arena where no mercy is given or expected. I asked, "Adam, why are you doing this to me?"

Adam jammed his dad's 10 percent up my ass. "Because you're a hack! I don't even know why my father handles you! Get off the stage and let a real comic on!"

I held the stage until they removed Adam, and then walked outside to Melrose Avenue. I thought about suicide, but I couldn't imagine dying without the *Tonight Show* credit in my obituary.

As soon as I set foot back inside the Improv, a frantic Budd Friedman came over to me. "Brucie, Johnny's too drunk to drive home. You're the only dependable person I know here." Maybe that was a compliment, but it was no consolation. No one wants to be introduced as America's most responsible comedian.

Budd put Johnny's car keys in my hand. My first thought was to reject this offer. How could I drive him home after just bombing in front of him?

Then I thought about it and said to myself, *Hey, this could be a second chance. I'll be real nice to Johnny, tell him a couple of jokes. Maybe I can turn this around.*

"Sure, Budd," I said. "I'll drive Mr. Carson home."

An hour later I was behind the wheel of Johnny Carson's car. He was in the backseat with this beautiful blonde who had laughed at my jokes. She might have laughed at me, but she was now making out with Carson like she was trying to win a reprieve from the governor.

I was driving thirty miles an hour so as not to lose Sandy Shire, who was my ride back, and also to give me time to rehabilitate myself with Johnny.

At one point the blonde came up for air and pointed at me. "Oh Johnny. He's so funny! You should put him on your show!"

I hacked my way into the moment. "Hey, I'm not doing anything next Tuesday."

Carson leaned forward and, for the first time, spoke to me. "Son, what is your name?"

"Smirnoff. Bruce Smirnoff," I replied.

"Well, Smirnoff, let me tell you something. You got no structure, your timing is bad, and your material sucks."

Things had gotten even worse. Before the car ride, he only knew that I sucked. Now he had a name to attach to that feeling of disgust.

We arrived at Carson's house in Bel-Air, where we were waved in by two guards with shotguns and 9-millimeter pistols. I guess ex-wives can be dangerous. I opened the door for Johnny and the girl, wanting this nightmare to end as fast as possible. But God wasn't finished laughing.

I saw Sandy waiting behind us in my car, but behind that was another car. And another! And another! Apparently Sandy had told all the barflies and hangers-on at the club that there was going to be a party at Carson's house!

There were eleven or twelve people just leaping out of their cars, ready to party down with Johnny. The guards ran over, and Carson got out and saw this giant circus happening around him. He turned to me. "What the *hell* are all these people doing here?"

I said, "Johnny, here's all I know: I told Sandy to follow me. I guess he told that guy to follow him, and—"

"Well, Smirnoff, get these people the hell out of here before I have you all arrested!"

There went the last hope that he might forget my name.

The following Monday, Irvin Arthur called to apologize for his son's abysmal behavior. The next day he called again, to drop me as a client.

The years have given me better perspective. Never appearing on *The Tonight Show* probably saved me the embarrassment of being heckled on national TV by my agent's other son, one of my family members, or even Ed McMahon.

YOU FOLLOW THE BURNING BUSH

✳ Bob Saget

I was working PJ's, a strip joint in Fairbanks, Alaska, in 1983. The owner told me I was going to follow the last stripper. So I was in the wings watching this girl, and suddenly she set her pubic hair and her nipples on fire. I don't think she actually lit anything on fire—she had some kind of a prosthetic pussy shield, like Lee Marvin's nose in *Cat Ballou.* Her rhythm wasn't too good, but who cares when your nipples and your bush are on fire? Her song ended— "Fire," by The Crazy World of Arthur Brown—and she blew herself out like a birthday cake. Then the DJ announced from offstage, "And now the comedy of Bob Saget."

When I walked onstage, it smelled of sweat and sulfur, as if an Olympian god had farted. I stood off to the side, yelling, "More!" I was certainly interested in seeing what she could do to top setting her pussy on fire, because I knew I wasn't going to follow her with my little bag of jokes.

High Times

✳ **Allan Stephans** One night on the Outlaws of Comedy Tour we ran out of booze. The hotel's night manager refused to sell us any more, so Sam Kinison ordered a fully stocked limo. When it arrived, we took out the booze, tipped the driver, and sent him home. Sam's quote for the night: "The party never has to end."

✳ **Andy Kindler** I was in Edmonton, Alberta, in the dead of winter. The other comics decided to have a gross-out contest. The winner peed down the heating vent. They thought it was hilarious. I didn't. Of course, the apartment smelled of urine for the rest of the week. Still not funny for me.

✳ **Argus Hamilton** One night I was supposed to be working with Ollie Joe Prater in Chicago. The club owner went down to the airport to get him and couldn't find him. Finally he was spotted going around on the luggage carousel. Ollie Joe was drunk. He must have sat on the edge of the carousel, passed out, and become part of the luggage parade. God knows how many times he went around.

✳ **Kevin Rooney** The club owners in the mid-eighties would give us cocaine because they wanted the comedians to be crazy. Who knows what wondrous entertainment a drug-crazed comedian might conjure for the paying customers? The drugs were free, but if you asked for a sandwich, they charged you. I can have a bag of coke, but no food. Funny people aren't nourished and happy. Funny people are insane, addicted monkeys, banging on the bars of the cage.

✳ **Greg Behrendt** In 1986 I was doing a string of one-nighters around Minneapolis with Ken Bradley and Mike Andolphie. After a show one night, I got really fucked up and slept with this girl who was *really* not attractive. The following morning Ken said, "Man, you were messed up. You got to really think about it. You've got a problem. I mean, you might as well have just slept with a dude." He was being really serious, coming down on me for being drunk and out of control, and I started feeling shitty. Then we walked out and saw that, in his drunken stupor, he had parked the car on the lawn of the hotel.

✳ **Pat Buckles** In 1986 I went to Caroline's in New York, when it was on Eighth Avenue. I ordered a chocolate ice cream sundae with extra whipped cream because I was pregnant. It tasted sour. The waiter brought me another one, and the whipped cream on that one was bad, too. When I complained to the waiter, he said it was impossible that both creams could be bad, since they were from different cans. Then he thought for a moment and said, "Oh, wait a minute. Belz was in this weekend."

Richard Belzer had sucked the gas out of all the whipped-cream cans before he went onstage.

A MODEST PROPOSAL

✳ Patton Oswalt

I'm emceeing at the Comedy Factory Outlet in Baltimore, Maryland. This is in 1990, and we're doing "Buck a Yuck"—six comedians for six bucks. Or, as Blaine Capatch called it, "Pack o' Hacks."

This drunk braces me and says he wants to propose to his girlfriend. I say, "Yeah, great. After the last comedian, I'll—"

"I want this done firs' thin'," he slurs.

"Um, it's better if we do the show first, and then—"

"THE...CUSTOMER...IS...ALWAYS...RIGHT." He spaces out the words and says them loud, like important people in the movies. Then he sits back down, in the front row.

The show starts, and I manage one joke before he heaves himself to his feet and sort of half-bends on one knee.

I get a look at his date. There's no way these two have been dating for more than a few months. This is a summer fling for her. She's pert and pretty, with ironic eyes and a better horizon. He's a carb-heavy, forty-watt schlump who's never going to escape the inertia of his next paycheck.

"Uh, um, Donna, in front of all these people at the show," he stammers, while Lou Reed's "Metal Machine Music" plays in my head. "At the, uh, comedy show, I want to ask us—you and me—you—to be married and husbands and wives."

"You know the answer is no," she says. She says it quietly, but not softly enough to not be heard by everyone in the room.

The schlump sits back down, roots around in his popcorn bowl, and I go back to entertaining a crowd whose collective soul has just swallowed a shot of pure sadness. "How you folks doing?"

SPARTACUS FINALLY GETS A LAUGH

✳ Steven Alan Green

The late Eric Douglas—Kirk's son—is onstage at Jongleurs, London's biggest comedy club, a place where office parties and hen nights go.

Eric's telling jokes, but not getting laughs. He's pacing and starting to sweat. Finally, some bloke in the crowd yells out, "Come on, mate, tell us a joke!" Douglas fires back with some aggressive put-down. Others join in, chanting, "Tell us a joke!" Forced back on his hind legs, Douglas gets very aggressive. "Do you know who I am?! DO YOU KNOW WHO I AM?!"

"No, who are you?" shouts a heckler, in an uninterested tone.

Douglas snaps back, "I'm Kirk Douglas's son! I'm Kirk Douglas's son! THAT'S who I am!"

Suddenly a lone bloke in the back row stands up and says very solemnly, "*I'm* Kirk Douglas's son."

Then another audience member stands up, puts his hand over his heart, and says, "*I'm* Kirk Douglas's son!"

Soon, hundreds of audience members all stand up, hands on hearts, solemnly repeating, "I'm Kirk Douglas's son!"

100% COTTON

✳ Mike Myers

In 1982, on my last day of high school, at the tender age of nineteen, I was hired by The Second City, a sketch-comedy/improv troupe in Toronto. I was part of the touring company, which was the apprentice version of the main stage company. After a year and a half, we began a Canada-wide tour. This was my first "real" tour. Though still living at home in the suburbs of Toronto, I was a punk rocker, obsessed with my own coolness—a baby-faced Sid Vicious and by far the youngest member of the cast, their average age being thirty.

The day before the Canada-wide tour, I had managed to leave my family-home nest in the suburbs and to secure an apartment of my own—one room, downtown, in a house with other artists.

Not only was I on my own for the first time, I was going to be on the road for the first time. I had many misconceptions about adulthood and life skills. My mother had told me to buy all one-hundred-percent-cotton clothing because it was "healthy" and it was "quality." I took her advice as gospel and over the weeks gathered an entire ensemble of one-hundred-percent-cotton socks, underwear, and T-shirts, spending every penny of my meager savings account.

The tour began in the Rockies of Canada, and it was a thrill to get out of Toronto and see the rest of my country.

We spent the first day in Osoyoos, British Columbia. On the border of the United States, Osoyoos is a peaceful little town whose one claim to fame is that it's "Canada's only desert town." It was crazy hot, in the high nineties, and although I had put off doing laundry (since I didn't know how to do laundry), it was now time, as my clothes were starting to get "rank." I did have rules, however. I deemed it perfectly civilized to go four days with the same socks, three days for T-shirts, and two days wearing the same underwear. It was day five, four, and three, respectively.

I went into Osoyoos's Laundromat. The water in the washing machines had a strange, though not at the time alarming, odor. It was a chemical smell, not unpleasant, but not "April fresh." Predictably, I underestimated how long the laundering process would take, and I was summoned to the tour van to head to our next destination with no time to change out of my odoriferous, hygienically expired clothes into my newly cleaned, one-hundred-percent-cotton wardrobe. I had so much to learn about time management.

That night, we played an art college just outside of Nelson, British Columbia. After the show, I got drunk on free-beer tickets, which, for some reason, none of the other cast members availed themselves of. I vaguely remembered reading some memo about our travel time not being until six o'clock the following evening, and I would, therefore, have the whole day to nurse my hangover before hitting the road.

My mature fellow cast mates piled into the van, eager to get back to the hotel, which was in town. I decided to stay and drink with some of the locals. This would later prove to be a big mistake. In *Apocalypse Now*, the golden rule was "Never leave the boat." When touring Canada with a comedy improv/sketch troupe, the golden rule is "Never leave the van."

I had recently bought a new leather jacket, and because of it, I was sweating through my already-stinky "day five" clothes.

While I was pogoing to the local punk band that had come on after us, a sultry female whisper came from behind me: "Nice show."

I spun around. It was an attractive, middle-aged, heavily tattooed-and-pierced punk-rock lady who, I felt, wanted to tadpole my punk-rock bones.

"Thank you," I said, nervously.

"Do I smell leather?" she asked, closing in on me.

I glanced behind the punk lady and, as though I were the lens in one of those rack-focus shots that Scorsese's very fond of, zoomed in on the middle-aged punk lady's biker boyfriend, who was about twenty feet away and appeared very unhappy about this transaction, displaying body language that suggested my impending murder.

"Yeah, it's a new leather jacket, and I'm kind of...sweaty, so... it...might...smell of...leather," I muttered.

The biker lady then asked, "Do I smell handcuffs?"

"No. You most certainly do not smell handcuffs!"

With that, I bolted out of the venue and onto the street, drunk out of my head, confident that the hotel was right around the corner. It wasn't. In fact, the town was a good ten miles away, accessible only by an unlit, two-lane highway that went through virgin and hostile wilderness. It was easily ninety degrees that night. I was drenched with sweat and my clothes were really, really starting to smell. I began my long walk. It was pitch dark, not a human being for miles. Just forest. Dark, foreboding forest.

I heard a noise behind me from the primordial woods. I pretended I didn't hear this. The noise got louder and closer. I finally looked back and saw a pair of ghoulish, glowing, retina-reflecting eyes. Then, another pair. Then another. It was a pack of wolves. There were eight sets of eyes now, and they had begun their gallop toward me.

I took off, running as fast as I could down the abandoned highway toward the safety of the town, now six miles away. I could feel that the wolves were gaining on me, when, suddenly, a headlight appeared in front of me, moving in my direction. I kept running toward the single headlight and began waving my arms. At first, I thought this was a motorcycle coming toward me, but then I realized it was a car with one headlight out.

Now, quick side note: When I was four years old, and our family was driving to Montreal for Expo '67, every time we passed a car with one headlight out, my older brothers would tell me that it was "Penetang Joe."

According to my brothers' invented legend, "Penetang Joe" had escaped from "Penetanguishene Penitentiary," which was a facility for the criminally insane in northern Ontario.

Supposedly, "Penetang Joe" had one eye and one headlight and picked up unsuspecting victims to steal one of their eyeballs. While it's true this was just a childhood tale, long since dismissed, at this moment I was drunker than Cooter Brown, and therefore susceptible to the possibility of "Penetang Joe's" actual existence. So I stopped my efforts to flag down the car. I turned around. The wolves were right on my tail. I had a choice: be eaten by wolves or have one of my eyeballs stolen by Penetang Joe.

There's more to this adulthood business than one would think, I thought.

The car pulled up to me. The man who was driving rolled down the window and in a very thick Canadian accent said, "You're not from around here, are ya?"

I looked closer. Two eyes. Thank God! I leaped into the car.

"There's wolves on this road, buddy," the man said. I said nothing, still unsure of the man's actual identity. Maybe Penetang Joe had since gotten a glass eye, I thought. I looked closer. Both eyes moved in unison. I was safe. He took me back to the hotel as the sun was coming up.

Still visibly drunk, I stumbled into the lobby to find the entire cast eating breakfast.

"I got chased by wolves!" I blurted out like a lunatic. "I almost got killed by Penetang Joe!" My neatly groomed, well-rested thirty-year-old fellow cast members exchanged looks among themselves— the kind of looks that I would exchange with my friends when crazy people on Yonge Street would come up asking us if we'd seen the "Christmas babies." We had not.

I noticed that everyone had their luggage beside them. "The van is leaving in half an hour," the stage manager said.

"But we're not leaving till six!!!" I screamed with far too much desperation. They laughed in my face.

"Six A.M., ass!"

I quickly realized my immature belief that "itineraries are for pussies" was coming back to haunt me. "Jesus, Myers, you smell like Sasquatch. What'd ya do, sleep in a pile of shit?"

More derisive laughter.

Enough is enough, I thought. So I dug deep, leaning on my years of improv training, and conjured up the following pithy response: "... Um ... No."

I was, after all, drunk.

I stumbled to the elevator, which was, of course, out of service, and I was forced to run up five flights of stairs. Stinking all the more, I took a quick and much-needed shower. Feeling like a new man and a paragon of self-care, I opened my luggage, which was filled with freshly laundered clothes. I noticed once again the chemical smell of the washing-machine water from the Laundromat in Osoyoos. Much to my horror, as I pulled on my underwear, they split pathetically in two, as if my undergarments were now made of Kleenex. All that was left was the elastic band around my waist. Had somebody slipped me acid?

I tried on another pair of underwear, and once again, they disintegrated. I tried on my one-hundred-percent-cotton T-shirt. My arms went through the sides of the shirt like a little person punching his way out of a rice-paper bag. I grabbed my one-hundred-percent-cotton jeans, and they fell apart as if they were made of laundry lint. All that was left was a pile of cottonlike powder on the hotel-room floor. Obviously, there was something in the water at Osoyoos that destroyed cotton, and, therefore, everything I owned.

Defeated, I put back on the soiled T-shirt, the sullied socks, and in a coup de grâce of humiliation, the fetid underwear. Still drunk, I went downstairs and entered the van, and because of my putrid state, was relegated to the rear of the van, between the last seat and the back door. I passed out beside the prop trunk on a makeshift mattress of garment bags.

I woke up, hours later, incapacitated and hungover, certain that this Fellini movie that I had begun to accept as my life had ended.

It hadn't. I found myself in a mountain town that was an exact replica of a Bavarian village. This town, the name of which has escaped me, was not only authentic in its German architecture, but we had inadvertently visited on its once-yearly "German Day" celebration. Everyone was dressed in traditional Bavarian lederhosen. Steins of beer. Pretzels in every hand.

My cast mates, who were strangely unfazed by the local customs, had decided that unless I changed my clothes, I couldn't ride in the van anymore. Unfortunately, all the clothing stores were "Closed for German Day."

A drugstore was my only option. There I bought a pair of plastic-bagged BVD briefs, size 38—six sizes too large—the only size they had. They looked like "before" underwear. The drugstore had only one pair of pants, which I bought—hippie drawstring pants—which, if we were to be honest with ourselves, were actually ladies' pants. I called them "hippie pants," only to the extent that they were in fact made to go over a woman's hips. The least offensive T-shirt I could find was a long-sleeve beer T-shirt that read *"Ich Bin mit Dummkopf,"* which loosely translates to the English "I'm with Stupid."

I went into a schnitzel restaurant and changed in their men's room. I had the presence of mind to recognize this as a threshold-crossing moment in my life. I had gone into that men's room an incompetent, wet-behind-the-ears young adult with no life skills, but I came out of that men's room an incompetent, wet-behind-the-ears young adult with no life skills and a pair of women's pants—the type of pants that Laura Petrie wore on talent-show episodes of *The Dick Van Dyke Show*. "I'm just a housewife, not really a professional dancer," Laura would say.

I went back to the van to the derisive cheers of my cast mates. For hours, I sat there, humiliated, nursing a hangover.

Finally, feeling a little better, I took the opportunity to look at the tags on my new clothes. They were not one-hundred-percent cotton. They were a cotton/polyester blend, more polyester than cotton, really.

I convinced myself that I'd learned some valuable lessons about adult life that day. One lesson was that I was going to have to figure out this whole "adult" thing on my own. Another lesson was that sometimes even the best self-care intentions, like buying "one-hundred-percent cotton," can disintegrate in your hands. I also learned that the world is full of wolves and every once in a while you have to rely on the kindness of strangers to help you out.

However, the most valuable lesson I learned was to never do your laundry in Osoyoos, B.C.

CHECK THE OIL AND CLEAN THE PUNCH LINES

✳ Kip Adotta

There weren't many comedians before the comedy explosion of the 1980s, so it felt special. By 1986 it seemed as if everybody was doing standup comedy. I was driving to a gig in the middle of nowhere. I stopped for gas, and the guy filling my tank said, "Hey, you're a comic." I was thinking he was a fan and told him, "Yes." He said, "Yeah, well I am, too. I do comedy down here at Bob's Beer Joint."

The Last Word, Part Two

✳ **Lenny Maxwell** In the middle of my act, some guy yelled out, "You prick!" I said, "Sir, someday you're gonna eat those words."

✳ **Jason Stuart** I was performing for fifteen hundred kids at Syracuse University. I was more worried about being over twenty-six than about being gay. Some kid screamed, "You suck." I took a beat, turned my head à la Jack Benny, and said, "You're right! And I'm damn good at it." The audience screamed.

✳ **Jim David** At one show I did, a bachelorette party kept yakking until I screamed at them to be quiet. They threw a plastic penis at me. At the end of the night they wanted it back, and I said, "No, you cannot have your penis back," which was the first time I ever used that phrase.

✳ **Red Buttons** I was working at a nightclub in Boston; it was during the baseball season, sometime in the late fifties. Of course, the Boston Red Sox and the New York Yankees had had a blood feud all those years. Regardless, like a schmuck, I did a line about the New York Yankees. A woman sitting ringside, accompanied by a guy who looked like one of the cast of *The Sopranos*, stood up and, at the top of her lungs, yelled, "Red Buttons, go fuck yourself!" There was total silence; it was as if a bomb fell. In those days there was no public use of vulgar language like that, especially by a woman. I stood there shell-shocked for a minute, and then I said, "Lady, if I could, I'd put it in my act!"

Rusty Warren I was being heckled at a gay bathhouse by this guy sitting in just a towel. Finally my manager, Eva, yelled out, "Would someone put something in his mouth to shut him up, please?" The joint went up for grabs.

Hugh Fink I was onstage in 1991 when this huge guy stood up and said, "Hugh Fink, you stink." I tried to ignore him, but he kept yelling, "Hugh Fink, you stink." I proceeded to completely destroy this guy, who stormed out of the room to audience applause. Four years later, when I was a writer on *Saturday Night Live*, I was introduced to David Wells, the Yankees' star pitcher, who was going to be appearing in a sketch. He said, "Hugh Fink, holy shit! Did you perform in Vegas at the Tropicana Hotel? You fucking humiliated me. I was drunk and I stood up and heckled you and you just fucking nailed me." I said, "You sure it was me?" He said, "Hugh Fink, you stink."

IT'S NOT DECAF

*George Lopez

Back in 1992, I was working in El Paso with two other comics—a man and a woman. Working the road as a comic meant you ate, slept, and worked with these two other comics you'd probably never met before that week's gig.

Everything the guy said was funny to me. One afternoon I was laughing so hard at lunch, I hit the table with my hand, flattened my sandwich, and broke the plate.

The woman had just the opposite effect on me. When she opened her mouth, my mind was instantly taken over by images of screaming dive-bombers, gored bullfighters, and my grandmother dancing in her underwear.

Part of the problem was that this woman's mouth was always open. She started talking about five minutes before she woke up, and didn't stop until an hour after she fell asleep. She only ceased babbling to take a drink from her coffee. I never once saw this bug-eyed girl without a coffee cup in her hand. For her, cocaine would have been a sedative.

This woman loved coffee so much she said her dream was to go to Colombia, meet Juan Valdez, and fuck him for all the pleasure he had given to her. It was the funniest thing she said all week—and she wasn't joking.

It's not as if she talked *with* anyone. She talked *at* you, *over* you, *around* you, all day and all night. No one could say anything. She just forced you to stand there. You didn't even need to act like you were listening. She only needed you to be in front of her while she rambled on.

The problem was, you heard everything she said. You could not block her out. She had one of those voices that caused whales to beach themselves. She didn't even listen to what she was saying, I don't think—I don't know how else to explain the fact that she re-peated the same stories so many times. She'd take a sip of coffee and start talking. Sip and talk. I have never seen such a relentlessly perky, nonstop talking machine. She reminded me of a hyperactive, yapping little Chihuahua, and I fantasized about having her hu-manely euthanized.

On Friday night I was onstage when I saw the middle act—the guy I liked—lead a woman into the comics' dressing room. After the show, he told me the woman he'd brought in there had blown him and spit his semen into a coffee cup.

We were laughing our heads off thinking about what a great profession we were in, when in walked the Caffeine Junkie. She entered, talking faster than a Las Vegas car salesman in debt to the mob. It all sounded like a single long word coming out of her mouth. She talked for so long, I checked the back of her neck for a blowhole. After about ten minutes of discussing each audience member that reminded her of a family member, she blurted out, "Oh. Here's my coffee."

She snatched up the cup containing the dose of male essence and drank. Now, maybe it would've been possible for us to knock the cup from her hand before she drank from it. Instead, we just watched in stunned silence.

Maybe God had her drink the sperm-laced beverage because the laugh we got out of it later was payment for forcing us to listen to her life story so many times.

We did the decent thing, and never told her what she'd drunk. Though, believe me, I wanted to ask her if it had tasted different—like maybe chicken soup.

CLASSY GIG

✳ Michael Patrick King

During the big comedy club boom, I was in a comedy team. We called ourselves "King and Mende." My partner, Lisa Mende, and I were considered a kind of poor man's Nichols and May. We were classy and smart and witty, and we occasionally played the comedy-club circuit—where "classy and smart and witty" does not go over as well as "dirty and dirtier and song parody." Basically, in the world of road comics, we were the Elephant Man—a freak Noël Coward–type act in a lineup of road-critter standups.

Needless to say, I always felt out of place on the road, always assuming I wouldn't fit in. Not so much in the clubs themselves, but in the comedy condos. And I had good reason.

The first time we actually stayed in a condo, we were booked at the Comic Strip in Fort Lauderdale. I was very nervous about who I'd be sharing the week with. Dom Irrera, who was my friend, my comedy partner's husband, and the headliner that week, tried to calm me down by saying, "You'll be fine, as long as we're not booked with Mick Lazinski."

I asked, "What's wrong with Mick Lazinski?"

Dom said, "He's a good guy, but last time he was at the condo, he took a dump in the pool."

Okay. So my worst feelings about this not being an Algonquin Round Table tour had been confirmed. Imagine my delight when I arrived at the Florida condo and the driver told me my condo mate would be Mick Lazinski!

My first thought: *I want to die.* My second thought: *Look at the bright side; I won't have to wait to use the bathroom because Mick shits in the pool.* My third thought: *Can I get in a quick swim* before *he arrives?*

Now, how was I going to handle this situation? I mean, what do you say to someone with that reputation? How does the topic even come up? "Morning, Mick, you killed last night, and how about not shitting in the pool today?"

I decided to ignore both the topic and the pool for the length of the gig. But Dom, the ballbuster of all times, was not so silent. He constantly said stuff to Mick about the story. Mick always laughed it off, and I began to get the sense that maybe it was just a "road legend" and not true at all.

In fact, over the week, Mick and I ended up having some laughs and a good time. And then one day he said to me, "You know, that shitting-in-the-pool story isn't true."

Relieved, regretful for my cool behavior toward him—and even more regretful for the time not spent in the pool—I responded, "I didn't think so. Who would actually shit in a pool?"

To which Mick replied, "Yeah, I *never* shit in the pool. I was drunk, I took a shit *near* the pool, and it fell out of my shorts and rolled into the water."

In my best Noël Coward, I replied, "Really? You don't say!"

A COMIC NO-SHOW

✳ Diane Nichols

I worked this club in Sacramento where they always sent the slowest-witted guy to pick up the comics at the airport. I would fly in and often he would say, "We have to wait about twenty more minutes for the opening act's plane to come in."

Well, one time I was at the luggage carousel, and I saw that the company van was already parked outside with the trunk popped. I asked him, "Don't we have to wait for the other act?"

He said very nonchalantly, "Oh no, not today. The cops shot him dead yesterday trying to attack some girl, so I can take you to the condo right now."

SAVE THE GOLDFISH

✳ Tom Arnold

When I first started out in standup, I knew I had to be different, to have a "hook," so I had trained goldfish in my act. Because I had these precious trained fish, I began attracting crowds with hecklers who were women. I could handle male hecklers by saying things like, "Let's go outside so I can kick your ass!" You know, clever comebacks like that.

One fish did an impression of the pope. Then I would take a sword-swallowing fish from the fish tank. I'd bring out a little cocktail sword and insert it into the fish's mouth.

At the end of the act, as a spectacular fish finale, I even placed one of the finned acrobats on a miniature fish-sized motorcycle and took him through a ring of fire, the ring having been fashioned from a tennis racket. It seemed very silly.

However, some animal rights activists started attending the show. They would freak out if I accidentally killed any of these goldfish. I wasn't killing them as a rule, but if I was drunk my visual acuity was not up to par. I may have poked a fish or two with the sword in some place other than their mouths (I was a little shaky back then).

My philosophy on fish mishaps: They're fucking goldfish, for God's sake! I'd seen worse. I used to work in a meatpacking plant.

So what do you do with crazy women coming up on stage, ten at a time? They carried colorful placards about animal rights and stuff. It was just a horrible, horrible situation; the wrath of women is still my biggest fear.

In addition, there was a fire-hazard problem as to how much

lighter fluid to put on a tennis racket. As a result, there were several fires during my comedy-fish-of-fire era.

However, I did need a blowtorch for my goldfish. Allow me to explain: Goldfish were so important to my act at that time that I carried them around with me in my car. The problem was if I went out partying after a club date, I'd leave the fish in the trunk. By morning, if it was wintertime, and it always was, the fish would be frozen solid, and I would have to find a local fucking fish store to replace the deceased fish in order to do my show that night.

When a couple times I couldn't find any nearby fish stores, being so dependent on my fish routines, I had to thaw out the dead, frozen fish and keep the water moving to pretend that they were active and alive. They basically do the same thing on Cher's endless farewell tour; electric wires set in the stage shock her into motion, giving the appearance of life.

So I bought a blowtorch to set my fish free from the block of ice. Spoiled by Wal-Mart, I tried to one-stop-shop for the blowtorch at the fish store. As if fish stores stocked blowtorches because so many goldfish were asking to be cremated instead of the traditional "burial at sea" salutes with a quick flush down the toilet bowl.

Eventually I caved and set my goldfish free, which meant that I actually had to write an act.

Still, I fear that when I die and go to heaven, God will appear as a giant goldfish.

Let's just hope that I don't end up in the other place—the one with the blowtorches.

DON'T HECKLE THE DRIVER

✳ Judy Tenuta

Back in the early eighties (that's 1980s, pigs!) I was a penniless petite flower and Love Goddess in Training. In order to spread my signature religion, Judyism, not only did I have to wake up at 8:00 P.M. to verbally abuse herds of mortal swine, I was also forced to be a road hog and travel with trolls cross-country.

So, one time, my opening act, Tommy Hack (now star of the hit TV series *Full Pants*), was driving me through the badlands of South Dakota to do a show at the Comedy Crevice. We were in his Pinto Blow-About with a hundred miles to go, and he said, "Hey, Judy, you saw my act last night, so what do you think of it? Be honest, what do you really think?"

I said, "Ask me when we get within walking distance of the town."

A TRAINED SMART-ASS

✳ Carl Labove

I did a one-nighter at the Cranston Bowling Alley in Cranston, Rhode Island, in 1999. It was "Bowlin' to the Oldies Night." You did a comedy show in the bar while people threw gutter balls to "Woolly Bully."

But they did pack that bar with about two hundred of Cranston's comedy fans. I was onstage doing this really heinous bit about a plane crash where fifty people died and the survivors went on to catch connecting flights. I did the gate announcement: "For those of you who weren't charred or severely burned, we have a flight leaving out of gate seven. For those of you who've lost loved ones or traveling companions, they're on carousel six in the baggage-claim area. Please bring your dental records for identification and pickup."

There's a reason why I dropped the bit.

Someone in the audience yelled, "Stop talking about plane crashes!" The show stopped dead. I heard someone crying; otherwise it was total silence. I'd known it was only a matter of time before this happened; somebody had lost someone in a plane crash.

I just said, "Look, you know, people die of a lot of things, I'm just gonna go on and do my cancer chunk now." That broke the place up, and I moved on to lighter material.

When you're a smart-ass, you've got to become good at getting out of the holes you just dug.

ARMED AND AFFECTIONATE

✳ D. L. Hughley

I was in Anchorage, Alaska, in about 1998. The phone in my hotel room kept ringing. When I answered it, this woman said something I didn't understand, and hung up. A few minutes later someone knocked on my door.

I didn't really want to answer the door, because I was in Alaska and I didn't know anyone. Besides, I looked through the peephole and saw that the woman standing there wasn't too cute. So I ignored her and she went away. A few minutes later my phone rang again, and the whole thing started over. This went on all day and night. This woman obviously knew when I was in the room, because as soon as I got back there, the phone rang, and then she knocked on my door.

Finally I called security and they said to call them next time it happened.

She called again and I phoned downstairs. Security hid at the end of the hallway, and when she started knocking, they grabbed her. They opened her purse and found a hatchet. Not a gun. Not a knife. A hatchet!

I didn't know if a hatchet is the preferred weapon for hunting comedians in Alaska, or if that was all she had. All I could think was maybe she saw one too many episodes of *Comic View*.

I do know this: if she'd been a little cuter, I might be dead.

IS THAT WHAT I THINK IT IS?

✳ Doug Stanhope

I think it was 1991, back in the days when I had hope and a mullet, and nothing could possibly go wrong. My friend Becker and I were new to standup comedy, rarely making more money than it took to keep us in a shared bachelor apartment and draft beer. But really that was all that mattered.

At that point in a male comic's career, your only real goal is to get enough laughs to trick someone into fucking you. A typical night would include an open mike at a mostly empty ASU jock bar or an Italian restaurant in Mesa, followed by trashing a karaoke night, maybe a stop at Becker's friend's house to do some coke, speed-talking for hours at some tragic titty bar, followed by a quick stop back at the karaoke joint to see if the fat girl left, and finally a drunken cruise down through "Whore Village."

Cruising the hookers on Van Buren Avenue was always like a drunken jungle safari ride. We never had any genuine intention of buying anything. These whores weren't Jamie Lee Curtis in *Trading Places;* these were the hookers that you see on *Cops,* riddled with meth sores and jailhouse tattoos. Their pussies smelled right through their pants. We'd look and laugh and heckle, hurling our most inventive insults out the window before doubling back down Washington Boulevard to repeat the process. It's all certified Satanic time-killing.

One night Becker and I pulled up slowly on a horrifically ugly black hooker, who was double-timing in our direction while looking apprehensively over her shoulder. She was right beside the passenger door when she noticed us and, without so much as an inviting glance from us, forced her way into the car. The ugly hooker was hysterical, screeching about someone with a gun chasing her.

We listened in terrified silence, then suddenly our uninvited guest jumped into a sales pitch: "I'll suck bofa yo dicks fo fifteen dollahs."

Now there was some question as to whether "she" was actually a "he," but when offered a seven-dollar-and-fifty-cent blow job, a drunk's standards dip pretty low. While my last two brain cells treaded water in a sea of beer and discussed whether getting blown by a transvestite counted as a homosexual act, the hooker yanked out my cock and started blowing me. It was a good way to close a deal in any line of work.

The hooker was sucking my dick like she was going for a world record. Becker and I were trying our absolute best not to laugh.

Anytime you get blown that close to your best friend, the tendency is to chuckle a little bit or make a suicide-murder pact. It occurred to me that my cock was in the mouth of a very ugly, angry crack whore. I stifled my laugh so as not to give her any reason to freak out and bite down.

At this point I felt her hand digging around in my pants, which were conveniently down around my thighs. I asked her, "What are you doing?"

"I DID NOT TOUCH YOUR WALLET!" She began rummaging around the floor of the Jeep for the wallet I hadn't yet realized was missing.

The hooker handed the wallet back to me, minus the fifty-dollar bill that had been living there. At that moment I realized why the hooker offered us two blow jobs for fifteen dollars: it was a loss leader, like when Best Buy offers the new *Star Wars* DVD for only fifteen dollars. They want to lure you into the store to buy the cheap DVD, hoping you'll buy a new plasma TV.

I demanded the fifty back. Of course, the hooker denied having it.

Now, here comes the real difference between a drunken comic and a street whore. I threatened violence; she actually responded with violence. She grabbed me by the hair and smashed me into Becker, knocking him out of the Jeep. He was probably relieved to no longer be in a small space with a big, raging man dressed as a woman. I kicked the hooker in the head, which only made him/her angrier.

At this point, any illusions that this was really a woman had left permanently. Time to sober up and lose the boner. I jumped out the driver's side, and the hooker jumped out the passenger's side. I still had my wallet in my hand and—for lack of a better idea—I positioned it over the top of the Jeep and aimed it like a handgun at her head.

"Gimme my money or I'll blow your fucking head off!" I said, hoping the pitch-black night would help my bluff.

This tactic worked to the extent that she believed that I had a gun, but not so much that she changed her story. "I ain't got your money!"

At this point I could only hope that Becker would intervene with some good-cop/bad-cop, but he was scrambling around like a spastic boy who's just found out he's adopted and doesn't know how to react. I finally managed some "Let's scram!" eye contact with him. Becker got back behind the wheel, and we squealed out of there without cash or dignity, but safe nonetheless.

We then reviewed our options: (a) turn back around and hit "her" with the tire jack, or (b) just try to run her over and rifle her pockets. Finally we were struck by the harsh reality that we'd been burned and there was nothing we could do about it. Head home, young soldiers. Live to fight another day.

The drive back to Mesa was the most silent drive of my life, humiliation filling in where adrenaline left. Finally, Becker realized that most of the shame was mine and began giggling and singsonging, "Aaaaaa-ha-ha! You got your dick sucked by a guuuuuu-uy!"

"Fuck you! *You* waited in line to get *your* dick sucked by a guy!" I said, and then, a beat later: "And where's my seven-fifty?"

There's no moral to the story, but if there's a lesson, it's this: If you're gonna get half a blow job from a dude, get the second half. At least that way you go home empty.

EVEN A POLITICIAN HAS TO PAY

✳ Earthquake

In 1995 I was the headliner, Sherman Golding the emcee, and Chocolate the feature for a nonprofit organization's fund-raiser. The dude who hired us was a city councilman for Fort Wayne, Indiana.

After we did a great show, the councilman said, "Come to my office tomorrow morning and you all can pick up your money."

I gave the other comedians my word: "Don't worry. He's a good dude. A city councilman wouldn't take our money, man."

We went down to his office in the morning, waited three hours, and finally his secretary said, "He left town."

I said, "Well, if he doesn't bring us our three thousand dollars, we're just gonna take all his shit out of this office."

He didn't show, so we took everything.

Chocolate was a saved woman, and she said she wouldn't take anything. I said, "You wanna get paid?" She dropped her religion and picked up a telephone.

I was laughing at her. "Okay, all this shit in here, and you grab a phone? He owes you three thousand dollars! That phone ain't three thousand dollars' worth of stuff." Me and Sherman was robbing like we was professionals. Hell, we tried to roll a big-ass copier machine out of there.

The gay dude who was his secretary was screaming, "You can't take this. You can't take this!" He was very flammable and getting red in the face and his voice was getting high-pitched. "I'm calling the poh-lice!"

I slapped the phone out of his hand, and you'd have thought I'd really beaten this mother. He just lay on the ground wailing.

We snatched computers, plaques, and even pictures of the councilman's kids. We piled all this shit into the limo and started for the airport.

Fifteen minutes into the ride for the airport, the police pulled us over. I told them the story and they took us to the station. The councilman, who was supposed to be out of town, was waiting there with our check. We released all his stuff. He dropped the charges, and we flew out of there.

Later my friend told me this councilman was running again. I went on the radio and told this story, called him a crook. He didn't get reelected.

SORRY ABOUT THE FUNNY

✳ Drew Carey

Around 1992 I was hired to do a show for a company's Christmas party in Maine. They sent a deposit (a percentage of my fee) and an airline ticket. When I talked to the corporate representative who'd arranged the gig, I asked her preference, the "clean" version or the "regular" version of my act.

The woman cheerfully told me, "Oh, just do the regular act. We're all adults."

I went out there and I started to do my regular act, which had a couple of swearwords in it—nothing too dirty. I got no response from the audience. Nothing. You could've heard a pin drop. Dead silence like a funeral. I started to imagine it was *my* funeral.

I continued talking and bombing, bombing and talking. I felt as if my skull were imploding, collapsing on my brain. All I heard were the death screams of a hundred jokes. One after another, my babies left my tongue and fell to their death on the stage in front of me.

In the midst of it all, I noticed this old guy advancing toward the stage from one of the front tables. He walked up to me, reached up, seized my mike hand, pulled it downward, and tugged me into a face-to-face confrontation.

The old guy said, "I'm the chairman of the board. If you swear one more time, you're out of here!"

Then the chairman of the board walked back to his table. Everyone else was just observing in total freeze-frame silence.

I can't remember exactly what I said or what they heard. I know I was mumbling as I clumsily placed the mike into the stand. "I'm really sorry, and this was a real mistake. I thought I was going to do one thing, and then…you know how it is…of course you don't. Just forget I was ever here. I don't want the rest of the money. I'll send you back the deposit…use it for another party. I need the plane ticket to get home. I'll see you, good night."

I went behind the curtain, ran back to my hotel, slammed the door, and took the phone off the hook. I half expected a mob from the show to kick down the door and toss me into the street.

That really taught me: no matter how good you are—or how good you think you are—you'd better know what you're in for.

By the way, I kept the deposit. That was their penalty for not giving me an honest assessment of what I was in for.

You should always find a reason to keep the deposit.

What a Joke

✳ **Jeff Stillson** I was working on a cruise ship with this guy who was truly terrible. Halfway through the act, an old man with a walker stood up and screamed, "Are you gonna end this, or do we have to?"

Another time, I performed with this comic in Long Beach. His wife was there with his in-laws, who never approved of his being a standup comic. They were sitting there watching him go down in flames. From his very first joke onstage, it was just wind. Finally it just became unbearable and his wife stood up and screamed at the audience, "Come on, people, laugh! This is funny! This is funny!" With that, the comic just sort of slinked off the stage and put an end to it. I'm sure he works for her father now.

✳ **Jeff Foxworthy** This guy who was a bartender at the club on my first trip through town became an opening act the next time I played there. The first night, I watched him do my act, word for word. This was early on for me, so I didn't have that much material. When he got off the stage I went up to him and said, "Garfield, you just did half my act!" He said, "Was that you? I am so sorry. I knew it was somebody's act. I didn't realize it was yours."

✳ **Jon Hayman** In 1982 I was working the Comic Strip in Fort Lauderdale with Joe Bolster. We had no idea who the third act was to be. We were sitting in the condo when in walked this woman. Before we could even introduce ourselves, the first thing out of her mouth was, "You should know that I sleep with a gun." With that, she marched off to her bedroom. Later that night we heard her screech out of her bedroom, "Oh my God, there's a giant bug in my room, help me!" Joe and I said at the same time, without even looking up from the TV, "Use your fucking gun." She later became a daytime talk-show host, a perfect fit.

✳ **Larry the Cable Guy** John Fox and I were working the Comedy Corner in Tampa. We got up Sunday morning around two in the afternoon to go to a 7-Eleven. The store was filled with parents, kids, and older people, who were all dressed up, obviously coming home from or on the way to church; John's in his pajama bottoms and a T-shirt, hungover, hair all messy. He practically yells at the clerk, "Gimme one of them *Oui* magazines." The guy doesn't speak English too well and keeps repeating "We? We?" John is pointing to the magazine behind the counter and spelling *O-U-I*. Finally the clerk spots the magazine and asks John, "How do you get 'we' out of *O-U-I*?" John snapped, "Just bag it up, Lester, you dumb fuck. I got a hard-on ain't gonna last all weekend." I was so horrified that I set down what I was gonna buy and walked out the door. I didn't look back. I didn't want to see the looks on those church folks' faces.

STAGE CLOTHES

✳ George Wallace

Some years back I was working for Smokey Robinson as his opening act. I would always fly myself to whatever town we were appearing in and meet Smokey there.

This one time I got off the plane, and after about an hour of watching the conveyor belt go in circles, I realized that my luggage was not ever coming out. It was a nonstop flight, and from my window seat I'd actually *seen* my luggage going up that little escalator into the plane. So, as I filled out the lost-luggage forms, I imagined my bag hitting a grazing Nebraska cow in the head.

I then told the lady I was appearing at the Valley Forge Music Theater and they could deliver the luggage there. My description of my one suitcase was eerily like the description of a lost child: "She was about this high, light brown, and had 'Samsonite' written in big letters on the front." I told the lady that my tux was in the bag and how important these clothes were to me, and that even if I was performing when they found it, they should bring it to me while I was onstage. I'd seen another comic once do the same thing and it had worked out pretty good.

At around seven-thirty, I was waiting for my luggage in my dressing room. I had nothing to change into, but in my entire life I've never had a dressing room that I didn't dress and undress in. I was so used to doing it that I actually took my pants off and put them on again, just to preserve a ritual that had worked for me for many years.

The Music Theater was a very classy place. The whole audience wore suits and ties, Smokey wore a tux, and it was beautiful. Finally

7:45 came, and I knew I was hitting the stage in jeans and tennis sneakers. Not beautiful.

I told the audience what had happened, and got a few laughs. Then, out of nowhere, someone yelled out, "Hey, George, you can have my suit." So I said, "Let me see it." Before I knew it, there were five different men and one woman onstage with me. I had the audience going wild. I had two thousand people voting on which suit would be right for me.

All of a sudden I looked and, yes, coming down the aisle was a guy carrying my bag! The guy stood there while I changed into my tuxedo, still doing my act. We passed a hat around for the delivery guy's tip. By the time I'd finished dressing in my tux, my time onstage was almost up. Out loud, I counted the money in the hat. It was over four hundred dollars. I gave the guy the money and said to him, loud enough for the audience to hear, "I'll see you tomorrow night in Tucson."

JOKE PIMP

✳ Joe Bolster

Back in the late 1980s, an agent in New York asked me to work a new comedy club in Myrtle Beach, South Carolina. I agreed, then asked how things had gone during the club's inaugural week. The agent mumbled something about the headliner having a "problem."

I asked, "What kind of problem?"

The agent replied, "Oh, you know, one of those opening-week kinks. Don't worry, your week's gonna be fine. I just need one of your head shots to send down there."

A few days later I boarded a jet bound for Myrtle Beach. After a short flight featuring a breakfast Danish that looked and tasted like a catcher's mitt, I landed in the South's premier beach resort and took a cab to the club. It was situated on the outskirts of Myrtle Beach and looked a tad seedy from the outside. The building had a string of colored lights around the roof, and a rusty mini-trailer serving as a marquee.

According to the sign, the current headliner was a comedian named "Joe Booster." (Remember, I'm Joe Bolster.) I walked inside, and there, on an easel in the lobby of the club, was my publicity photo—lying sideways. I walked over to the bar and identified myself to a ruddy-faced gent with bloodshot eyes. Instinctively I knew this man was no stranger to the demand "License and registration, please." Mr. DUI took me to an office behind the bar to meet the owner, another scruffy character, who looked like a drug mule for the Allman Brothers.

Scruffy stuck out his hand and said, "Dave. Pleased as hell to meet ya."

His warm greeting was followed by a number of concerned questions about my welfare. "How was your flight? Didja get a drink? 'Cause any liquor you want, it's yours. Hey, we're all real excited to have ya at the club!"

I was then taken into the comedy room, a bare, boxy venue with long tables and plastic chairs sitting on a bare concrete floor. It was a school cafeteria with a liquor license.

Ruddy the bartender gave me a lift to the comedy condo, where I was joined by the other comics, Greg Ray and Mike Fechter. The condo was in pristine condition, except for a massive divot out of the living room wall. It looked like a SWAT team had taken a few pokes at it with a battering ram.

Our show that Tuesday night was not well attended. In fact, the audience consisted of a table of fifteen men sitting a fair distance from the stage.

Evidently, Mr. Pleased-as-Hell had expected more of a crowd, because there were about twenty waitresses lolling around the bar. When I left the stage at the end of my act, I noticed that only five of the men remained and most of the waitresses had gone home.

The next night it was more of the same: small crowd, lots of waitresses, not enough laughs.

When the show ended, Pleased-as-Hell motioned the three of us into his office. "You know what," he said, "this comedy shit ain't workin', so I'm closin' up shop. I'll pay you boys for the two shows, but that's it. You can stay at the condo tonight, but I need your asses out first thing in the mornin'."

I later discovered that Pleased-as-Hell had an extensive criminal record and, as a felon, was not allowed to have a liquor license.

It also turned out that the club was a de facto whorehouse. The "waitresses" were really hookers, and their potential customers were our audience members. When a "waitress" scared up a client, she took him back to our condo while we entertained his friends.

The "minor problem" with the opening week's headliner was that he'd discovered the scam. He'd returned to the condo after the first night's show to find fresh wet stains on his sheets. His response had been to take a heavy ashtray and slam it over and over against the condo wall—hence the humongous divot.

His week had consisted of one show; we'd managed to log two shows. They shouldn't have given up. Things were improving.

There's one more twist to this tale. About two years after the Myrtle Beach gig, a comic told me that the club owner had moved on to producing porn films. Some time after hearing that tidbit, I ran into a comic who had just returned from staying at a comedy condo that had been stocked with porn films. One night he popped a tape into the VCR, and something caught his eye. Following a lesbian munch-fest, the camera moved away and eventually stopped on my publicity photo—taped, I'm sure, over that hole in the wall.

As P. T. Barnum said, "There's no such thing as bad publicity."

MOTORCYCLE MAYHEM

✳ Jimmy Shubert

The year was 1985. I had moved to Los Angeles the previous year. I was working on becoming a paid regular at The Comedy Store, but until I could get the big pay of fifteen dollars a show, I settled for a job as one of the club's doormen. It wasn't a bad place to pass the time as I worked on my craft. This was just before the huge comedy explosion of the eighties, and The Comedy Store was a hotbed of activity. I was starting over, basically, and I spent most of my free time there hanging and making new friends, watching and learning from the likes of Jim Carrey, Damon Wayans, and of course Sam Kinison. I knew all these legends, but it was just casually. That was about to change.

Monday night at The Comedy Store was always a freak show, a real carnival of souls that all seemed lost. The Original Room, the Belly Room, and the Main Room were all packed with people. The place had an energy about it. It was alive and buzzing. The standups went on to a very hungry comedy audience. The crowd stayed basically to see the last act of the night, which was Sam Kinison, who had a cult following of porn stars and celebrities, and was not even close to being famous yet.

I showed up at The Comedy Store late one night when Sam

was already onstage and had been on for a while. I wheeled my motorcycle into the backstage area behind the curtain and was sitting on it, smoking a cigarette and talking with two other comedians.

The manager was running around backstage, screaming and yelling (he was from Thailand), "He get off now! It getting too rate!" He was oblivious to the fact that a comedy genius was working his trade.

One of the other comedians looked at me on my motorcycle and said, "Why don't you ride out there and tell them it's last call?" Then he said, "You know, that's never been done before!" That was all he needed to say to a young comedian eager to prove himself.

Then the other comedian said, "Just drive out, say it's last call, and tell Sam, 'By the way, your ride's here.'"

I started my bike and gunned the engine several times as I worked up the nerve. *Am I really going to do this?* I asked myself.

They pulled the curtain back and I went skidding down the three little steps, coming to an abrupt stop at the edge of the stage. I was wearing a long trench coat and mirrored sunglasses. I looked at the audience and said, "It's last call," and then I turned to Sam and said, "By the way, your ride's here!"

Now, I didn't know this at the time, but Sam was deathly afraid of motorcycles. But we were in front of an audience that was going nuts, and I have to give him credit—he didn't even bat an eye. He said in his signature scream, "LET'S DO IT!! AAAURGHHHH! AAAAAAUUUURGGH!" And he mounted the motorcycle. I turned the bike and gunned the engine, popped it into first gear, hit those three steps with just enough juice to climb them, and we were through the curtain. I could have stopped there, but I dropped it into second gear and kept on going through the doorway and down the hallway, past screaming comedians diving for cover. I was yelling, "Get out of the way!" I never saw so many middle acts move that fast.

Sam had a death grip on my rib cage as we barreled out the back door and onto Sunset Boulevard, and still I kept going west on Sunset to La Cienega. As I made my U-turn, Sam finally loosened his grip and screamed above the loud engine, "You're a crazy motherfucker!"

As we drove down Sunset past The Comedy Store, we passed about thirty-five people who had come running out to see where we went, and as we drove by, they applauded and waved. I pulled over, and Sam got off the bike and gave me a look like he was sizing me up. I said good night and drove home.

I didn't see Sam for about two weeks, until I showed up at The Comedy Store on a Monday night, walked into the back bar, and heard someone yell, "Jimmy Shubert, you crazy motherfucker! Get over here!" It was Sam. He was standing with Randy Quaid, and Laraine Newman from *Saturday Night Live*. He introduced me and told them the story of how I'd driven him offstage on my motorcycle. I didn't realize how cool it was until I heard him tell the story.

A Tough Crowd

✳ **Rondell Sheridan** Mike Langworthy was onstage having the worst set of his entire life. Lawrence Taylor from the New York Giants was in the front row and finally yelled, "What do we have to do to get you offstage?" Langworthy didn't even hesitate. "A hundred dollars and I'm outta here." I saw this huge black arm come up with a hundred-dollar bill in it. Langworthy snatched the money, leaned into the mike, and said, "And the next comedian . . ."

✳ **Frank Poynton** I was waiting to do a set at a comedy club just outside of Chicago. The comic onstage was doing a bit about a "crazed Vietnam vet," when a prosthetic leg, complete with sock and shoe, landed at his feet.

✳ **Marc Maron** The stage at the San Francisco Punch Line was elevated. I was in the middle of my act there when a guy climbed up there with me. I thought he was going to kick my ass, so I said, "What's up, dude?" He said, "I'm just cutting over here to get to the bathroom." He thought it quicker to go across the stage than work his way through the tables and people. Interrupting my act just wasn't in his equation.

✳ **Steven Wright** I was playing a theater-in-the-round in upstate New York. The stage slowly revolved. Suddenly a fight broke out that went on for several minutes. Each time I revolved on the stage, I wondered what point the fight was going to be at by the time I came around the next time. It was exciting not knowing who was winning the fight till I spun around to face it each time.

✳ **Wil Shriner** My second time I was ever onstage, a woman in the very front turned to her friend and said, "Oh, I've seen this guy before." My attention went her way as she continued, "And he sucks." I spent the rest of my set wondering where she could've seen me before.

FOLLOW THAT

✳ Chrissy Burns

I was doing a corporate show for a feed-and-seed company way out in northwestern Iowa, really in the middle of nowhere. Every year the company invited all its customers—farmers and their wives—to come out to a banquet hall, have dinner, and see a little comedy show.

They asked me to come early so I could have some food and meet people. When I showed up, there were about two hundred people there, two-thirds of them in their sixties and seventies. They gave me some food and showed me to a seat they'd saved for me at a table of old people.

The guy seated beside me said, "So *you're* the pretty lady comedian they've been saving this seat for. I'm one lucky guy."

I said, "Well, that just proves you're more of a comedian than I am!"

He laughed and said, "Oh no, sweetie, I love buxom redheads!"

I laughed, he laughed, the table laughed. Then I started talking to the people across from me.

While I was involved in conversation, the lover of redheads next to me fell facedown into his plate of food. And I, startled, stupidly asked him, "Sir, are you okay?" Well, of course he's not okay! He's facedown in his au gratin potatoes!

He was dead. He'd simply dropped dead, right there at the table. So they called an ambulance, but the paramedics refused to take him, saying, "There's nothing we can do for him." So they had to call the coroner, who instructed us not to move the body. So the dead guy sat there for a while as we waited for the coroner to come out from the big city. The coroner arrived and, well…when you die, you lose control of your bodily functions, so they carried him out with potatoes and corn on his face and his pants soiled on both sides. Death is not pretty.

As they were getting the poor old man on the gurney, people were cleaning up the mess he had made at the table—feces, urine, etc. They got it all cleaned up just as the body, now covered with a sheet, was headed out the door. The coroner loaded it into the black station wagon, the door closed, and over the speaker I heard, "Well, we have a comedian here tonight. Please welcome Miss Chrissy Burns!"

JOKES FOR AN ORGY

✳ Rick Overton

It was 1978 and I'd just parted ways with my partner, Roger Sullivan. We were "Overton and Sullivan," but it was just one check per show—you do the math. So I was on my own, and I was pretty scared about whether I could cover my own act. My reflex to twist my head to the left had to be worked out somewhere in small rooms. I had to work wherever I could, so when Plato's Retreat—the sex club in Manhattan—tried a comedy night, I was there with my little note cards and my notebook of jokes. I was performing for a bunch of sad-sack shmoes who'd just done too many passes at the crappy buffet and had to sit down. By force, gravity made them watch my act.

I was doing my act and one guy was throwing these little pimientos from inside the olives at me. He couldn't get the distance for them to hit me, so I just watched them land at my feet. Well, anyway, I got through a hellish set of creepy silence, and then they told me I could stay for the party afterward.

I won't lie. It wasn't all about the stage time, but also about seeing some bizarre debauchery.

They had these "starter girls," prostitutes that got activity groups going. I got involved in one of the activity groups with a starter girl. It was really appropriate, because I was just beginning in my comedy career and she was just getting into the sex trade—a couple of newbies kind of groping around. We were both wearing our little paper trainee hats, as it were. Then, to cap things off, I pounded down two bottles of cheap champagne and wandered around wearing flip-flops and a towel around my waist.

I stood at the edge of this huge pool, which was now drained of water, its bottom covered with blue mats. It had become this sea of bobbing asses and heads, a naked mosh pit. I thought this moment to be the most surreal thing I had ever seen, when comedian Professor Irwin Corey's head popped up from the writhing mass of flesh. He inhaled deeply and dove under again like a dolphin breeding. I thought, "Okay, wrong again."

MY MOM LOVES GEORGE CARLIN

✳ Dennis Blair

I'd been George Carlin's opening act for about ten years when we performed at the Count Basie Theater in New Jersey in 1998. My mom, who is slightly insane, lives in New Jersey and came to the gig.

My mother has seen me perform at least a hundred times. She almost always brings a very old, sickly, or close-to-dying friend with her to my shows. My mother believes I am the comedy version of Elisabeth Kübler-Ross, that the sick and dying need a good laugh and I should be the one they see before they move on for their eternal rest. What could be better then having the giggles when you meet God?

But on this night, my showbiz-obsessed mom came alone. When she saw George, her eyes lit up. She walked up to him, flung her arms around him, and said, "George, you look good! I could really go for you!"

My life and career passed before my eyes as I quickly dislodged my eighty-four-year-old mother from George's neck and hustled her away. Fortunately, George took it in stride and didn't fire me on the spot.

I deposited my mom safely in the audience and did my show. When I came offstage, George appeared in his doorway and said, "Hey, Dennis, your mother just gave me a great blow job in the dressing room."

SWANEE, HOW I HATE YA!

✳ Kathy Griffin

I accepted this corporate gig, a thing at which I notoriously bomb. Still, I can never resist corporates because they pay so much money. There was some guy in Arizona who owned a place called Rawhide. It was described to me as a banquet room, where they intended to hold a very classy benefit, and they wanted me to perform.

I got there and went inside, where I met the woman who was organizing the event. The problem was, she loved me but no one else did. She was gushing, "Oh my God! You're my favorite comedian! I just *love* you! I had to *fight* to get you here!"

I thought, *Honey, you're gonna get canned so fast after this!*

They brought this guy backstage who had Lou Gehrig's disease; the event had been organized for him. He was clearly disabled and was saying, "Oh, I'm looking forward to seeing you perform! I really miss you on *Saturday Night Live.*"

I said, "Well, that's nice, but I was never on *Saturday Night Live.*"

At this point it was about fifteen seconds before I was to go on. The sound guy looked over and said, "Wait a minute! You're not Sheri Oteri?"

I said, "No, I'm—I'm Kathy Griffin."

The sound guy said, "Ah, great!" He threw his hands in the air and walked away.

Then the curtain opened and I went out onstage. What my agent had described to me as a black-tie table banquet was actually a fair. The floor was all dirt; there was a snow-cone machine crushing ice, a popcorn machine popping. Not too far away, a gunfight show was audibly in progress.

I started my act, and it was just a disaster. People stared at me, some with confused looks, as if they thought, "Ain't she supposed to be...? She don't *look* like the lady from TV."

I was thinking to myself, *Oh God, I gotta contractually fulfill my sixty minutes.* I looked at my watch and realized I was only a minute and a half into this disaster.

The experience was so horrible that I had actual flop sweat. The clock seemed to be going backwards.

Just when it seemed matters couldn't get worse, this little kid climbed up onstage with me. The kid, who was about six years old, stood in front of me, a big grin on his face. I was in the middle of telling some story about how irritating Julia Roberts is, when the six-year-old kid started singing "Swanee" and doing a soft-shoe. No one was helping me; no one was getting the kid off the stage.

I snapped and said clearly into the mike, "Can somebody get this fucking kid outta here?"

With that, the room went silent. I could hear people making gasping sounds.

I thought, *Oh God!*

I had presupposed that the crowd would laugh at the comment and that the mother was going to call out, "Timmy, come down, bad boy!" But the kid was still dancing and singing "Swanee." That being the case, I had no choice but to kick the kid off the stage myself.

I finally finished the gig and was just covered in sweat. The girl who booked me came backstage and said, "I think you're great anyway!"

I said, "I really need my check now."

THE JOKE IS IN THE HOUSE

✳ Paul Mooney

I was opening for Eddie Murphy in 1987 when Whoopi Goldberg first came on real big. I was calling her "a fugitive from a pancake box." It got back to her, and she started showing up every night to hear me say it. Security would tip me off: "Whoopi's here. Leave it out." And I would.

One night we were in Philadelphia and she snuck in. I was doing the joke about her when I saw something coming at me in the shadows. I thought it was security. It was Whoopi. She grabbed the mike and said, "I look like what, motherfucker?" The place went fucking nuts. I said, "Well, I'm busted."

And ever since then, she and I have been friends.

DOING RON WHITE

✳ Frank Lunney

In 1987, Ron White and I were starting off, doing the Dallas Improv on Monday nights. Ron was developing really well, booking some gigs, getting a little ahead of the rest of us, and maybe starting to get a little bit of an ego. I guess I was feeling ornery one night when I told the manager of the club, Tom Castillo, to put me on before Ron.

I got onstage and started doing Ron's act: "Hey, folks, good to be here, I haven't been here for a couple of weeks. You know, I bought these pants today just for this show. And I asked my wife, 'Honey, do these pants make me look fat?' And she says, 'No, I reckon it's that big ass of yours.'"

I heard Ron in the back. "What the hell's he doing?"

I did five more of his jokes. And the comics were dying, 'cause they knew what was going on. The audience was laughing, 'cause half of them had never seen me or Ron.

Ron yelled from the back of the room, "Hey, why don't you just do another one of my jokes?"

I said, "Thanks, Ron, I will." I did the rest of his act and stepped offstage.

Ron's a big boy, and he was livid. I went out around the side of the club to avoid him, but he didn't have enough time to clobber me because he had to go up onstage.

Like me, Ron was new, so he didn't have much material and wasn't very good at ad-libbing. When he went up there, all he could do was what he knew. "How you doing, folks, you know, I bought these pants, ah, shit!" Then he started, "You know, my wife ain't the greatest cook, in fact, uh, oh Goddammit!" He tried to start four or five jokes, but he realized I'd already stepped on them all.

I had to hide from him for about two months, because he wanted to kill me.

THE FIRST RULE OF A SHOW

✳ Steven Wright

One of the weirdest things in my history of the road happened in the early eighties about an hour from Boston, in a town called Leominster. It was one of these places that did comedy one night a week. It wasn't an actual comedy club. At the time, it was mainly for disco. Three comedians drove out, and we were in there sitting at a table waiting for the time. And the thing was, the audience didn't know there was going to be comedy. That is not good. That's one of the basic things that should be happening the night of a show, that the audience should know that there is going to be a show.

There's disco music playing and the lights are flashing and people are out on the dance floor. It's a Friday or a Saturday. And then all of a sudden, at some hour—eight or nine, I don't remember—

they just shut the music off, the lights stop moving, people are looking all around and they just walk off the dance floor. They didn't know what was happening. And a guy walked out with a microphone in a stand and he said, "Now it's time for the comedy show." There was no adjustment. And then he says, "And here's our first guy." And I don't remember if I was first or what number I was, but it didn't matter. It was absolutely horrible. It was the worst that I ever experienced.

I remember standing on the dance floor starting to go into my act and it was just like two or three minutes of just horrible silence. And I left. I actually left. I just left the stage. I've never done that. I've always tried to do the time I was supposed to do, but it was just too bizarre. It was too bad. It was a survival thing. Psychological damage.

A LITTLE COMEDY FROM THE AUDIENCE

✳ Vic Henley

I was working at The Comedy Store in London, which I think is one of the best comedy clubs in the world. It's a showcase format, with a host and five comics doing sets, with maybe an extra guest thrown in from time to time. This particular night was sold out, so about 450 people were enjoying a fine show.

Sean Meo is hosting. I'm lingering near the stage door because I'm on next. The other comics and I are talking, so we don't hear what Sean says, but we all hear the showroom go dead silent. I crack the door open and we realize that Sean has done some jokes about midgets and now someone's yelling at him. "I'm a midget and that's wrong and I can't believe you're making fun of us. The proper thing to call us is 'little person.'"

We're laughing our asses off backstage because we're a bunch of dicks who always enjoy other people's misfortunes, especially a fellow comedian's. Looking into the crowd, we can see a very angry little person standing in the aisle, letting Sean have it. "It's my birthday and you're ruining my birthday!" The audience is silent. All you can hear is the shouting and our muted howling backstage.

Scrambling to save the situation, Sean says, "Well, how about we sing 'Happy Birthday' to you? Would that make it better?" He launches into "Happy Birthday," and to our surprise the entire audience joins in. When they get to the part of the song that's "Happy Birthday, dear so-and-so," all 450 people sing out, "Happy Birthday, dear MIDGET, Happy Birthday to you!"

HOOKED ON LOVE

✳ Steve Wilson

In 1997 I met this girl, Rose, in Columbus, Ohio, when I was opening for the singer Brian McKnight. It was just a booty call, a one-nighter, but we kept in touch with each other. Every now and then I would fly her out to some city where I was performing.

The next time I came to Columbus, she came to see me, we had a good time, and I asked her, "Why don't you just move to Buffalo," where I was living at the time.

She said yes. That should've been my first hint that something wasn't right. I know I ain't *that* good to get a girl to leave Columbus for Buffalo.

The next weekend I took a couple of my boys and we drove to Columbus and moved her to Buffalo. It was like the happiest day of my life. Later I was sitting on the couch. She came out of the shower completely nude, and we made love on the couch. By now I was so happy I wanted to die, because I knew the shit doesn't get any better than this. My dick was screaming at me, "Marry this woman, right now!"

I was still inside her and she started coming clean to me, saying, "You know, you are the best man I've ever had in my life." I was just feeling like the biggest man in the world, saying things I'd never thought before, like, "I will make you happy."

She said, "Good, because the last guy, my pimp, used to beat me."

Maybe as a comedian I was thinking it was a joke, so I laughed. Then I noticed she was crying, and she said it again. "You're the best man, uh, I'm glad I don't have to be a prostitute anymore since I've met you. I'm changing." And then she said, "All right. Since I'm cleanin' my, my whole space, uh, I used to be a crackhead."

I didn't know what to say, but my dick was screaming, "Get me out of here!"

I think I tried to play it off, all cool, like I heard it all the time: "Oh, so you used to be a prostitute and a crackhead?"

She was letting it all out now: "And I knew this was love and I took a chance to come here, 'cause I'm not supposed to leave the state of Ohio 'cause I got three felonies." I wasn't saying nothing, because all my brain could manage was a big blinking sign that said, YOU'RE FUCKED NOW, MOTHERFUCKER.

Then she said something that set off a brushfire in my head: "I gotta make some money while I figure out what else to do, so I've got a package of dope coming in the mail."

"You're gonna do what!?"

"It's just weed. I got a package coming tomorrow. We're not

gonna do drugs, but we, um, you know, I'm just gonna sell 'em out of the house."

So I picked a fight with her. I couldn't tell her it was about the crack-ho thing. So I went off about her leaving the cap off the toothpaste, or some such shit. I just went off, cussing and quoting the Bible, just acting the fool—whatever it took to get her out of my house.

That was the last time I used my frequent-flyer miles on a crackhead.

NOT THAT KIND OF GIRL

✳ Mike Preminger

Bachelors Three was a big club run by a guy named Bobby Van. It was owned by Bobby, Joe Namath, and another guy; hence the name Bachelors Three. I worked there several times, opening for the Temptations, the Four Tops, and Blood, Sweat and Tears.

To get onto the stage you had to walk down a long, thin aisle from the back of the club. Blood, Sweat and Tears would come single-file down that aisle, playing their instruments for their opening song, "Spinning Wheel." The last guy in line would be their lead singer, David Clayton Thomas, who'd hit the stage just in time to belt out the opening words of the song, "What goes up..."

But the fourth night of the gig, the band just had to keep repeating the opening instrumental, because there was no David at the end of the line.

I was standing in the back of the club when the band's road manager ran to me and said, "Where's David?"

I said, "I don't know if you've been paying any attention, but there's an opening act before your guys get up there, and that's me. Recognize me? How the hell do *I* know where he is? I was onstage."

Road managers only know how to badger whoever's within reach until they get what they want, so he continued, "You don't know where he is?"

"No, I don't know where he is."

"You gotta know." His implication was, *I don't know, so you have to know, because I get fired if I don't know.*

Meanwhile the band was playing the beginning of the song over and over, like a broken record.

The road manager shifted from harassment to his only other gear, panic. "We have to find him. Help me find him."

I said, "Yeah, that's my job, to help you find David."

Then I remembered that before the show, some girls had come into the band's dressing rooms. This one girl had been sitting next to David, so I said, "Maybe he's with this girl."

But they weren't in the dressing room. The road manager was too panicked to think. "Where could he be?"

I didn't care, so at least I could guess. "Do you know where David's car is?"

We walked to the car and saw two pairs of bare feet hanging out the window attached to two naked bodies.

The manager said, "David, you're onstage."

David didn't even slow down. "Give me a couple of moments."

The guy was yelling at him. "Get in there!"

I said, "Maybe you should let him finish. You don't want him trying to sing with blue balls and a hard-on."

The road manager couldn't hear anything but himself yelling, "Get in there! Get in there!"

David ran entirely naked through the parking lot, getting dressed on the run. Most guys only drop their pants for a car fuck, but not David. He took everything off. That shows respect for the girl. That's class.

The girl was lying there in the car naked. I guess in his sleazy way the road manager wanted to do something nice for me in return for finding his singer, because he said to her, "While you're down there, why don't you do Mike?"

She didn't try to cover up or anything, just looked at him and said, "The comedian? What kind of girl do you think I am?"

THE LAUGH IS ON ME

✳ Helen Kearney

I did this show in Lancaster, Pennsylvania, in 1993. This one guy was sitting by himself and just sort of smiling, but I could never really get him to laugh. As we comics sometimes do when this happens, I focused on him as opposed to the other people who were obviously having a good time. He was definitely not heckling me or being rude—he just wasn't laughing the way I wanted him to, so I sort of homed in on him and started talking to him, but he was sort of evasive, so I moved on.

He came up to me after the show and thanked me and told me he'd had an amazing time. He told me his wife had passed away a few months before, and that this was the day of their wedding anniversary—his first anniversary without her. He said I'd helped him get through the day. I'd thought he wasn't enjoying the show, but I couldn't have been more wrong.

Watching the Pros Do It

✳ **Jim O'Brien** Ollie Joe Prater always brought along his own opening act. This one guy was driving in Tennessee with Ollie Joe on the passenger side. Out of nowhere, Ollie Joe punched his opener/driver in the face. The guy nearly lost control of the car. He finally regained control and said, "What the fuck did you do that for?!"

Ollie said, "You're startin' to ad-lib on stage. And I don't like it."

✳ **Harris Peet** Sometime around 1981, Richard Pryor was writing a new act and working it out nightly at The Comedy Store in Los Angeles. One night Pryor was due up next and waiting in the hallway. There was Ollie Joe Prater, who was already stretching and limbering up, though he had at least an hour and a half before he'd be going on after King Richard.

Ollie Joe was moving his head back and forth, loosening his neck, and said to Richard, "Yeah, Richard, I'm on after you, and I don't even know what I want to do."

Richard said, "Why don't you do your best joke first and find out if you're any good."

✳ **Mark Cordes** I worked with Dave Attell at the Riviera in Vegas and saw him come up with a bit. It was the first time he'd ever been to Vegas, so of course we ended up at a strip joint. This nude girl leaned down to him and he said, "What do you know about Candy's murder?" She said, "What?" He handed her a ten and said, "Maybe this will refresh your memory."

✳ **Mack Dryden** I was working The Comedy Works in Philadelphia with Dennis Wolfberg and Jerry Seinfeld back in 1983. A blind piano player warmed up the audience. Dennis was the emcee and didn't know the piano player was blind. So Dennis introduced Jerry, then led the blind man toward the back of the stage, figuring the guy would walk behind him and through the doorway. Instead the blind man walked face first into the wall. Jerry got onstage and said, "Good job, Dennis. I've seen dogs do better work."

✳ **Robert Wuhl** Rodney Dangerfield would try out new jokes on my answering machine. The amazing part was hearing him pause for the laugh before moving on to the next joke.

✳ **Hiram Kasten** One Tuesday in 1982 found me working with Dom Irrera and Peter Fogel at some godforsaken hell gig in Jersey. While waiting for our turns onstage we ordered our dinners, which, in the case of this cheap gig, were just sandwiches. The food took a long time to come, arriving just as Fogel was being introduced. Never getting a bite, he ran for the stage. During his twenty minutes, Dom and I began to eat and laugh and bitch and all was normal, until Dom thought it might be funny to lift the top slice of the rye on Fogel's sandwich and rub his dick along the top of the exposed pastrami. Anything for a laugh. Fogel finished his act and rushed hungrily back to our table. He grabbed the funny half of the sandwich and was just about to bite into it when he looked up to see our faces. He stopped for a second and said, "Oh yeah, Dom, what did you do, rub your dick on the sandwich?" Then he took a big bite. Anything for a bigger laugh.

THE ONE-HANDED CLAP

✳ Jim O'Brien

Back in 1982, at the Dallas Comedy Club, this one-armed millionaire used to come in every night with a different hooker. None of the hookers ever wore underwear. The guy would sit next to the stage with the prostitute next to him and have her flash the comic the whole show. There was a mirror along the wall opposite the guy and his "date," so half the audience saw what the comics did.

Onstage I'd say to my blind partner, Alex, "Do you smell anything unusual?" The crowd always knew what I was talking about, so they went crazy, and the one-armed guy would slap his forehead to clap.

The hookers always had a great time, too. They were getting paid to entertain the crowd, but working far less than the comics.

A FOOL FOR THE ROAD

✳ Larry the Cable Guy

When I first went on the road in the late eighties, I was so stupid. I was dumber than Rain Man on no sleep. The road can be a comedy boot camp, where you're toughened up by smart-ass drill instructors.

In 1986 I'd been booked on one of my first paying gigs. The afternoon of the show—I was scheduled to go on at eight o'clock that night—the other comics snuck in my room while I was asleep and reset my alarm clock three hours forward. Then they had somebody from the club bang on my door and say, "Dude, where you at? We got a show. You need to get down here!"

I looked at the clock. It read five after eight. I hauled ass down to the club. Of course, there was nobody there because it was only like five-thirty.

A month or so later I was working in Milwaukee with a comedian named Dak. He saw me doing laundry and told me that I needed to throw starch in with my clothes or they wouldn't get clean. I told him I didn't have any starch. He said, "Well, just cut up a couple potatoes and throw them in there."

So for the next couple of weeks I did all laundry with potatoes in it. You know someone at one of those public laundromats had to have seen me cutting potatoes and dropping them into the washing machine, but nobody said anything. They were probably afraid I was some sort of psycho homeless guy saving a buck by cooking his potatoes in his laundry's hot water.

ANY PUBLICITY IS GOOD, BUT...

✳ Tony Robinson

I was working in Portland in 1987 and had a girlfriend who lived there. One night she came to the comedy condo to spend some time with me, and brought a sexy little piece of lingerie, a red teddy.

The next day I put the teddy on, ran out of the bedroom, and jumped into the arms of the feature act.

My lady friend had a camera and started taking pictures. Being comics, we hammed it up and had a good laugh.

The following week I walked into the San Jose Comedy Club. The sign read, AN EVENING IN RED WITH TONY ROBINSON. And there were the pictures from Portland of me wearing red lingerie, being held in another man's arms. Everybody who attended the show saw those pictures on their way into the club.

The emcee gave my introduction, "Please welcome your headliner, 'Red.'" The entire audience began to chant, "Red, Red, Red, Red…"

Those pictures became the hardest act I ever had to follow.

FUNNY AS A GUY

✳ Mishna Wolf

The drunken girl at the bar at Giggles was spilling her apple martini all over my cowboy boots, and she was practically in my lap at this point. I was between shows, and a hostage.

I sat there trying to remember how I'd gotten into this ridiculous conversation, with no end in sight. Oh yeah, she'd told me, "My boyfriend's dad just died a month ago and he hasn't laughed in a month, and you made him laugh." I should have known by that too-intimate opener that she was crazier than a shithouse mouse, but instead I'd said, "Really, he liked my act?"

Now she was opening up to me about all sorts of shit that I just shouldn't know. She continued, "I mean, you know—men are dogs! I didn't have sex for like a year, and when I finally did, it was with a guy who hit me." Yipes! Heavy! Too heavy!

Jesus, I thought as she blathered on about her tattoo, *what is it about me that gives her the feeling I want to go do the next show with her psychic jizz all over me?*

She unknowingly answered my question: "After watching your set, I really feel like I know you. You know?"

I mentally reviewed my set to see what bit could have possibly said, "Hey! I'm off my fucking rocker, so if you are too, come talk to me after the show!" I thought they were just dick jokes, but apparently there's a hidden subtext in them that you can only hear if you're off your meds.

Maybe it wasn't my set. Maybe it's because, as a woman, I seem more approachable than the guy comics. Or maybe men deal with it, too. But as I listened to the drunk girl at Giggles, I thought of some of the male comics I knew, and was sure that by now they'd have shut her down or at least had her blow them in the walk-in fridge.

It must be me. I seem to attract the one girl in every audience with no boundaries who really needs to talk. I've heard it all: drug addiction, car accidents, herpes, cancer, Satanism, breakups, gang bangs, near-death experiences, psychic powers, and Wicca.

I asked my fan if she needed to get going, to which she replied, "No, I'm staying for the second show. I want to watch you again." I told her there wouldn't be any new stuff in the second show, but she didn't seem to mind. She just looked at me with her Charles Manson eyes and said, "You know, there really are no coincidences."

Finally the show started and I pointed her into the showroom. She reluctantly went in, and I started looking over my jokes, trying to forget all the things she'd told me. While I counted my blessings that she hadn't tried to get me to exchange numbers with her, I heard a commotion coming from the showroom. Clearly an opener was being heckled, but I ignored it and went back to my notes as the show moved along.

The commotion kept getting louder, so I popped my head in the showroom to see my drunk girl being escorted out by the manager while shouting at the comic onstage, "You're not funny! You wouldn't know funny! If it was funny, you wouldn't know it! You don't know funny!"

I went back to the bar, trying to distance myself from the situation. But as they dragged the girl by me toward the door, she made eye contact with me and screamed, "That guy wasn't funny! *You're* funny!"

As they took her out the door, I noticed that the heckled opener had come offstage and was standing at the bar, watching me. He looked at me dubiously for a moment before saying, "Friend of yours?"

WHERE THE TUSCALOOSA

✳ Dobie "Mr. Lucky" Maxwell

Every comedian who's climbed the ladder of the business has been booked for a gig for which he or she is just not ready. It's natural; moving up the ladder requires more experience and material, and one has to get that experience somewhere. Most of the time it involves going to a different part of the country to cut your comedy teeth. Why people think you're funnier if you're from far away has always been a mystery to me, but it's true. If you're from somewhere else, it's a big deal.

The first time I was booked to close a show at a Ramada or Holiday Inn was in Tuscaloosa, Alabama, back in the late eighties. After a long, hot drive from Chicago in a rattletrap car with no air-conditioning, I pulled up to the hotel. I noticed there was a radio-station van with a trailer parked in front of the show lounge. I walked over to the lounge and introduced myself to the person in charge, a guy named Dave, who had a ponytail and an earring and a few tattoos. This was long before that look became commonplace, and he really stood out. He was a good guy with one of the thickest Southern accents imaginable.

Dave shook my hand and his face got serious. "You got a tough'n tuh-naght, Yankee."

"What? I've got a tough one tonight?" I had to repeat everything he said to make sure I understood it.

"Well, yuh see that table fulla people over thar? They work at the radio station and they all got fahrd today."

"Fahrd?" I asked.

"Yeah, fahrd." I was still at a loss.

Then it hit me. "Oh, you mean *fired,* right?"

"Yeah, that's what I said. Fahrd."

The whole staff of the radio station sponsoring the comedy show had just been fired, and they'd started drinking at about 3:00 P.M. for a 9:00 P.M. show.

When I came back to the lounge at 8:45, the radio station people were still there, and much drunker. The back of the bar had some pool tables, where some players from the Alabama football team were drinking beer right out of the pitchers while steadying themselves on cue sticks. The rest of the crowd was just starting to turn up the rowdy.

Dave started the show at about 9:15 and brought up the opening act, a black comic from Texas. The black comic started to do his act, but the rednecks in the back of the room dropped the *n* word on him, and he left the stage after about three minutes.

Dave went back up and acted like nothing was wrong, introducing the next act, who was supposed to do between thirty and thirty-five minutes. The crowd was loud and not paying much attention, so this guy did about twelve minutes before he bailed out.

Two comics gone, and we were only fifteen minutes into the show. It was supposed to be a ninety-minute show, and I was supposed to do forty-five to fifty minutes.

Dave went back up onstage and gave me an introduction I'll never forget. Try to add the thick accent on your own.

"Fuck those two pussy motherfuckers. We got a guy here from Chicago who's gonna do two and a half hours of kick-ass comedy for y'all."

Then he forgot my name. He asked me to tell him and I tried, but he didn't hear it. "Doobie? What kind of a pussy name is thay-at? Ah, just get your little Yankee ass on up here and make 'em laugh."

I walked through the crowd with my heart in my throat to a smattering of applause that had died out by the time I reached the microphone. I tried to just do my act, and actually it started to get some laughs. I felt great. Within five or six minutes, though, I felt myself losing the crowd. I felt bad. I went into survival/whore mode.

I remembered that there were Alabama Crimson Tide football players in the crowd, so I yelled out their cheer, "Roll Tide!" It got a huge yelp of approval from the crowd. I went on with my act, but after five or six more minutes I felt them drifting off again. I knew I was in trouble. There was no way I was going to do the forty-five-minute show I was scheduled to do, much less the "two and a half hours of kick-ass comedy" Dave had promised them.

All I could think of was to say it again, so I did. "Roll Tide!" It got another yelp of approval, but this time one of the drunken football players with an allergy to crowd-pandering yelled, "Go back up north, Yankee. You ain't no comedian."

I snapped. The controls for the sound and lights happened to be on the stage, so I cranked up all the lights and turned the sound up as loud as it would go. What I didn't know was that I also had turned on all the speakers in the hotel hallways and parking lot. It was some kind of emergency broadcast system or something.

I was so angry about the whole situation that I said the following sentence, which I don't think had ever to that point, or has ever since, been uttered in the state of Alabama.

I said, "I just want to say from the bottom of my heart...FUCK BEAR BRYANT IN HIS DEAD CANCEROUS ASS." If you don't know, Bear Bryant was the legendary coach of the Crimson Tide, who died of cancer. I was proud of myself for packing such a wallop into one sentence on the spur of the moment.

I've never seen such a large group go silent so quickly. It was eerie. They didn't boo. They didn't talk. They didn't do *anything*. There was just stunned silence. At this point I was so angry I just kept going.

"I'm going to dig up his dead, rotten corpse and take a big shit in his hound's-tooth hat and wipe my ass with his death certificate. He's DEAD, and you're LOSERS. You can't win football games and you sure as hell can't win a war, either. Oh yeah, and fuck NASCAR, fuck rasslin', and double-fuck grits and corn bread, too.

"You people ought to be ashamed of yourselves, you rude Civil War–losing inbred sons of bitches."

I learned one thing from my biker father, and that's when you're in a war of words, go right for the malady. Hit the soft spot and hit it hard and take them out of their game. I did just that until I couldn't think of anything else, letting loose a verbal Nagasaki blast that stunned them.

When I was done insulting them all, I went back up onstage and said, "For those of you cousin-fuckers who didn't hear it the first time, I want to say it again. FUCK BEAR BRYANT IN HIS DEAD CANCEROUS ASS. I'm going to go back up north, marry a darkie, and pound out lots of little half-breed babies, and we're all going to ride on the front of the bus down here to your FUCKING

FUNERALS. From the bottom of my Yankee heart...GO FUCK YOURSELVES, YOU ALABAMA MOTHERFUCKERS." I figured if I was going out, it was me who was going to light the fuse.

I slammed the mike down and three security guys walked me to my room in complete silence while my heart beat like it was going to leap out of my chest. I knew I was in big trouble.

There was no applause, no boos, no catcalls, *nothing*. They just sat there and took it in silence. I've never seen anything like it before or since.

I hadn't realized that my little diatribe had been playing in the halls and the parking lot of the hotel. People were coming out of their rooms to see what all the fuss was about. I was sitting in my room thinking I was going to die in Tuscaloosa.

The phone rang in my room a few minutes later. It was Dave. "You in some DEEP shit, Yankee. Don't leave your room. Wait for my knock."

The knock came and it was Dave, along with the three security guards. The tension was very thick as he sat down and counted out my money on the bed. I was very surprised that he paid me. He didn't look me in the eye as he counted out the cash. Suddenly he looked at me dead-on with a stern look.

"Boy, I am a proud Southerner, and I have hated Yankees my whole life. But, I have to tell you, you had some BIG OLD balls to do what you did in there tonight. I don't like it, but I sure do respect it."

I expected him to shoot me at any moment.

Instead, he looked me in the eye and got real serious and real quiet. "You're in a LOT of trouble, boy." I knew that already. Then he got even quieter.

"They gonna kill ya."

I couldn't believe how matter-of-factly he said that. It still chills me to this day. He said it again, just to make sure I heard it, I guess.

"Yup...they gonna kill ya. You got to git yer shit...and git."

I packed my things and got out of town.

I drove all night to the next town I was booked in, which was Biloxi, Mississippi. I slept in my car in the heat because I couldn't afford another hotel room with the money I was making.

For months afterward I got calls from other comedians saying, "Did you work Tuscaloosa recently?" I told them I had.

"Well, Dave has your picture right above the stage and told us that you started a riot in his club."

Over the years, the story has grown to the point that the cops were there, and I spent the night in jail. I want to set the record straight: none of that happened.

But I still cheer for Alabama to lose every football game it ever plays, and I'll do that until my dying day.

KEEP THE CROWDS DOWN

✳ Kenny Kramer

In 1976 I had just finished opening for the jazz drummer Tony Williams at the Cellar Door in Washington, D.C. I didn't have another gig for a few weeks, so I decided to try to get some work in Washington. I saw this place called Lou's Tavern at 14th and K, across the street from the Silver Slipper, a famous strip joint. I walked into this bar and said to the boss, "Hey, I'm a comedian. I just finished at the Cellar Door. Here's the review of me. They think I'm pretty terrific. How about giving me a gig here, let me do some work?"

The guy said, "Okay, kid, yeah, you're in."

I asked for a hundred bucks a night. He said, "No problem, no problem. You start tonight."

This place had go-go dancers on the top level, working the pole, and the bottom floor was a strip club, with featured strippers. The boss said, "You're going to be the emcee. You just go out there, fool around, do what you do, but as soon as you see the red light go on, bring out the next girl."

Before I left, I gave the guy a picture. "I have a bit of a following here in Washington. Maybe if you advertise that I'm playing here, I could do some business for you."

"Oh, that's terrific, kid. That's terrific."

My first night the club had five or six strippers for an audience that never reached double figures. I went out and kibbitzed for like four minutes, and then on came the red light. Boom, I had to bring out the next stripper. That was the routine all night long.

I was there four or five days when I said to the boss, "Listen, I gave you a picture. Why don't you put a little ad in the paper or something? I'm sure we could do some business. Put my picture out in front here. Maybe people walking by will recognize me."

"No problem, kid, don't worry, I'm on the case. I'm taking care of it."

The following week, nothing was happening—no advertising, and never more than eight people in the club at a time—this in a place that seated about eighty-five people.

One night I was doing my little thing, waiting for the red light. I hit five minutes and no red light. Ten minutes, fifteen minutes, and still no red light; I'd never been on this long. Twenty, twenty-five, thirty-five minutes. I was in new territory, out of my material and just winging it. Two of the six guys in the audience walked out in disgust, because I was struggling. No sooner had a third of my audience walked out than I got the red light. I brought on the next stripper and went right to the bartender who controlled the light. "What was the deal with the red light? How come I was on for so long?"

He said, "Ah, those two guys who left were vice squad. I just wanted you to bore them to death so they'd leave."

I asked him, "What's going on? How come this guy doesn't want to advertise me?"

The bartender poured us both shots before he leveled with me. "You jerk. Don't you know what's going on here?"

I said, "Someone has to be losing his ass here."

He said, "What kind of business you think we do? How much do you think we take in a night?"

I said, "I don't know, maybe $500."

He said, "We're taking in between $35,000 and $45,000 every night. Don't you get it, jerk? This is a laundry here. He don't want customers here. He just wants the registers to ring with lots of money coming in so he can use this money legally. Don't you see what's going on? He don't want no business."

I stayed there for the month until my next gig. I took three grand out of there and a few bored strippers. Not a bad deal if you don't mind not getting any laughs. Of course, that was why I left for another gig—without those laughs, you're just a liquor pimp.

BUDDY HACKETT'S LATE-NIGHT DINING

✳ London Lee

I was on the road opening for Connie Francis, and Buddy Hackett was working at a theater nearby. The three of us were hanging out one afternoon, and Connie said, "Why don't we all have dinner tonight?"

Buddy said, "My show doesn't go on till ten. I never eat before the show, so we'll have dinner at one o'clock in the morning."

She said, "By then everything's closed."

Hackett said, "We'll go to the Holiday Inn."

I said, "What the hell are we gonna do at the Holiday Inn?"

Buddy was insistent: "It's beautiful; you'll love it."

So, at one o'clock in the morning, the three of us were in Buddy's limo, heading to the Holiday Inn for dinner. We got out of the car and immediately saw they had a thick chain on the restaurant door.

Buddy was real nonchalant. "Don't worry about it. I can handle that."

He walked over to the limo and returned with a gun in his hand. He kept saying, "No problem," and shot the lock off the door. Just like in a movie. Then he grabbed the broken chain, tossed it aside, and walked into the restaurant. Like sheep, Connie and I followed him into this pitch-black dining room. We didn't want to hurt his feelings—after all, he'd just gone to the trouble of shooting off the lock so we could eat.

He turned on the lights. "Okay, let's get a chef to cook for us."

I said, "Buddy, it's almost two in the morning. He went home already, or he ran out when he heard you shoot off the lock."

"We'll get a chef. You got the Yellow Pages with you?"

"What are you, crazy? I don't carry the Yellow Pages with me."

Just then the manager of the hotel walked in. I guess he'd heard all the noise. He recognized us, and Buddy told him we wanted something to eat. The manager was so happy to have us there, he set the table and cooked us a great meal. He then had us sign a bunch of menus, and Buddy gave him a fistful of money before we left.

We were driving back to our hotels as the sun came up, and Buddy said, "I'm still hungry."

Both Connie and I said, "Uh-uh, Buddy. We're done for the night."

HERE'S LAST NIGHT'S SHOW

✳ Mike McDonald

I was working with Dom Irrera at Garvin's in Washington, D.C., in about 1984. The last night of that gig was on the Fourth of July. Harry, the guy who owned the place, thought that because the fireworks at the Washington Monument were ten blocks down the street, people would walk by the club and want to come in: "Hey, hon, now that we've seen a ten-million-dollar fireworks display for free, let's see a couple of comics we've never heard of for fifty bucks."

So, of course, three couples showed up that night. Dom actually tried to do his act and he was dying, because there were all of six people in the audience. Harry wasn't even there yet to see his grand scheme go down. So, when it was my turn, I put my giant boom box on a stool, placed the mike in front of it, and introduced the tape from my Saturday-night show: "This was a sold-out show, a killer crowd. I hope you enjoy it."

The tape started and I lip-synched the performance. It got a little chuckle from the three couples and the staff. After about five minutes I walked off, leaving the tape running, and went back to playing pinball.

I finished a game and out of curiosity walked into the showroom; those couples were still watching my boom box. I sat in the front row and heckled the boom box: "Hey, I suck! Do something new!" This got another chuckle out of the couples.

Again, I went back to playing pinball, leaving the tape running for those three couples.

Harry walked in, saw me, and said, "Hey Mike, aren't you supposed to be onstage?" I said, "I am."

He walked in, saw the three couples watching the boom box, and exploded, "What the fuck? You can't do this in Washington. You don't know who these people are!" Of course, he was afraid they might be some government big shots or, worse, IRS agents. A club owner would rather you fuck his wife than face an IRS audit.

I said, "Look, I'll pay the couples' tabs and tip the waitress. You don't have to pay me for this show."

All of a sudden the whole thing was the funniest thing in the world to Harry. The tape ended and the couples gave the boom box a standing ovation. I considered sending it to my next gig.

THE JOKE WAS ON ME

✳ Rodney Carrington

In 2002, my buddy Barry and I were on tour and we stopped off at a truck stop somewhere. There was an adult bookstore right next to the truck stop, so we decided to kill some time by pulling a practical joke on my tour manager, Gary. We were going to get a blow-up doll and stick it in his bunk on the bus.

I guess it must have been a busy week, because they didn't have any woman dolls left, only "Leon," a big black male doll. Leon did not come cheap. He was $170.

I bought the doll and started blowing it up inside the adult bookstore. A couple of truckers walked in and one of them said, "Hey, look at this som'bitch. He can't even wait to get it home."

I said, "No, this is a joke!"

Then the guy said, "Whatever, pervert."

Barry was laughing his ass off, standing on the other side of the store, acting like he wasn't with me.

I finished blowing it up and finally ended up with this five-foot-ten-inch black doll with a big ol' black pecker hangin' off it. I said, "I can't run across that parking lot with this thing."

The clerk at the store gave us some trash bags, and we covered up the top and the bottom of the body, but the bags weren't long enough to reach the middle of Leon, so his pecker was poking out.

Barry opened the door and I took off running. Just as I reached the tour bus, a highway patrol car pulled around and hit me with its headlights. I was frozen like a deer in this police car's headlights, holding a big black blow-up doll. The cop just shook his head in disgust and drove away.

After the initial joke was over, this thing just kind of became a throw pillow for about three weeks. Then this girl came along and asked if she could have it. We gave it to her. Last I heard, she and Leon were still happy in Omaha.

MAKING FRIENDS WITH KENNY G

✳ Mike Rowe

It was the early 1980s and I was in my early twenties and new to the business when I got the chance to open for Kenny G at the legendary Bottom Line music club in New York City.

When I got to the club, there was a buzz in the air; a few celebs were there, Mason Reese and the sax player from Billy Joel's first band. I was ushered into my very own dressing room with the traditional lighted mirror and a private toilet with a stall. The place was bigger than my apartment.

I looked down to the other end of the hall and saw Kenny G's dressing room. I was hoping to meet him and maybe get an autograph for my mom. I couldn't help but notice that there was a huge party going on in his dressing room; it was filled with smoke and music and wall-to-wall people. I saw a huge buffet loaded with ham, strawberries, pasta, every food you could imagine.

I looked back into my room. Nothing.

Suddenly I saw Kenny himself pop his head out. He spotted me looking at him from inside my empty room and smiled knowingly. Suddenly he was coming toward me. Kenny G was coming to invite me to his private bash!

He introduced himself. I let him know how excited I was to be working with him.

There was an awkward pause; Kenny looked around to see if the coast was clear, and then, in a hushed tone, asked, "There's a lot of people in my dressing room. Is it okay if I take a shit in here?"

For me there was no party, no pasta and strawberries, just a lingering, acrid stench from the nation's number-one smooth jazz horn player.

SHE DEAD IN MY BED

✳ Doug Williams

Back in the early nineties I worked with this hypnotist in Huntsville, Alabama. I asked him to teach me hypnotism because I wanted to get coochie with hypnosis.

The guy said, "Yeah, yeah, I'll teach you. But look, man, you can't use it for those purposes. You know, nobody's gonna do anything against their will."

I was thinking, *Well, you know, you just had a person up there crawling around like a dog and barking. Who's gonna wanna do something like that?*

So he showed me a few tricks. Toward the end of the week there was this fine young white girl in the audience giving me the eye, and after the show, we went back to my hotel room.

When you hypnotize someone, you get them to relax their breathing, to slow everything down by imagining they're on an island, or going down in an elevator, or sucking slowly on a big black dick.

This girl had been drinking, so when I did this stuff to her she went into something like a coma. I could *not* wake her up. It scared me shitless. I was this twenty-three-year-old brother in Huntsville, Alabama, with an unconscious white woman in his room. I had done my last show, so I was thinking I should just leave. This was before all the *CSI* shit, so I didn't think they could tell anything had been done to her. Like the autopsy would just read "died a natural death," not "died from some funky-ass hypnotism by a horny brother."

I snapped my fingers till they bled. I poured a gallon of water on her face. She was still alive, but in a deep, deep sleep. I sat there the whole night looking at her.

She woke up the next morning. "I don't know what you did, but that was the best sleep I have ever had!" She felt so good about the good night's sleep, she gave me some pussy anyway.

I never hypnotized anyone again. From then on, if my comedy didn't do it, I went home alone and hypnotized my dick into relaxing.

Classy Gigs

✳ **Jim David** I played a pigeon owners' convention, and there was a constant cooing throughout my show. I would say something, then hear, "Cooo. Cooo. Cooo."

✳ **Shelagh Martin** One gig in England was in a cellar bar that had flooded to a depth of about an inch. We still went ahead with the show, because otherwise the club would have lost a lot of money and we wouldn't have been paid. Also, the British audience was too polite to leave.

✳ **Sinbad** In Tampa, around 1982, this club owner was losing it all to cocaine. He didn't pay his light bill, so they turned off the electricity in the middle of the show. He was so terrified of having to refund money, he handed me one of those red table candles to hold in front of my face and told me to keep going. I did my bit, and when I introduced the next comic, I handed him the candle. It didn't bother me, because the crowd was laughing and I didn't care about anything but getting laughs.

✳ **Judy Tenuta** It's the winter of 1981 in Chicago, with maybe ten people in the audience, when a rat (the four-legged kind) runs across the stage. Suddenly the club owner takes out a gun and blasts it, then motions for me to continue with my show.

✳ **Lewis Black** My opening night at this club, the emcee ended with a piece about watching his wife in the delivery room. Anybody who knows comedy knows how the next five minutes went: how her vagina gets bigger and bigger and bigger, and how the baby's head pops out and he's looking at this and goes home that night thinking about how much he loves to eat that pussy, but now he's gonna get down there licking and "that pussy is so big now it'll snap right over my head. And now, ladies and gentlemen, here's the comedy of Lewis Black." Not even a pause. Pussy snapping over your head and "here's the comedy of Lewis Black."

DON'T ASK HIM TO DO A SECOND SHOW

✳ John Fox

In Chattanooga, Tennessee, in 1987, my opening act was this magician named Bingo. His whole act was only five minutes long, concluding when he threw a bird into the air and it landed on top of his head.

On a Saturday night, with the place packed with four hundred people, Bingo threw his bird into the air and it flew straight into a ceiling fan like a feathered kamikaze pilot.

Maybe the bird was sick of showbiz—the lonely life of a bird on the road—and saw his chance to end it, once and for all. If so, he went out in the grandest traditions of showbiz, because those audience members not covered with bird meat and feathers were going nuts. A crowd hadn't reacted with this kind of screaming and howling since Jesus did his water-to-wine bit.

Nobody even noticed that poor Bingo was on his hands and knees, sobbing and picking up pieces of his former magic act. When he realized that the audience was laughing and applauding, he started yelling, "Stop it! Stop laughing! You're sick! It's not funny!"

The audience thought this, too, was part of the act, and laughed harder.

I was watching this at the bar. The waitress standing next to me said, "You know, if he could do that every night, he'd be a headliner in Vegas."

THONGS

✳ Jennifer Rawlings

A few days before I went to Iraq to perform for the military, I had drinks with a friend of mine who gave me the heads-up on how absolutely filthy dirty Iraq was, warning me about the tents, the Porta Pottis, the whole shebang.

So before I left for the Middle East I went to Victoria's Secret and bought a brand-new thong for every day I was going to be gone. That way I could just abandon my underwear instead of packing it.

The first night I spent in Iraq was in Mosul, and the next morning I got up, "showered" in a trailer-type canister, put my worn thong in the trashcan and put on a new one.

Well, one of the male comics I was traveling with saw me do this and had a fit. "Jennifer, these poor soldiers have been over here for a year. We could auction that baby off."

I wasn't interested in putting my thong on "military eBay," but I got the point. From that day on after every shower I carefully placed my thong on my army-issue cot, in the army-issued tent, and left for the next camp.

We must all do what we can to boost the troops' morale.

HEEEEERE'S DAVID

✳ David Steinberg

One of the greatest thrills of my life was the first time I hosted *The Tonight Show* in 1968. I was twenty-six years old and in my suit I looked like I was going to my bar mitzvah. In the sixties Carson wasn't as tired yet, so there weren't a lot of guest hosts back then.

I'd done just two guest spots when Johnny asked if I wanted to host the show. I thought he was joking with me. It was the equivalent of starting delivering phone books for AT&T and two days later being made vice president.

My first guest was Paul Simon, who sang one song, sat down, and immediately started criticizing my monologue: "You know, if you would've done this first and that second, it would have been funnier..."

I was hosting for the first time, completely out of my mind and filled with angst, and my first guest was explaining how my joke placement was off. We laugh about it to this day.

I was finally about to start my interview with him when there was a huge response in the audience. I was thinking nothing big just happened, but the audience was screaming and clapping like crazy. I was even more freaked when I spotted Alan King standing at the curtain in a tuxedo. He did a walk-on, joining Paul on the couch. In those days, walk-ons were extremely rare. There were only three networks at the time, and the shows pretty much stuck to their formats.

Alan couldn't get over how young I was. All I remember him saying, over and over, was the word *young*. Every time he said "young" and laughed, I felt a little smaller behind the desk. He sat there with his big cigar, got a big laugh or two, and left. I felt like my head was barely above the desk and my feet couldn't touch the floor.

I started talking to Paul Simon again when there was another incredible response from the audience. I looked over, and standing there in a tuxedo was Milton Berle. It was some bizarre tag-team match of comedy giants. Milton sat down and did his rapid-fire shtick. Paul Simon and I were going nuts—Paul Simon's a fan of all of those comics. Milton got some huge laughs and he left.

Paul Simon left, and I was just about to bring out my next guest, Muhammad Ali, when I heard the biggest response yet. It was the great Jack Benny. All he was doing was standing there staring at me, and the audience was laughing its collective head off. He was also in a tuxedo. He sat down and was as funny as a human can be. He told me he and Alan and Jack had stopped by on their way to a roast upstairs at NBC.

Jack Benny left and I brought out Muhammad Ali, who was brilliant. He was funny and handsome—fast with his hands and faster with his mouth. *The Tonight Show* at the time was ninety minutes long, so each guest hung out with you for a while.

Finally I had about twenty minutes of the show left. And then all of a sudden there was an explosion of applause and laughter. The audience was making so much noise I was afraid to look over to see who it was this time. I was thinking with this applause it had to be Jesus and Moses, coming back as a duo. At this point I was afraid I'd have a heart attack. I felt like I couldn't take any more surprises.

I looked over and it was Carson in a tuxedo. Carson himself walked out on my first time hosting to say hello! Of course, he was brilliantly funny, and he had planned all of this. Just 'cause, you know, I was a young kid and he had everyone come down to help out.

Then Johnny left, and I remember sitting across from my third guest—I can't remember who it was—feeling so all alone. It felt so anticlimactic. I said to the audience how excited they all must be to know that they're just left with me for the next fifteen minutes. I could hear TV sets clicking off all over America, but it didn't matter, because I had hosted *The Tonight Show* with Paul Simon, Alan King, Milton Berle, Muhammad Ali, Jack Benny, and Johnny Carson—and some guy I can't remember, because he came out after Johnny Carson blew the last circuit in my mind.

TRAVELING WITH MY FATHER

✳ Mark Schiff

When I found out my dad was dying of cancer, I spent a lot of time in New York with him and my mom rather than in Los Angeles, where I was living at the time. One of the good things about being a road comic is you can live anywhere and book yourself out of wherever you are. Road comics have no office. So New York became the base I booked myself out of.

My dad loved my act. He thought I was the funniest person in the world. I guess you *are* the funniest person in the world if someone thinks you are. My dad and mom came to see me at least a hundred times before he died in 1988. He would come and see me wherever I was doing a show. And he always got dressed up for the show. I would say, "Dad, you don't have to wear a sport coat. I'm at the Comic Strip, not the Copa."

"I don't care. If I'm going out on a Saturday night with your mother, I'm not going to look like a slob."

I remember him asking me to do certain bits about my mother. He loved it when I talked about how they'd been married so long she'd sucked the brain out of his head.

"She loves when you talk about her. Do me a favor. Do that thing about her cleaning the house." My dad really loved my mom. He was just so proud of her. And with me being an only child, we were his life.

I remember that my dad had just gotten out of a hospice where they'd sent him back home to die. The night he came home, I had a show to do. I said, "Dad, maybe I should stay home instead."

He wouldn't hear of it. "You go and be funny." I did.

About three days later I had this gig about two hours away, in upstate New York. That afternoon we were all sitting at the dining room table when my dad said in the weakest of voices, "Can I come with you tonight? I'd really like to see your show." I knew what he was saying. He was saying, "I really want to see you one more time before I die."

I asked my mom what she thought. "If you think you can handle him, then fine." My dad was very weak, but he could go a short distance if you helped him. I said, "Yeah, I can do it."

That afternoon as we were leaving, my mom said, "You boys have a nice time tonight. I've got things to do here at home. Call me when you get there." So off we headed to my gig. It was a cold winter day, and a light snow fell for most of the drive. We didn't talk much on the way up. As I remember, my dad slept most of the way anyway. I kept looking at him as he slept in the car. I cried most of the way up, but that was okay. I was with my dad.

When we got to the hotel parking lot, we noticed that it was empty except for three or four cars. "Hey, Marko," my dad said, "can I drive around the lot?"

My dad loved to drive. He was the one who'd taught me to drive just a few years earlier in empty parking lots on Sunday mornings. He'd done every single bit of the driving for the thirty-nine years he was married to my mother. She never drove once. Now he was asking me to let him drive. "Sure, Dad," I said.

So I got him around to the driver's seat, and for two minutes he drove very slowly around the lot. "That's great," he said.

I helped him park, and we checked into the hotel and went to our room. It was still early, so I helped him off with his pants and he took a nap. I then called my mother, told her we were safe, and she started crying. "Take good care of him. I love him."

I said, "I love him too, and I also love you."

At about eight o'clock that night we went over to the club, which was attached to the hotel. Before we went in, my dad said, "Thank you for taking me."

I said, "You're welcome. Thank you for being a great father." Then he asked me to do the routine about my mother that he always liked. I did them all for him.

A few weeks later he died. About a year later, my mother came to see me work. On the way to the club, she asked me to do the routines about my father. I kissed her on the head and said, "Sure." I also did the ones about her, because I knew he would have wanted to hear them.

THE LOST FISHHOOK

✳ Joan Maurer

I remember making a road trip with my dad, Moe Howard of the Three Stooges, back in 1932. I was five, and my dad was on the bill with Larry and Curly at a theater in San Antonio. Over the weekend and in between shows, my dad took me for walks to a nearby park.

One day as we moved along, hand in hand, he explained he had a surprise for me. His vivid imagination had come up with a scene right out of *Tom Sawyer.* Although we had no fishing poles, he explained we were going fishing. Like Tom, we did have kite string and a safety pin, although my fishing attire was a far cry from Tom's straw hat and tattered pants. My mother had dolled me up in a pale blue wool jacket with matching tights and cap.

For the next two hours we stood by the river and he kept yelling, "You see that one go by?" Whenever I thought I had a fish, I pulled up my empty string. He would tell me that a giant fish had probably come by and pulled my little one free. It was so exciting.

When we finished fishing, dad removed a small rock from the stone embankment that bordered the river. Inside that hole we stuffed the roll of kite string and our makeshift hook. I listened carefully as he explained that one day we'd come back.

Periodically, I dreamed about his promise. But Dad and I never went back.

Fast-forward sixty-five years, when a friend and I had occasion to go back to San Antonio. This time I was invited to speak on a panel about the Stooges. The park where Dad and I had fished was so close, and I knew I'd never get back there again unless I went this time. I set off to find it. It was amazing. I not only found the park but I also found the stone wall. Someone, during the years that ensued, had given the park a face-lift, cementing together the stones that formed the wall, burying forever our safety pin and kite string.

Even now I have tears in my eyes thinking about my road trip with my father and our fishing trip. There is nothing like going fishing with your dad, especially if you're on the road and he happens to be one of the Three Stooges.

KILLING AT A FUNERAL

✳ Vicki Barbolak

It's always my policy to say yes to any work at all, so it was no surprise to me when the comedy club's booker told me they needed to send a comic out to do a funeral and they'd decided to call me.

The deceased woman was Sylvia Kaplan, and I called her family to express my condolences and discuss my fee. Sylvia's daughter told me her mother had been a great fan of all the legendary comics and had also written a few jokes herself. Sylvia's mother had been killed in one of the Nazi camps, but Sylvia had survived and come to America as a young child. That was everything I needed to know about Sylvia. Then we argued about my price for about ten minutes before I accepted the job.

Of course, there was the worry of being upstaged by an urn, and the problem of what to wear. I'm a little on the voluptuous side, and I like to make the most of it. I always wear sexy short dresses made of stretch animal prints, because I also have a highly refined sense of taste and style. This look is perfect for the stage or for shopping at Target, but when dressing for comedy at a funeral, one must perfectly balance respect and dignity with glamorous, starlike presence. I decided on a sleeveless, leopard-print pantsuit.

Then all I had to do was plan the show.

I really wanted to do a good job for Sylvia, so I decided, in the tradition of Milton Berle, one of Sylvia's favorite comics, to steal the jokes of all the other comedians Sylvia had loved. I did George Burns, Phyllis Diller, and Jack Benny. I closed with two jokes Sylvia herself had written. The mourners were laughing. Everything was going better than I'd dared to hope. I looked out at Sylvia's daughter. Her face was a mix of tears and laughter. I didn't want to mess this up, but as I stood there, safe in the jokes I hadn't written, hiding behind George Burns one-liners, I battled an inner voice that wanted me to slip in a comment of my own. It was a naughty little thought, and I tried to fight it.

The rabbi was sitting directly behind me, the only other person on the dais. His chair, which could have been placed anywhere, was directly behind my leopard-spotted behind. I was sure I was hiding him completely from the audience, and finally, against all reason, just when things were so perfect, I broke away from the script and turned toward the rabbi and said, "Enjoying the view, Rabbi?" There was a moment of acute silence, which seemed to me to last about four years, and then the rabbi bent down in his seat and convulsed with laughter. The whole group followed suit, and a giant sense of relief washed over me, the kind that can only be matched by a call from Planned Parenthood saying the test was negative.

After I sat down, a short film featuring Sylvia was played on a large screen. In every frame of the film she was smiling, and her joy was infectious. Her children and grandchildren shone in her presence. She'd come here as a child, an orphan of genocide, and she'd carried nothing but love and laughter in her heart.

Watching the film made me remember Sylvia's daughter telling me about her mother riding the bus to work, and how she'd loved telling jokes to the bus drivers, who Sylvia often said were in need of a little cheering up. The last part of the film featured Sylvia, in her seventies, reading her funny poems on the local PBS show *Seniors Speak Out*. She had the host laughing to the point that tears were falling, and the audience was going wild. I was so grateful that I didn't have to follow that film.

Sylvia was an impossible act to follow. Sometimes when I think things could be better, I remember Sylvia and am reminded that we all have the choice to live a life filled with laughter and love, no matter what our circumstances.

LAUGHS IN BOSNIA

✳ Bernie McGrenehan

In April of 1998, I went on a three-week Department of Defense tour of a war-shattered region of Bosnia. Comedian René Sandoval and I were to perform one show per night at each of the twelve American military camps throughout the region.

The agent guaranteed there would be no risks or danger involved. This one went the way of most such promises by agents. Upon arriving at the first camp, I was greeted with a flak jacket and helmet to wear at all times. I'm sure my agent would have told me they were just expecting rain. In fact safety was a concern, for the war had ended in the previous couple of years, but was still fresh enough for possible unrest and upheaval.

The tour was extremely disturbing and challenging from a

creative standpoint. Escorted from camp to camp in a private bus accompanied by a driver and a military chaperon, we were flanked by two Humvees, one in front, one behind, with machine-gun-wielding soldiers standing in the roof hatches.

The devastation of the country was heart-wrenching and painful, destruction and death everywhere. There were cemeteries every half-mile, with tombstones carrying the names of children ages one to twelve, lined up in long rows. The locals would run from their half-blown-apart homes to wave and greet these American soldiers in our convoy as we passed, offering us fruit and single daisies from their yards. What had these poor people seen and endured? How can humans do this to one another? I'd have only moments to reflect, for in a few hours I'd have to be funny again.

At each camp, the audiences were anywhere from a couple hundred soldiers to a thousand, and their response was amazing. Soldiers would line up to meet you, buy a CD, and tell you that they had not laughed in six months. "Thank you for reminding me how to laugh again."

There was one show—the final stop on the tour—that would change my life.

We were informed that there were twenty soldiers atop a mountain, guarding an electronic tower, and they would be there for three months. They had no stoves or sleeping facilities, just tents and sleeping bags. Food was picked up twice daily from the next-nearest camp, two and a half hours down the mountain via Hummer, the only vehicle tough enough to drive over the unstable terrain. Isolation doesn't begin to describe the situation of these twenty-year-old soldiers. We were asked if we would be willing to take a Black Hawk chopper ride to the top of this peak and perform a show for these men. Without hesitation, we said yes.

The force of this Black Hawk thrusting off the ground was too amazing to describe. With headphones on, I spoke to the pilot throughout the entire journey, as he described the history of the wreckage that lay beneath us. The chopper cleared a line of trees and we saw a muddy field, where we were dropped, splashing water and dirt up to our knees, as we ran for the tents in the distance. We were greeted by the colonel and sergeant of the unit and met the men, who lit up like Christmas trees, like kids who'd just seen their first Tonka Toy.

From the inside of a tent, twenty by twenty feet, no stage, no lights, no microphone, we were introduced. René did his set, and then I did mine. I gave it my all that night. I could see how important and freeing these laughs were to these young men. When the show ended, we were photographed, patted, and hugged with joy and exhilaration.

When we shook hands to say thank you and good-bye, their faces changed. I could hear the Black Hawk over my shoulder, and turned to see it appear over the tree line in the distance, approaching to remove us, but not them. As the chopper touched down in the mud, the copilot jumped out, blades swinging overhead, waved to us, and said, "Let's go." We silently shook hands one last time, and ran against the wind toward the chopper.

As that Black Hawk blasted us off the mud and into the sky, we peered out the window and down on those twenty men below. They were looking back up at us. Standing at full military attention, with one hand over their hearts and one above their heads, they were saluting us! René and I looked at each other, and just lost it. Not a word was spoken between us, the feelings too overwhelming to describe.

I realized, then and there, what it was for me to be a comedian. It was not about having your name on the marquee in Vegas, or getting a standing ovation from two thousand, or having your own sitcom on a major network. Being a comedian was about the sound of joy and laughter coming from those twenty young American soldiers on a hilltop somewhere in Bosnia.

ACKNOWLEDGMENTS

When two old road dogs get a book published, a lot of people help. They're giving us the light at two pages so here we go.

We must thank the paying customers. Unlike any other of the performing arts, standup comedy can't be performed without an audience.

Ritch thanks his children, Savannah, Sierra, and James, who fuel his ambition, light his shadows, and thankfully take after their mom. He also thanks Ronna Dragon for a second chance that never gets old.

Mark thanks his family, Nancy, Jacob, Eli, and Noah, who inspire his best material and provide his biggest laughs.

We'd also like to thank:

Our agent, Dan Strone, and his assistant, Alison Masciovecchio, at Trident Media Group, who masterfully steered this book to the best port.

Steve Ross, who said yes to the book and no to our request for more money. You were right, it made us stronger.

Our editor, Rick Horgan, whose superb talents enhanced the book, and whose guidance showed us how a deadline can cure ADD.

Our audacious editorial assistant, Julian Pavia, who answered more dumb questions than Custer's scouts.

Jay Sones and Laura Quinn, who got the word out in a big way.

Fred Toczek, lawyer extraordinaire and teacher of the really important stuff.

Ralph Seymour, full-time webmaster and part-time superhero.

Bill Rich at BillRichPhotography.com, who could find the Elephant Man's good side.

Rick Messina, Jimmy Miller, John McDonald, Lee Kernis, Tim

Sarkes, Pat Buckles, Judy Orbach, Rory Rosegarten, Marc Pariser, George Shapiro, and Bruce Smith, who were so generous with access to their clients.

Laura Fairchild, Kate Fennerman, Sonia Vaughn, Holly Bonnette, Janice Frey, Judy Englander, Kali Londono, Douglas Miller, Aimee Hyatt, Helga Pollock, Graham Gordy, Cheryl Gunter, Stacy Mann, Melissa Tempone, Maria Surovoy, Rhonda Schock, Jessica Zajicek, Ilene Waterstone, Joceyln Pickett, Peg Warner, Alexis Ramer, and Jody Gluck, for getting us through.

Kay Urbant, Ruth'e Korelitz, Pam Yager, Katherine Rogers, Judy Kain, and Maria Ferrari, who somehow got a lot of mumbling on tapes onto the page.

Mike Lacy, the owner of the Comedy Magic Club, for feeding comics, abandoned animals, and starving egos.

Author Judy Carter, Judy Gruen, and Cathryn Michon, who unselfishly shared with us their hard-earned lessons of the book world.

Alan Shapiro, Dan Pasternak, and Mike Abrams, who connected us to some of the great cornerstones of comedy.

Jerry Seinfeld and Kevin Dochtermann, for letting us know this would happen no matter what.

Mitch Julis, who stepped up to the plate before the ballpark was even built.

Louis Faranda, who handed us the city that never sleeps.

Jackie Martling, a fifty-thousand-watt guy who always goes beyond the call.

Hillary Winston, a funny woman and talented writer who spent an afternoon listening to road stories, suggested a book, and swore never to do standup comedy.

Bill and Bob, for helping us get the joke.

Every comic who gave us a story, and a laugh.

About the Authors

✳ **Ritch Shydner** has been a standup for years and has written for numerous television shows, including *Roseanne*, *The Jeff Foxworthy Show*, and *Mind of the Married Man*.

✳ **Mark Schiff** is also a long-time standup and has written for *Mad About You* and *Roseanne*.

Both Ritch and Mark have appeared on *The Late Show with David Letterman* and *The Tonight Show* with both Johnny Carson and Jay Leno.

To learn more about the book,
visit www.standupstories.com.